Dancing Through Fire

DANCING THROUGH FIRE

A Journey of Transformation Through Ancient Teachings of Indigenous Wisdom

By Robbie Warren, Otter Woman Standing

with Susie Spies

Dearest Sue,
Thank you for all
you do in the world! Keep saying yes.
Robbie WA
Otter Woman
Standing

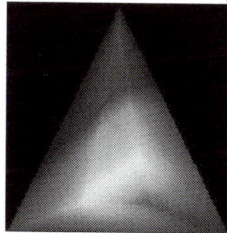

PRISM LIGHT
PRESS

ISBN 978-0-9898066-3-3

Published by
Prism Light Press
PO Box 625, Tallahassee, FL 32302
www.prismlightpress.com

Manufactured in the United States of America.

I dedicate this book to love.

To all that is and all that will be.

Trai, you are that for me.

Table of Contents

Foreword

"Come to the edge," he said.
They said, "We are afraid."
"Come to the edge," he said.
They came. He pushed them.
And they flew.
— Apollinaire Guillaume

To walk the road of a visionary is not easy. Nor is it a choice. If a person has been given a vision to fulfill, one born from a dream that is seeded and gestated in the womb of the soul, then when its time of birth arrives, it shoots through the canal of Universal Consciousness to arrive into a single heart, a single mind, all in the blink of an eye as though Awareness itself is born in the split of a second. The person to whom such a sacred seed is given then awakens at a level he or she might never have imagined or thought possible.

Throughout history there have been countless brave women and men who have taken great risks to follow the visions they received: Plato, Leonardo da Vinci, Madame Curie, Galileo, Einstein, Gandhi, Yogananda, the Wright Brothers, Amelia Earhart, Steve Jobs, are only a very small fraction of the visionaries who, in one way or another, have inspired and contributed to the ongoing evolution of Humankind.

What makes today different from all the other eras is that
we have come into a time where the survival not only of
humanity is at risk, but all of life on Planet Earth as well. Even
with the visionary wisdom that has guided humans through the
centuries, choices have been made that threaten all life here
on Earth.

With well over seven billion human beings now in
existence, each requiring a certain amount of Earth's
resources to survive, our beloved planet is quickly being
depleted and drained of those very elements that give it life,
and in turn give humanity and all here, life.

What we see happening then is the dawn of new
visionaries coming into being, each with a piece that if, the
world listens, can show us a way through the chaos into a
higher level of consciousness, ensuring the survival and
enrichment of all life. The Dalai Lama, Joseph Rael, Astronaut
Edgar Mitchell, Former Canadian Ambassador James George,
Matias de Stefano are a small sampling of those extraordinary
visionaries presently living who are helping the mass
consciousness to awaken.

When you read Robbie Warren's book, it will become clear
that Robbie is one of the new visionaries. In her story, you will
travel with her through the journey of discovery as she
awakened to the vision of the Fire Dance that was given to
her, a vision that would help all who danced this sacred
ceremony wake up. A dance to help raise the vibration of the
mass consciousness.

Robbie's struggles and triumphs are wonderfully described
in such a way that you easily can empathize with her in the low
valleys of her journey and then can turn around and celebrate
the power and beauty of that moment her vision is born.
Robbie's willingness to share so personally of her experiences
as she grows into her vision is courageous and uplifting. It is a
story to inspire the masses and bring hope to a world moving

into a future of unlimited possibility. It is a story of transformation.

— Jeanne White Eagle,
Author and Visionary
May, 2015

The Fires of Awakening

The fire in the middle of the arbor reached seven feet high, and the flames danced against the night sky. Four other fires burned steadily in the four corners of the arbor — east, south, west and north. The fire keeper fed the flames of the fifth fire, which got hotter and hotter.

"Dancers, come to the center," I called out. The twelve dancers circled around me. They were cold and wet, and they hadn't eaten for more than twenty four hours, but their eyes were lit with an inner fire to match the blaze we had set.

I explained that when the wood was burned the fire keepers would create a bridge of coals, and that it was up to Spirit to decide if each dancer would walk across it that night. I told them to ask Spirit for guidance and to honor Spirit's command. I looked around at their faces — old, young, black, white, male, and female. Each one was on a journey, a journey of transformation.

The dancers returned to their individual spaces in the arbor, waiting for the moment when they would decide whether or not to cross the coals. Whatever Spirit told them, their transformation was inevitable. I knew this. I knew this because I had been given a vision of this dance. And it had utterly transformed me. I was no longer the woman I had been back in September 2001 when a different kind of fire propelled me onto this journey.

I was driving to work when it happened. I was most likely on my cell phone with a client or a vendor or some other associate because that is what I usually did. I turned on the radio and heard a news bulletin, reporting that a plane had crashed into one of the twin towers in New York.

The way the radio announcer described it, I thought perhaps a small private aircraft had crashed into one of the towers. At first it sounded like a hoax. The 'go to' position in my head was that it had to be a joke, because everything had to be okay in our world. How could it be real? I wondered what was special about that particular day. Was it April Fools' Day? Was the same thing happening as when "War of the Worlds" went on air and people thought the earth had been invaded by aliens?

I continued my drive to work and made whatever phone calls I needed to make. When I arrived at work, however, something felt different. The staff cars were there, but the front door was locked, which was unusual. I unlocked the door and went in. I noticed, with some irritation, that small things that were supposed to have been done by my staff had not been done. As I went through the office, I performed the routine tasks that should have been done already. I switched on the showroom lights, turned the 'open' sign on the front door around, and picked up the mail and took it to the offices in the back. There was no music playing, so I turned it on.

When I walked past her office door, one of my designers called out to me, "Have you heard?" I asked her what she meant. She said something about the plane going into one of the towers, and I told her it had to be a joke and kept walking. A few moments later one of my assistants asked if I'd heard, and once again I dismissed it, saying we shouldn't worry, that it must be a hoax. I went to a place of complete denial.

A few minutes later another of my assistants came in and said that her brother worked for one of the companies in the tower that was hit. I could see on her face that it was real, and it began to dawn on me that it was not a joke. As more of my staff arrived, I realized I had to deal with their emotional reactions to what was happening. I had a television in the presentation room that was not connected to a television network — it was used as a teaching tool. We turned it on, and although the reception was poor and the images were snowy, we tuned in to a morning news show.

By the time my staff gathered in the presentation room, it must have been close to 9 a.m. At that point I was still dismissive and I felt frustrated because my mind was on work and getting things done, and no one was doing any work. I kept coming and going between my office and the presentation room, to make phone calls and write emails, and my staff stayed huddled around the television, clinging to the snowy picture for any new bits of information. I was becoming more and more exasperated because no one else was doing any work.

I happened to be in the presentation room, looking at the television screen when the other plane flew into the second building. I actually saw it. I saw it happen live. Amid the shock, reality started setting in. Some of my staff members were in tears. The person who had a family member in the first tower stood back so that she could make calls to her family to find out if her brother was okay, but she couldn't get through to any of them.

Nineteen of us crowded around a blurry screen, watching the grainy pictures of smoke billowing out of the towers. The images on the television told us that everything in our lives was shifting as we speculated about who had done this and who was flying the plane. Was it military? Was it commercial? Was it manned? Was it unmanned?

The cameras stayed glued to the burning buildings, and suddenly we saw someone leaping through a window. Immediately the focus shifted from who was responsible to the fate of the people who were trapped above the burning sections of the buildings. People were throwing things through windows to break the glass so that they could jump out. They must have known they were jumping to their deaths, and I could only imagine that they were desperate to save themselves from burning alive.

It was horrifying to witness it over and over as the pictures kept being repeated. I could not just stand there and watch. I stepped back and tried to reach out to Sam, a friend I had recently met, but she didn't pick up her phone. I was reaching out to her for some kind of answer.

A little later we heard that a plane had crashed into the Pentagon, and I remembered that Sam's father worked there. I tried to call her again and still couldn't get through. That's when it felt real; it was touching someone that I knew.

We all stayed around the television, and couldn't stop watching. We saw the first building collapse. We could hear the people around the cameras screaming and yelling, and we saw people running away from the building that was coming straight down on itself. I thought about the people who had jumped out of the building and the others who were still in it, and that all of them ended up in the same place, underneath it all. Some of the people in the room screamed in shock, and I may have been one of them. I don't know how long we stood and watched. Then the second tower went down.

I felt, in that moment, that it was not going to end; it was going to continue happening. Buildings falling, planes falling. The people on my staff were crying, and I didn't know what to say. I didn't know what to be for them. I told them all to go home and do what they needed to do for themselves.

I stayed. I sat in my office in the big empty building. I kept seeing those images through the snow on the screen, over and over in my head. It was dark when I eventually locked up the building and went home, completely worn out. I didn't even turn on the radio in my car.

Something deep down inside me shifted that day that I couldn't explain at the time. I knew I needed to understand what I had witnessed. I couldn't figure out how to make sense of it. The news reports speculated about which faction or terrorist group or country might be responsible. Soon it was blamed on a terrorist group from the Middle East that I didn't even know existed. I was so removed from world news and all of this. The news reports were talking about it as if I should have known who this person, this terrorist, was. I kept thinking, 'How could I not know? How could I have been so oblivious? How could I have been so focused on myself, my business and my clients that I didn't know what was going on in the world?'

Looking for Answers

In the days after the towers went down, the whole country shut down, and my business did, too. I asked everyone not to come to work for a few days, mostly because I didn't want to go to work. I learned with relief that my assistant's brother was okay because he hadn't been in his office that day.

I listened to the media coverage. One commentator said, "Oh, it's the Muslim extremists," and another said, "The Muslims hate the Christians." I wondered how the Muslims knew that building was full of Christians? Or that the planes were full of Christians? If it was all about religion, why bomb a financial center and not a church? How could it be about religion?

Some days later I found myself standing in a book store in the religion section. I was looking for something that could help me make sense of what was happening. I bought books by the armful: books on Buddhism, Hinduism, and even an encyclopedia of the world's religions. I thought the encyclopedia would tell me what I needed to know, but when I opened it up and found a religion called the 'John Smith religion' I had to laugh.

It occurred to me that somewhere over in the Middle East there could be a Muslim woman who was trying to do the best she could to create her life in a good way, or the best way for her, and maybe she was looking at all that had happened, and maybe she was also looking at an encyclopedia of world religions, trying to figure it out. What made her any different from me? What could possibly make her so different in her life, so different from me that she would say, "Yeah this is okay. It's okay to fly planes into buildings."

I couldn't think of any reason why her life should be different from mine. We were all just people trying to make the best of our lives. There are so many different ways to see God. How could it be about religion?

Up to this point in my life, I had concentrated on my work and my business and little else. I had a Harley Davidson motorcycle that had become my life outside of work. I spent most of my weekends either with Sam or on my motorcycle. I had met Sam through the Harley Owners Group (HOG Club). I had been riding with that group for a few years because a former boyfriend got me into motorcycles. Sam was the editor of the Club newsletter, and I had just been elected as the President of the Ladies of Harley. We began talking at these gatherings and started going on some rides together. She was easy to talk to, and I felt drawn to her. She was not like the other people in the club.

Sam had deep brown hair that fell in thick soft waves half way down her back. She almost always wore her hair in a pony tail, and she was strikingly beautiful – not the kind of beauty that comes from make-up or from fussing with herself. I don't think she even knew how beautiful she was. While she was tough and could be rowdy with the best of the guys in the Motorcycle Club, she also had delicate features and a softness that went with her strength. Her hands were quite small, and I remember thinking how delicate they looked on the throttle of her motorcycle. It seemed such an odd combination. Although we had only just met about a month before, by the time 9/11 happened, we were already close.

Sam had previously shared some of her spiritual beliefs with me; many of these ideas were completely new to me. She told me about different ways of thinking about spirituality from around the world, and that made me think about my own spirituality. My grandfather was a Baptist minister in Alabama, and I grew up going to a Baptist church. Although my family was in the south and Baptist, we were not part of the Southern

Baptist Convention. I always had questions and my mother taught me that it was okay to question and to think for myself. Sam introduced me to writers and thinkers like Marianne Williamson, Deepak Chopra and Eckhart Tolle. Now I felt a sense of urgency to understand what it all meant.

It was a few days before I saw Sam again. When she came to my apartment, she was tired and I could see that this had taken an emotional toll on her. She stepped through the door, and we hugged, no words, just an embrace that I felt in a new and different way. I didn't really understand these feelings. I had never thought of being in a relationship with a woman before.

We sat on the sofa, and I turned the sound off on the TV. It seemed that the TV was always on now. She told me that her father was not in the Pentagon when the plane crashed. He had been called away to another location and he was safe. Because the phone connections were down, she didn't find out until about twenty four hours later.

"I just don't understand this, Sam. How can this be about religion?"

"Because people are lost," she said. "Religion has blocked so many people from themselves and from God. It's crazy."

We sat in silence and watched the TV screen to see, for the millionth time, the towers falling and the dust engulf the city. It still didn't make sense. But something inside me was yearning to learn, to understand, and to grow. Something had shifted not just in the world, but inside me, and there was no turning back.

Ground Zero

During 2001 I had been going to New York City once a quarter for interior design workshops that were being given by a world-renowned interior designer, and I was one of the few designers selected to be part of her mentoring group. It was a huge honor to have qualified for this. I was due to go to the third workshop in October 2001. Sam and I decided to go together on that trip and take a couple of days off for some down time and sightseeing. It was during the planning stages of our trip to New York when 9/11 changed our lives.

In the weeks after 9/11, I carried on reading the books I had bought, and others that Sam had been sharing with me. I was reading books and authors like Caroline Myss, the Dalai Lama, and titles like *The Tao of Pooh*, and many more. I just could not get enough of it. I was still in a place of exploration, of being open, for the first time, to what it means to be human and to have a connection to God, and what that connection might mean and could look like.

The weekend trip that Sam and I planned in New York was scheduled to take place exactly six weeks after 9/11. I debated about whether or not to go. At that point we were still being bombarded by news and information and the media was still showing the same footage over and over. Things were still uncertain and scary, and even the thought of getting on an airplane frightened me. I tried to get back into my work as best I could and decided that going to the seminar was a way to turn my focus back inward and stay connected with my work.

When Sam and I spoke about going to Manhattan, she said she felt strongly that a powerful force was pulling us to be there. I trusted her. She seemed so much more tuned in while

I felt like a novice just learning what it meant to be connected spiritually.

I purchased the plane tickets two days before the workshop, and we got on a plane to New York. I was so used to seeing Manhattan and the city to the right as we flew in from Charlotte, but when I looked out of the window something seemed off, eerie even. I was trying to put my finger on what was wrong. I didn't recognize the city, and I didn't know why until Sam said, "You can't see the towers." The iconic landmarks of the Twin Towers were gone and seeing the skyline really brought it home.

We landed late on Friday afternoon; by the time we got into the city, it was getting dark. My seminar started on Sunday, so we planned to spend Saturday at Ground Zero. Sam was to fly home on Sunday morning while I stayed for my workshop on Sunday and Monday.

We landed, took a taxi to the city, and got settled into the hotel in Midtown. It was surreal to walk out of the hotel the next morning and see everything seem so normal. It was a crisp but warm fall day, and the sky was a clear blue. We passed a street fair with vendors and hot dog stands and people crowding the street. Life seemed to be just moving along. In the back of my mind, I kept hearing and seeing the news footage, and I thought, 'Don't you people know what just happened here?'

We took the subway to lower Manhattan in the financial district, to get as close as possible to Ground Zero. I didn't really understand those words; I guessed it was a military term. It took on a different meaning for me that day. The subway usually goes all the way down to Battery Park but between it and mid-town was the destruction of the twin towers and the buildings that were around it. We took the subway as far as we could go and went up out of the tunnel, emerging maybe only thirty blocks from where we started. We walked out into what felt like a completely different day.

It wasn't crisp and clean with the new fall season coming in. There was no blue sky, even though the sun was shining, because we were engulfed in dust rising from below. It was grey and dingy, and everything was dusty.

Hundreds of people milled about. They seemed to be in a daze. Most were moving slowly in the same direction, craning their necks to see into the center. Some people were taking photographs.

As we got our bearings, we realized we were just a few blocks from the northern part of the perimeter line that had been set up around Ground Zero. We walked up to it and noticed that the perimeter blockades continued as far as we could see. We decided to go left for no other reason than left felt like the right direction to walk. We stayed on the perimeter and followed it to where it turned right, and we continued next to it, going south. Sometimes there were alleys we could look down, and we stopped to try to catch glimpses of what was closer to the center.

We stopped where a few people were standing at a barricade in front of a wider gap between the buildings and looked through the chain link fence. I don't know what I was looking for. It was almost as though I was trying to see something that would make sense. We could see big chunks of cement and bars – just rubble everywhere. Further down the alley, I saw green army tents with the side flaps down. I couldn't see into the tents but printed in the distinctive military style type lettering was 'Morgue D' which must have meant that it was number 4. I knew that meant there were three morgues in front of that one, somewhere, and I wondered how high they went – to 'M' or even 'Z'?

I realized that they were bringing into the tent morgues anything that could be used to help identify someone. Maybe it was shoes, maybe it was a briefcase, or maybe even people, or what was left of people. There were military people going in and out, who I assumed were the military reserve and National

Guard. They all had masks on to protect them from what they were breathing. Even far away from where the towers had stood, everything was covered in dust. I remembered what it looked like when the towers came down and the big cloud of dust billowed through the streets. That's where we were standing – in that cloud of dust.

I don't think I have ever felt as alone in a crowd of people as I did that day. There were so many people walking around the perimeter. The air was thick with grief, dust, and sorrow. I had never felt anything like it. At that point all I wanted to do was to do was get out of it. Instead Sam and I stood there, unable to say anything. We looked at each other but couldn't speak. Like many other people, we'd brought a camera with us, and we thought we would capture some photographs, but neither one of us could take pictures at that point; it didn't feel right. Nothing made sense.

The perimeter fence was covered with pictures and posters of people who were missing and notes from family members begging for anyone who might have seen this person or that person to please call a particular number.

At one point we came to a bicycle attached to a lamp post with a chain. The courier bags were covered with grey powdery dust, and there was a little sign attached to the back wheel that said, "My son was a courier and he went into the towers on 9/11. If you have seen him, please call me." That bicycle had just been left there. No one, not even the police, had moved it out of the way. It had become a memorial to a young man, a bicycle courier who happened to go in to deliver something in the towers. I cried as I stood there and wondered how did any of this make sense?

At one point we had to stop so that the military could escort mourners for a memorial service into the barricaded area. We couldn't see if it was a civilian service or what but it must have been one of many such services. All we could see was about a hundred people in a blocked off area.

We kept walking, and when we walked down another block, I asked Sam, "What are we doing here? Why are we here? It's heart-wrenching to be here and to see this."

"We are here to pray," she said. "We are going to walk around the whole perimeter and pray."

"Okay," I said, feeling suddenly that there was some kind of purpose. Even though I didn't understand it, I agreed.

We walked some more, and I began to feel an urgency that I really needed to see what was going on in between the buildings and in the center. Every time we came to a fence, I just stood there holding it, looking, and trying my best to see inside, to see what was happening and who was there. Were they pulling out anyone alive? What was going on in there? I couldn't tell. We were blocks away from the center, and it was too far away to see anything.

The perimeter turned right again, and we found ourselves on the south side of the towers. We kept walking, and at each of the perimeter points, we saw policemen or National Guardsmen telling people to keep people moving.

I looked up another alley and saw policemen helping a woman down the alley. She was carrying a sky blue suitcase which looked like it was from the sixties. I guessed that she lived in a nearby building, where the glass had been broken and it was no longer safe. The authorities had probably let her go back in to get something. I watched her walking down the alley toward us with her suitcase in her hand, and I wondered what was in it. Clothes? Photographs? What was so precious that she went back to get? It was the strangest thing. Everything was grey, and her suitcase was the only bit of color I remember from that whole day down at Ground Zero.

We came to West Highway, which is the main road that went into the twin towers and the heart of the financial district. It was the same road that was being used to take the debris out and away to an off-site location where they would sift through it, piece by piece. They had to get the debris off-site so that they could continue to dig down. There were barricades across four lanes. We watched three or four flatbed trucks filled with all kinds of debris drive out, all dripping wet. It struck me as odd, and I thought, 'Why are these trucks wet? There's no rain.'

We stood at the barricade. The police kept telling people "Let's go, let's go!" as they tried to get people to cross the street, and then they would stop and wait when another truck came out.

I turned to Sam and said, "I want to be up there. I need to go up this street."

"So let's go," she said.

"How can we get up there?" I asked. "We can't just walk in there."

"Yes we can!" she said. "Just follow me, and don't say anything. "

She started walking and I followed, right on her footsteps. We walked right up to and past the policeman and he didn't say a word. We walked a little further. Two more policemen were talking to somebody else and they didn't say a word either. We kept walking, and when I turned around I saw four or five people trying following us, but the policeman stopped them and said, "No, you can't come in here!" and made them go another way.

A block further there were no more policemen. We were at the place where the National Guard soldiers were stopping the trucks. People in white hazmat suits with full face-head masks used fire hoses to wet the trucks down before they left Ground Zero. That's why the trucks that I saw earlier were wet. They were hosing down the trucks so that the dust wouldn't fly through the city as they drove through. People were wearing hazmat suits because it wasn't just building debris that was in the dust. People had been turned into dust, and the work crews didn't want to breathe that in or take that out.

We stood there for a few minutes, watching this process, and no one said a word to us. We decided to walk a little further in and saw more National Guardsmen with rifles in their hands. I got really scared.

"Just keep walking. Don't say anything," Sam said.

We walked right past them. I don't know how these trained soldiers did not see two civilian women walking into Ground Zero, but somehow they didn't. The closer we got to the center, the louder the noise level became, and when we reached center we saw why it was so loud. Trucks and cranes sifted through rubble, and people were everywhere. Right in front of us was a shower area where the people could shower before they left. I realized that we were standing right next to what was the sky walk that went between the three buildings. It was down on one side and still up on the other, at an angle. As we went underneath it, fully into Ground Zero, the noise was almost unbearable.

I looked up and recognized the steel girders that had become such an icon, sticking straight up out of the center of Ground Zero. I could tell they were the framework for one of the towers. Those metal bars had been in so many photographs in the newspapers and magazines and on the Internet. There we were, face to face with the symbol of the destruction.

I looked down at my shoes. When I left the hotel, they were brown, and now they were completely grey because they were covered in so much dust. We were standing on what felt like a big mound of earth. 'There shouldn't be soil here!' I thought. Then I realized it wasn't soil — it was debris. We were standing on a mound of debris.

"Now what do you want to do?" Sam asked.

"I need to pray," I said.

For the first time in my life, I prayed out loud from my heart. It wasn't the reciting of a memorized bed time prayer taught to me by my mother or a passage that my father had asked me to read from the Bible. It was the first time that I ever felt a true connection to the God Source.

When I started to pray, I couldn't hear anything. I couldn't hear the machines or the cranes. I couldn't hear the people. It was utterly silent in that prayer. I prayed out loud in full voice. I prayed for the people who were killed in the towers. I prayed for the people who were on the planes. I prayed for the people who took over the planes. I prayed for them and for their families and for the people who thought that it was the right thing to do. I had never prayed for someone who I felt had done something wrong before. I realized, in that moment of prayer, that it was not up to me to judge right or wrong. It was up to me to hold the intention of love for everybody. That's what I prayed for. I prayed for love.

As soon as I finished the prayer, the noise came back so loud it was like a jolt of lightning. It felt like it knocked me through my chest. Almost immediately somebody out there yelled, "Hey you two! How did you get in here? What are you doing in here?"

We had not been seen at all up to that point. And now suddenly we were visible.

Sam grabbed me by the arm and dashed out, not the way that we came, but out between two buildings to the side. We jumped over a barricade and the policemen yelled, but we kept running, and nobody came after us. I guess nobody cared what two women were doing inside Ground Zero at that point.

Sam and I did not consciously make ourselves invisible that day. She explained to me later that it is possible that someone with a higher vibration may not be as easily seen by someone with a lower vibration because the higher vibration is no longer a match for the lower vibration, and vice versa. When the prayer was over and our work was done, we were snapped out of it, and in an instant someone saw us. It was not an invisible Harry Potter cloak. We were there. Some people had even tried to follow us, but nothing stopped us from our mission. It was a phenomenon that I had not encountered before that day.

We continued to walk around until we got to the place where we started. We found our way back to the subway and went back to our stop in mid-town. When we came up out of the subway, we were back in that ordinary day. It was blue and clear, and there were normal city noises, and vendors, and people were still shopping. The difference between the two places was jarring and I felt disconnected.

That day in Ground Zero wasn't just about what I saw. It was about what I felt. It wasn't only my emotions that I was feeling. It was humanity's feelings. The whole world was focused on what was happening there. All that attention and energy, the world's fear, anger and sorrow, was all coming to a point at that one spot right there.

I think that something happens when that many souls are released so abruptly. People around the planet who were open and ready felt it. My experience of 9/11 wasn't special. I think many people had a similar experience. I made sense of it in my head but I felt it in my heart. That was the first time that I tuned in that way, to feel what I felt. It's hard to describe. It is different from seeing the truth of something — which I can do. But feeling it is different. I believe I had to step into the center, into the vortex, in order to be able to do it.

Before 9/11 I wouldn't have cried for some Muslim woman sitting on the other side of the world. I knew something was different in me and I knew it was different because of 9/11, because of what happened. I knew my heart had opened up. It would be a long time before I could put words to it. But I knew that I was not the same person I was when I left Charlotte, and I knew I could never be the same person again. And that scared the hell out of me.

I had to figure out who I was. I had to throw away the shoes that I wore that day — perhaps it was a symbolic letting go of my old life, and finding a new way to walk through the rest of my life.

Life is Fragile

It was the strangest thing to walk back into my office after going to Ground Zero. After having seen what I had seen, I tried to sit at my desk and answer emails and talk to clients on the phone. I tried to answer questions that my assistants asked me. I tried to go over projects with my interior designers. How could I sit there and carry on as if this horrible, horrible thing had not happened?

I tried to come back into my life as it was and put things back together, to act as if nothing had happened, to run my company and take care of my clients. I tried to do my work and do the things that I needed to do to make a living and keep my career on track. Yet, there was something that was so completely different that I couldn't put my finger on. How could I continue as if I didn't have this awakening? How could I sit at my desk, answer emails and stare at the same walls and pretend they were the same?

The truth is, nothing was the same. Nothing in my life was the same. I had woken up somehow and recognized and realized there was so much more to this existence on this planet than just working and creating a living. I couldn't wrap my brain around it and I couldn't fully understand it, but I knew to the depths of my soul that there was so much more to life than just building a career and doing this work. I was constantly distracted, thinking about the experience that I had at Ground Zero. I recalled how we got beyond the barricades and how we were not seen even in broad daylight. I thought about how silent and still everything was when I was saying my prayers at Ground Zero. It was as if the whole universe was just waiting to hear that prayer.

It did not make sense that I should be sitting at my desk focused on architectural designs and designing kitchen cabinets and choosing drapes and creating window treatments and picking out furniture and working with clients when everything was so different.

During these moments of awakening, my connection to Sam grew stronger and there was something between us much deeper than friendship. It felt like recognition on a soul level. It felt so real and so natural and so beautiful. I allowed myself to consider the possibilities even though I had never before thought of a relationship with a woman. At the same time I was exploring new ideas of spirituality, of who I was, and of what love was. All these new ideas were coming together and gelling at the same time. It was powerful and I was deeply grateful for the awakening. It was also scary. Yet I allowed myself to be completely open to it. At night I went home and kept reading the books that Sam passed on to me, trying to understand what had happened.

Sam understood my confusion and my 'waking up'. She tried to help me through that process which was confusing and gut-wrenching and yet also beautiful. There were nights that I just cried because life felt so fragile and so tender.

During the day I put everything I was feeling aside and got my work done. At the same time, however, I felt a deep sadness that I could not quite explain. Other people noticed it as well, and someone suggested that I was feeling my connection to the physical energy and experience behind the barricades at Ground Zero. The idea that I might be carrying something energetically that really was not mine or my own creation was something completely new to me. I had never heard of such a thing before and I was intrigued. I saw that it was quite possible that I was 'carrying' some energy that may or may not have been mine and that these feelings, although real to me, may not have been my own.

One evening Sam and I were talking about this possibility, and she said "You know, a sweat lodge might help you to release these emotions."

"What is a sweat lodge?" I asked her.

"It's a ceremony that takes place in a small hut called a lodge. Stones are heated in a fire and carried into the lodge and water is poured over the hot stones, releasing steam. It's a way for people to pray to let go of things that no longer serve them. I went to several sweat lodges at the Center for Peace in Tennessee when I lived there."

I thought about that for a moment and then said, "I'm willing to try anything that can help me shake these strange feelings."

Purification

Sam called Perry Robinson at the Center for Peace and explained what had happened to us. He agreed that a sweat lodge might be the best course of action to help us move through the emotions that were coming up for us. He said it could also be a way to solidify our own feelings and our own experiences. Perry suggested that it should be a private lodge, not open to anyone else. Perry and Sam arranged for a date to hold the ceremony about a week or so later.

I enjoyed the scenery on the drive to Tennessee, the lush trees and rolling hills that were full of life. Unlike the vivid greens of summer, the fall colors looked like fire on the mountain. I soaked up the beautiful range of colors and enjoyed being away from the hustle and bustle of my daily life.

The conversations that Sam and I had on the drive were mostly about what we had experienced at Ground Zero. We spoke about walking around there and what we had felt. It seemed surreal and far away, yet I could feel the depth of sorrow coming up around it. It felt odd to be experiencing such deep emotions and to be surrounded by the beauty of the turning of the season in the mountains.

I couldn't help thinking forward to what the lodge would bring. Even though Sam had told me about it and explained what I could expect to experience, I couldn't picture or imagine it. She was really good at helping me to understand, but for some reason I couldn't just pull together in my head what this experience was going to be. I decided to just enjoy Sam's company as we drove through the mountains on a new and different adventure. I would do my best to stay open to whatever the rest of the day would bring.

The Center for Peace was about half an hour outside Knoxville, settled way back in a hollow in the mountains. I was surprised to find that it was just a house, a home. I expected to find a center, so to speak, or some kind of big church. It made me feel so much more at ease to go to someone's personal home rather than a large commercial structure. Perry opened the door. He was a tall man with a full head of steel grey hair and the most loving, kind blue eyes I had ever seen. He grinned behind his big beard, and opened his arms to hug us. I immediately felt at ease.

After we sat down in his living room, he asked if we had any questions. Sam had already spoken to Perry about what we could do in exchange for the sweat lodge, and he told her that there was no charge for the ceremony, but that we could make a donation to the Center for Peace towards their on-going efforts. He also said that it was appropriate to bring a gift of tobacco for the lodge leader. I could not think of any other questions to ask. We came prepared to honor Perry as our lodge leader with a gift of tobacco and to make a donation to the Center for Peace for all of the work that they do in the world.

Perry said we would go to the sweat lodge and prepare ourselves for the ceremony. As we drove down the mountain into a meadow behind his home, I realized this was much more than just a home. In the meadow was a beautiful wooden circular structure, and although I couldn't imagine what it was for, it felt powerful. We drove past it and went to a place in the woods, on the side of the mountain. Walking along a path into the woods, I could see smoke drifting up through the trees. It was comforting.

When we reached the area where the sweat lodge was I could see that it had been used often. In the clearing I noticed a low, round structure shaped a bit like a turtle shell. It was about three feet high at its center point and maybe ten feet wide. It was covered completely in blankets and wraps, and it looked completely light-tight. It had a little opening in the front that I guessed to be the entrance. Suddenly I felt afraid because I realized that was the lodge and that's where we were going. We were going to go down on our hands and knees and crawl into that small, dark space.

The area was situated on a slope. The lodge sat downhill about ten feet from a fire. On the far side of the fire, on the uphill side, opposite to the lodge was a wall of small stones in a horseshoe shape, open towards the lodge, forming a protective wall.

A man stood with the fire. He was a striking figure with long grayish-brown hair pulled back in a ponytail. He was wearing a hat that you'd expect any Tennessee mountain man to be wearing, something akin to a Grizzly Adams leather brimmed hat. He stood there quietly, looking down at the fire, and didn't even look up at us when we approached. It was almost as if he were mesmerized by the fire, and even though I didn't understand what he was experiencing I somehow knew not to approach him

Perry sat down next to the lodge, which we could see clearly from our vantage point, and we waited on a bench on the uphill side. Even from that point we could feel the heat of the fire. I could see the door to the lodge, but it was completely dark inside and I couldn't see into it. I sat quietly and took in the scene, the trees towering over us in the clearing. It was cool in November up in the mountains, and I enjoyed feeling the warmth of the fire on my face. I could see the love and care that the fire keeper was putting into that fire.

A while later Perry told us to come towards the lodge, so we walked around the fire and down some stones set in the ground that made steps down the slope to the level of the fire. We stepped through an opening to the fire circle and to the lodge. I watched the tall man with the long hair work with and tend the fire. Then Perry went down on his hands and knees and crawled into the lodge and disappeared into the dark. A familiar fear came up in me. I become a little afraid if there are one or two too many people in an elevator, and it is a bit too crowded, or if I feel that I might be stuck inside a small tight space. I don't know that I would say I am claustrophobic because it's not a true panic that comes across me, but I would really rather not be in a confined space.

What had I got myself into? Sam could feel the fear coming up in me because she reassured me, saying, "You know, it's okay. This is a safe space."

I breathed deeply and watched the man with the long pony tail cover the opening to the lodge with blankets. I knew in that moment that it was pitch black inside the lodge and that Perry was in there by himself. I wondered what he was doing alone in the dark when I heard his voice, softly, from inside the lodge. I couldn't make out the words, but as his voice became clearer the man with the long pony tail knelt down at the door and bent his head and I could tell he was honoring what was happening inside the lodge. As his voice became clearer, I could hear that Perry was in prayer, preparing himself inside the lodge, and I knew he was preparing the ceremonial space for me and Sam to go inside. The fear I was feeling slowly started to ease, and the little knot in my stomach got smaller and smaller. Then Perry said in a loud voice, "Fire keeper, open the door please."

The man with the pony tail and the hat lifted the blankets up, and I could see steam coming out of the lodge.

"The lodge is ready for them to come in," Perry said in a loud voice.

The man with the hat and the pony tail held out his hand and offered to help us down the few steps around the fire to the entrance to the lodge. Sam, having done this before, went first. She got down on her hands and knees at the entrance to the lodge and put her head down to the ground and kept it there for just a moment. I didn't understand what she was doing.

As she was going into the lodge, I realized that it was my last chance to run and get away from this place and not do this. The man with the pony tail reached his hand out to me. I had a choice to make: to say no, or to say yes. I took a big deep breath. Then I put my hand in his, and he helped me down the steps and to the entrance to the lodge.

The only thing I thought to do was to mimic what Sam had done. I got down on my hands and knees at the entrance to the lodge. I didn't even look inside. I had my eyes closed. I put my forehead on the earth. I felt the coolness of the mud and the earth on my head; it felt so soothing and calming. I breathed in deeply, lifted my head, opened my eyes and looked into the lodge. In the few seconds that I had my face in the doorway, my senses were heightened and I took in the scene. I could see Perry sitting immediately to the right. Sam sat all the way on the opposite side of the lodge facing me. In between the door and Sam, stones glowed in a pit. I realized they must have been in the fire. I could feel their warmth on my face. I could smell some kind of herbs and the earth, and I could still feel the earth on my forehead.

I breathed in deeply again and crawled in. As I crossed through the doorway into the lodge, the last little knot of fear in my stomach was left outside and did not come inside with me into the lodge. I crawled around to the left and found a place to sit next to Sam. I could feel the coolness of the earth on my skin and the warmth of the stones in the air. The smell of herbs was stronger as Perry placed the herbs onto the stones. It was a pleasing smell. I took a deep breath and closed my eyes. In that moment I realized this was not the first time that I had experienced being in a sweat lodge.

My soul felt such a connection to this place, to this ceremony. My soul absolutely remembered being in a sweat lodge, feeling the warmth of the stones and smelling the herbs placed on the stones. I could feel the tears welling up in my eyes. I had never experienced anything like this before. I didn't know what to do with it.

I looked across the pit of glowing stones to the other side of the lodge, and in the dim light from the glowing stones I could see Perry and his gentle sweet smile and I felt at home. For the first time in as long as I could remember, my soul truly felt at home. I knew this is where I belonged.

Perry asked for more stones to be brought in. The fire keeper went to the fire and moved the logs to pull out stones one by one. Through the door I saw him take a cedar branch and gently brush off each stone with loving care. One at a time he placed the stones on a pitchfork and brought them to the door of the lodge. Once there he announced the presence of the stone and that it was now ready to come into the lodge. Perry acknowledged the presence of each stone as it was brought into the lodge on the pitchfork.

Perry used a pair of deer antlers to pick up the stones from the pitchfork and move them into the hole in the center of the lodge. I don't know how many stones were brought in this way. I didn't count. Each glowing stone was welcomed into the lodge, and Perry explained to me that he was using sage, sweet grass and cedar to bless each one. I felt gratitude and a connection to the stones as they were brought into the lodge. I could understand why each stone was held in such high regard. As the stones increased, so did the lovely smells. The only way I can describe it is that the lodge was full of love.

When all the stones were in, Perry asked the fire keeper to close the lodge door. I took a big deep breath and let go of the last little bit of fear that I saw sitting outside the lodge as the door was closed.

When the door was sealed and the blankets around the door were tucked tightly around the opening, the only thing I was able to see was the red glow of the stones. I took a deep breath in and I felt the expansion of the universe in that moment. I was no longer inside a tiny little structure that had boundaries and walls. I was floating in the cosmos. As the red glow of the stones got dimmer, I realized I was truly connected to the cosmos, to All-That-Is. For the first time I felt a deep and powerful connection with Creator energy moving through me, and I felt completely safe. Tears started rolling down my cheeks. I knew something that I didn't know before. For the first time in my life I knew what it was like to be completely held in the arms of love – to be completely held by the Creator.

As the tears rolled down my cheeks, Perry started to pray. He said prayers for the direction of the East, and he acknowledged all the gifts that come from the East. As he was doing this, he poured water onto the rocks and the lodge filled with steam. He gave us an opportunity to say prayers and so for the second time in my life I prayed out loud, from my heart. I released things that I was holding onto. I released emotions that I didn't even know that I was feeling. I felt so connected to the earth yet so completely held by the cosmos. It was the most amazing thing I had ever experienced.

When our prayers were said, Perry ended the first round and asked the fire keeper to open the door, and then to bring in more stones. Once the stones were inside, Perry asked him to close the door again, and this time he offered prayers to the direction of the south. When those were over, he ended the round and repeated this for the west and then lastly for the north. With each of the rounds, my prayers felt more connected to each other and more connected to all of creation. I felt wholeness within my body and within my soul that I had never felt before. When all of our prayers and all the words that needed to be spoken had been said and all the words that needed to be heard were heard, Perry asked for the door to be opened. Then he said, "This lodge is complete and you can leave." I didn't want to move. I wanted to be enveloped in that love and completely held in that heat. I didn't want to let go of that feeling of being completely renewed and pure and open.

When I crawled out of the lodge, I once again put my head onto the earth. I felt the coolness of the damp soil against my forehead and I wanted to remember that feeling and hold onto it for the rest of my life. The man with the pony tail was standing there with his hand stretched out to help me stand up. I didn't quite realize that I would need help getting up. But I found myself a little light-headed and dizzy, and so I was grateful for that helping hand. He pointed over to where I could sit to regain my strength, my thoughts, and my senses. Sam came out of the lodge behind me the same way.

The door was once again closed with Perry inside. I could hear his voice again, and although it was muffled I could hear that he was once again in prayer. I could tell that he was giving thanks for all of the experiences inside the lodge. I held my gratitude in my heart for that experience, for the feeling of coming home, for that feeling of something which my soul remembered.

After Perry came out of the lodge, we returned to the house and shared a meal. About thirty minutes later, the man with the pony tail came up to the house, too. He introduced himself as William Charles and said, "It was my honor to be the fire keeper for your lodge." That night I heard the term "fire keeper" for the first time.

I thought, what a beautiful man, what a beautiful, beautiful task that he took on. I told him how grateful I was for all that he had done, even though I didn't understand what it was that he had done.

We remembered that Perry also told us that it was appropriate to honor the fire keeper with a gift, and we realized we had not brought anything for William Charles, so we asked if it was appropriate to gift him with money and Perry said we could do that. When we had finished our meal, and we were ready to leave, Sam took some money and gave it to William Charles as a way to say thank you for the hard physical work that he had done to help us. It wasn't much, but I watched William Charles accept it with gratitude and humility and immediately turn around and place it into a basket that was for the Center for Peace.

Here was a man who had spent hours and hours working hard with the fire, dedicated to his task, and the little bit of

money that was given to him in exchange for that he gave
back freely to the Center.

The Long Dance

Things had moved quite fast for me. Six weeks after 9/11, in October, I was at Ground Zero. Two weeks later, in early November I was in the sweat lodge. It was quite incredible to go into the sweat lodge and feel one way, and come out feeling completely changed and different. I can't even explain how freeing it was to go into a sacred space and offer prayers. I had never been in nor witnessed such a ceremony, and it whet my appetite for more. I wanted to explore and understand more about the connection that I felt to the sweat lodge and everything about it. I wanted to understand it and I didn't want to miss out on anything. I wanted all I could get of this. I wanted to understand it and the memory that I experienced inside the lodge.

At the Center for Peace, Perry told me about some of the events that were coming up, one of which was a medicine dance. Using the term 'medicine' in this way was completely new to me. Sam explained to me that in Native American spiritual practices, or paths 'medicine' speaks to your spiritual connection, your character, and your own personal being in the world. Used in the broader sense it is another word for spiritual path.

In the wake of 9/11, I was intrigued with the idea of being able to create peace through spiritual practices. I had always looked at peace as having to come through the political arena and from the "powers that be" coming to agreement. I had never thought of peace coming from spiritual practices.

Curious about the medicine dance, I asked Perry about it. He explained that the Long Dance was one of three medicine dances given to a man named Joseph by Spirit, or Creator, or his spirit guides while in a vision. Each dance carries its own message, its own teachings, and its own blessings.

"Who is Joseph?" I asked

"Joseph Rael, Beautiful Painted Arrow. He is a Native Medicine Man who has shared his teachings and ceremonies with us over these last years."

"Where is he from?" I asked, thinking he must be Cherokee since we were in the Tennessee mountains.

"He is Ute and Picuris Pueblo. He grew up in the Pueblo where he was taught the medicine ways of his grandmother," Perry continued. "Joseph believes that teaching others about the medicine of his people is a way to bring about peace on the earth and to create peace. Just come and dance with us, you'll see."

Sam and I decided we would dance in the Long Dance. I didn't really understand the details of the Long Dance and how it worked. I just knew I had to be there. The lodge had spoken to me in such a profound way, and so surely this medicine dance that lasted all night would connect to me on a deep level, too.

Before the Long Dance, I met Perry's lovely wife, Jeanne Robinson, a deep soul who carries her wisdom in an open and giving way. Her long, thick silver-grey hair fell half way down her back. She kept the front of her hair pinned back on the sides to frame her face. She wore glasses with large frames and peered at me over the top of the frames as she spoke to me. She shared so much with me about Joseph and his teaching, and in learning more about him and the Long Dance, I felt a connection and a need to meet him, to get a clear picture of his work and be a part of what he was teaching.

We came together in the Peace Sound Chamber at the Center for Peace for the dance, and the drummers were positioned in the center of the round structure, nearly 30 feet in diameter. As the drummers played and sang the songs of the Tiwa Native tradition, we moved around in a clockwise direction weaving our dance with the other dancers and the rhythms of the drums. While we moved in the physical space, our spirits lifted in meditation. The space was lit by candles on small shelves on the walls, creating an odd feeling as the shadows and the light danced with us on the walls.

While I was dancing that dance, I did feel a beautiful connection to it, but it was not a deep calling. In fact, it only really scratched the surface. However, it did open a door for me to Joseph's teaching, and I felt a longing to meet him, but I didn't know how I was going to do that.

Sometime after the Long Dance, I received a message from Jeanne Robinson that Joseph was coming to the Center for Peace in February and that he would be doing a Mystery School teaching and sharing about his work. I had never heard of a Mystery School before, but I was intrigued. She explained that Joseph, as a Medicine Man and a Mystic, teaches from his own visions and knowledge and experiences. It is called a Mystery School because he teaches about the mysteries of life and you never know what he will talk about! She said it was open to anyone and everyone who wanted to come. I knew immediately that I needed to be there, to be in his presence and meet him. I told Sam about it, but she did not feel drawn to meet Joseph. Although I did not want to go without her, I was unable to stay away, so I decided to go on my own.

Mystery School

The Center for Peace was about a half hour drive from any hotels. I didn't know anyone there, and so I wrote to Jeanne Robinson and asked her if it was possible for me to stay with them in their home. They had a basement area that I knew they used for storage and I asked if I could camp out in it; I said I would bring a sleeping bag and a cot.

I offered to do a work exchange by seeing to the food and taking care of other visitors who were also staying in the house while Joseph was there, and therefore Jeanne and Perry would not have to take care of these tasks. I was happy to cook meals and clean up after everyone had eaten and do what was needed to make sure everyone was taken care of. To my surprise and delight, Jeanne and Perry accepted my offer.

I drove to Knoxville and the Center for Peace on Friday evening, arriving at dinner time. Perry answered the door and greeted me with his big beaming smile. He invited me in, and as I walked up the stairs into the living room, I could see they were all sitting around the dining room table for dinner. Jeanne Robinson welcomed me in and motioned for me to come in and sit with them, which I did.

There were three other people at the table, besides Jeanne and Perry: a Native American man, who I knew must be Joseph; a woman who was obviously his wife; and another woman with long grey hair that fell in gentle cascades down her back. She acknowledged my presence as well without saying anything to me. Her name was Brenda Sue Whitmire Taylor, and she was a long time student and helper of Joseph. She traveled with him, helping with the Dances and serving as his Moon Mother for many years. A Moon Mother, I later learned, is a woman who is clear in her connection to Spirit and works directly with dancers in the Arbor. The work shows up as support and encouragement, loving gentleness and even tough love. She stays with the dancers as emotions come up and helps the dancer process what is happening. She is a mother to all the dancers in the Arbor. Brenda Sue was also the Visionary of the Women's Web of Life Dance, which would later have such an impact on my life.

The only two people who spoke to me at dinner were Jeanne and Perry. I don't even remember Joseph looking up other than just giving me little nod of acknowledgment that I had come into the room. I enjoyed dinner with them and felt like a fly on the wall as they had a fascinating but complicated conversation about mystical things and energies. I hardly understood any of it and, quite honestly, most of it went right over my head, but I just stayed with it and listened.

After dinner everyone retired to the living room, and I cleaned up. I cleared away the leftovers, cleaned and packed away the dishes, and then I put hot water on to boil to make hot tea. I took some tea into the living room and found Perry and Joseph sitting in a pair of recliners.

The two men were strikingly different. Perry was about six foot three or four, with long grey hair that always looked a bit messy, a beard, bright blue eyes, and a wide smile. Next to him was Joseph who is not tall at all. He was perhaps five foot five, with dark hair, dark skin, and brown eyes. Apart from also having grey hair, he was a complete contrast to Perry. There they were, the pair of them, sitting in their chairs with their feet up, continuing their deep conversation about things that I did not understand. I felt so honored just to be there, pouring their tea. It was quite a moving experience.

Shortly after that I went down into the basement to bed. Earlier, when he was showing me around and explaining where the light switches were, Perry reminded me that their two dogs, Red Wolf and Dayska, would be let out and they would probably make their way through the basement where I was. I love dogs, and so that was fine with me. I didn't find out until later that Dayska was a wolf and Red Wolf was actually a dog.

It was a bitterly cold February night up in the mountains. I was grateful I had brought Sam's army sleeping bag, called a mummy bag, to sleep in. I had put it onto a cot ready to use. Every sleeping bag I had been in up to that point had a zipper that went on the side. What I did not know was that with a mummy bag the zipper goes in front, and there is a little hole for your face to stick out. The mummy bag goes around your head a bit like a sarcophagus and you are completely encased in the bag. I tried to get myself settled in the bag with the zipper to the side, and I could not understand why I had to turn my head to the side instead of facing forward. I got myself completely zipped up in the bag with its strange hole in the side and found that if I turned my head just right my face would peek out. I hunkered down in the cold and the dark, completely comfortable and finally drifted off to sleep.

Sometime in the middle of the night I woke up with my head inside the sleeping bag and heard a strange, heavy breathing sound in the room with me. I turned my head quickly to the right and managed to get my face out of the little hole on the side. I clearly heard the breathing sound behind me. I thought, 'Oh, God, there must be a spirit in here with me, or something.'

I lay still and kept listening to the deep guttural breathing sound. It seemed to be getting closer and closer. I had no idea what was going on. I thought if I screamed I would wake everyone up, including Joseph and his wife.

'What am I going to do?' I wondered.

Somehow I managed to wiggle my way around, grab my flashlight, and stick my head out of the hole. I slung the flashlight around and shone it in the direction of the breathing. There was a wolf leaning over my cot, breathing right on top of me. Unless you have ever been woken up in the middle of the night by a wolf breathing on top of you, you have never experienced such a fright. Luckily Dayska, as big and as powerful as she was, was one of the most loving, dear and sweet animals on the planet. I reached out to pet her and she settled in, and I realized I had a wolf protector while I slept there in the basement.

The next morning I woke up bright and early. I went upstairs and made sure dishes were ready for breakfast and that coffee was ready. I saw to it that people were fed and that everyone was taken care of before going down to Joseph's teaching for the day. I was also able to set a time with Jeanne to have a private session with Joseph on Sunday. I was last on the list, and I had to wait until the end of the day after he had finished seeing everyone else.

Saturday's teaching was beautiful, but honestly, like the conversation between Joseph and Perry over tea in the recliners the night before, I really didn't understand a lot of it — it went way over my head. Yet I allowed myself to just be with it as I listened to Joseph talk all day. I listened to people ask questions that didn't make sense to me. I knew on some level I was soaking it in and that I was exactly where I needed to be.

I spent another night in the basement with my trusty friend Dayska who slept peacefully under my cot. I felt protected.

When I woke up the next morning, I realized that I had to wait about ten hours to have my turn for private time with Joseph. Up to that point, I had not had any one-on-one time with him. We had not exchanged a word. We had barely even exchanged a glance with each other. Throughout the weekend it felt important for me to stay in that mode of being a fly on the wall, to not interrupt, to not ask questions, to be seen and not heard.

The day went by so quickly. I spent most of it looking through Jeanne and Perry's books, and I was fascinated by many of them. Once in a while Jeanne came in and checked up on me and made sure I was okay.

When it was my turn late in the afternoon, Perry came and took me up the stairs to the office. He pointed for me to walk down to the end of the hall and in through the door at the end where Joseph was.

As I walked down the hall, some fear came up. What was I going to say to this man? I didn't have a list of questions for him. I didn't have something that I needed to know. All I knew was that I needed to be in his presence and that I needed this time with him. I needed to understand something, but I didn't know what it was that I had to understand. So, how did I know what my question was going to be?

Joseph's Answer

I tapped lightly on the door that was cracked open a few inches and I heard a voice behind the door say, "Come on in." I pushed the door open and for a moment I stood there, half in and half out. Joseph grinned impishly at me and looked directly into my eyes for the first time that I knew of all weekend and said, "So, you're a medicine woman."

Those words shot through me. They caught me off guard. I had heard the term "medicine woman" before but I didn't know what it meant. And I certainly didn't know what it meant coming from him.

I couldn't take my hand off the door knob. I stood there, with one hand on the door jam and one hand on the door knob, halfway in and half way out, and he just kept grinning at me. Then he said, "Come on in and sit down."

I walked in, closed the door behind me, and sat down. I asked, "What do you mean?"

"Well, you are a medicine woman," he said. "I saw it in your eyes when you walked in on Friday night."

When I arrived on Friday evening, they were so deeply engrossed in their conversation and what they were sharing with each other that I had no idea Joseph had even realized that I had walked into the room. For him to say this to me on Sunday afternoon, after a whole weekend of pouring hot water for tea, fixing coffee and clearing the table, blew me away.

So I asked him again, "What exactly does that mean?"

"That's what you are going to figure out. That's the path that you are on, to understand what that means to be a medicine woman," he said.

What I realized about Joseph then and there was that I wasn't going to get a direct answer out of him. It wasn't going to be that easy. He wasn't going to make it easy for me, so I asked him, "What do I do?"

"Well, you need to make a medicine belt," he told me.

"Okay. What is a medicine belt?" I asked

"Well," he said, "A medicine belt is whatever it is to you." He grinned at me again, and I had to laugh and shake my head because I had no idea what it meant to me.

He answered the question that I didn't even ask when he said, "You will know."

"How will I know?" I asked

"You need to take a journey," he told me. I thought he meant I needed to go on a trip somewhere, but he explained that I was to hold that question in my mind while my friend played her drum.

"I don't have any friend that has a drum!" I told him.

"You will," he told me.

"Okay," I said and then I asked, "What do I do — just sit there and my friend will play her drum?"

And he said, "Yes, and your answers will come. It is as simple as that."

In that moment there were a million other questions I could ask him but I had a feeling that I wasn't going to get a straight answer. I wasn't going to find out everything I wanted to know.

The only other question that I could come up with was, "Who is going to teach me these things? Who will be my teacher?"

Joseph said to me, "You will not have a teacher."

That confused me even more. I had heard people speak of having a teacher, someone who showed them and taught the spiritual practices of this path. Brenda Sue, for example, was a teacher for several of the people at the Center for Peace, and I could see the bond she had with her students. It was strong and even a little scary. Learning the Medicine way is not an easy undertaking and to have a dedicated teacher seemed to be such a blessing!

I was disappointed to learn that I was not to have a teacher. At first I thought it meant that I didn't deserve a teacher, and that I didn't deserve to have someone take the time to teach me these things. I thought about that for a few minutes and then Joseph said, "You don't need a teacher. You just need to remember."

His words went right into me, and I felt them settle into my heart. I thought about how I felt when I got into the sweat lodge the first time, how I had remembered being in a lodge. I remembered the smell and the heat. What Joseph knew, but what I didn't know at that time, was that I do carry those memories. I carry them in my DNA. It is a soul memory. Joseph recognized that.

Joseph and I didn't talk much in that hour. In fact, we talked little. I sat there, mostly stunned, soaking it all in and trying to understand it. At the end of the hour, Joseph looked at me and said, "I would like to give you your wings." I had no idea what that meant, but I was learning to keep saying yes to Joseph. So I said yes.

"Stand up and turn around," Joseph said and showed me his eagle wing. Just the sight of his wing took my breath away. It was a single wing of an eagle spread out and fixed at full extension. It must have been about three feet long, and when he held it, it was as if it was part of his own body. When he moved it, I couldn't tell where Joseph ended and the eagle began.

Joseph stood with me and said a prayer over me. He spoke in his own language, Tiwa, and he spoke in English, my language. He put the eagle wing against my back, and I felt something move through me. I felt some *thing* move through me.

"You have your wings," he said. Then he turned me towards the door and gave me a little push, and I realized that my time with him was complete.

The Drum

Now I had the task of creating a medicine belt, whatever the heck that was, and I was supposed to have a friend with a drum who would play the drum while I sat there and got instructions on how to make the medicine belt. How crazy did that sound?

When I was sitting in Joseph's presence, it sounded perfectly reasonable to me, and as I was driving home from Tennessee, it sounded incredibly crazy. There I was with a weird set of instructions on what to do and no way to understand how to make that happen. I decided to chalk it up to experience and hold onto the feeling that I had when I met with Joseph.

I went back to my daily life of working and running my business and earning income by creating beautiful houses and living spaces. My days were filled with vendors and suppliers, builders, furniture makers and drapery work rooms. Along with all that day-to-day stuff, my relationship with Sam was becoming stronger and deeper.

Sam and I decided to go to Asheville, a lovely little mountain town in North Carolina to relax and not have any pressures for a few days. We spent Saturday exploring a nearby town called Chimney Rock and planned to stop at a small mountain river where we could put our feet in the icy water for fun and maybe even have a picnic.

We came across a tiny store called Feather Heads in Chimney Rock, filled with rocks, stones, feathers, and everything Native American. It also had a whole lot of other things that had nothing to do with Native American culture but had everything to do with being on a different kind of spiritual path. We spent hours in that store, looking at the bones, beads, feather fans and other things, asking questions, playing flutes, and making singing bowls sing.

As we were about to leave, Sam looked up and saw a beautiful drum hanging above one of the counters. She asked one of the people working there if they would get it down and let her see it. Sam took the drum and was given a drum stick, and as she started to play, tears came. I stood there watching her play the drum, clearly moved and unable to put it down, obviously feeling so connected to it.

Within minutes she was paying for the drum, and we were walking out of the store with it. As Sam walked out hugging her new drum closely, I remembered that Joseph said that my friend with a drum would play for me, and when I'd said I didn't have a friend with a drum, he had said, "You will."

There I was, with a friend who had a drum.

Medicine Belt

I explained to Sam what Joseph had told me and asked her if she was willing to play her drum for me so that I could understand what my medicine belt was and what I was supposed to do. Of course she agreed, adding that although she didn't really know what that meant, or what it looked like, she would love to do it.

At first we couldn't figure out what to do. It seemed like it had to be something bigger than her playing the drum and me sitting there. It felt like there needed to be more of a ritual, but I had no idea and so I was trying to make it up as I went along. We had a mutual friend, Janice, who did some healing energy work with her hands. I didn't know how it worked, but I thought that if she was working on me at the same time that Sam was drumming, it might help.

We went over to Janice's house, and I got on the massage table. She started working on me, putting her hands on my back. I had no idea what she was doing, but I was open to it. Sam started playing her drum, banging with a steady rhythm.

I found myself drifting into a sleep-like state but I was not asleep. I don't know how to explain it. In this waking-dream state, a man came up to me. He was made of stone, almost like the Michelin tire man but instead of tires he was made of stones. Little stones piled on top of each other made his legs, and bigger stones made up his body and his head. He came up to me and started telling me things. I was amazed and looked at him thinking, "This can't be real!"

The moment he finished, I sat bolt upright and said, "You are not going to believe this!"

I started explaining to Sam and Janice about the stone man that had shown up in my dream, and they both looked at each other in disbelief, trying to figure out how I was dreaming when I was lying there wide awake. I told them what he had told me, that I would no longer cry tears of sadness and only cry tears of compassion and that I needed to be steadfast and strong like the tree. I repeated the other messages the stone man gave me that had to do with the moon and the stars and the trees and the mountains and the waters. Sam and Janice looked at each other again and Sam said, "You know, we've only been doing this for about ten minutes, so there's something wrong here. We must have been doing something wrong. This doesn't make any sense."

"Okay," I said. I didn't know what this was supposed to look like, but I figured Sam and Janice knew more than I did about what it was supposed to be. So I took a deep breath and said we could try again another time. After that Sam and I left.

I was talking to Sam about it a few days later and told her that the little stone man talking about the trees wasn't making any sense as far as the medicine belt was concerned. I said that instead of being in someone's healing room or office, maybe I should be out in nature. I asked Sam if she would go with me to my family's house in the mountains. I thought of the place my dad used to take me that was close to the house where there was a huge boulder that he and I would sit on for hours. It was a special place to me and I said that perhaps if I sat there at sunrise while she played her drum, then maybe I would get the information that I was supposed to get in order to understand how to make my medicine belt. Sam said she thought it was a good idea.

The next weekend we packed up and headed for the mountain house. We were prepared for a few days, thinking that it would take that long. It was March and still cold up in the mountains. Before sunrise on Saturday morning, I wrapped myself up in blankets and went out and sat on the rock. Sam brought her drum and sat about twenty feet away from me so that she would not intrude on my process or meditation.

Sam started to play the drum and I closed my eyes. Almost immediately, who shows up, but the little stone guy again!

I said, "Dude, what are you doing here? I am trying to get past this to something deeper and more profound, and you keep showing up here!"

"Yes," he said. "I've got this information for you and you need to listen to me."

"Just tell me what you need to tell me so that I can get past this and get on with my medicine belt," I said.

Once again, he gave me exactly the same information about being like the waters of the earth, crying only tears of compassion for others, remembering I am like the trees in that I can root myself into the earth and still bend and sway with the wind. He told me about being like the moon and that as the phases of the moon change, so can I. He talked to me of the mountains and the protection that they offer and how old they are. He spoke to me about the sun and the heat of the sun and how it nourishes our planet.

In a flash, I saw the medicine belt. I saw it as clearly as it if were in my hands. I knew I had to create it. It was a beaded belt and on it were symbols of the sun, the moon, the trees, the waters and the mountains – because all of these things are part of who I am and how I am to be in the world and that is the medicine that I carry. I saw it as clearly as if I had just finished making it myself and I snapped awake, quickly, and I said to Sam, "I've got it!"

She looked at me and said, "It's only been about fifteen minutes, what do you mean you've got it?"

"I've got it," I said again. "I see how I am to make this belt."

"How can I help you?"

I told her exactly what I needed. I needed a piece of wood that was two by six that had nails slightly driven in near each end. I knew I had to go to the bead store and buy sinew. Sam kept asking me, "How are you going to do this? How are you going to create a belt with a two by six piece of wood?"

"I don't know, but I know," I responded.

While I was creating my medicine belt, Sam kept asking me how I knew how to make the loom, what to do, and how did I know the pattern that I was going to create. I had no answers for her. The only thing I could say is that after the drumming and after asking for the information, it was as if I knew something that I did not know a minute earlier. It was as if this information downloaded into my DNA and I understood what I needed to make the belt, what beads I needed, and I couldn't really explain it. I could not put words to it, other than I just knew what I needed to do.

Actually, it was a bit scary. I was asking myself the same questions. How did I know how to make that loom? How did I know how many beads of what color to use and which beads to string next to create the design on the belt?.

Sam was patient. She got all the things that I needed and drove the nails into a four-foot long piece of wood exactly as I instructed her. She created a surface where I could weave the belt with sinew and beads.

I took the sinew from nail to nail, back and forth, until I had what looked like a loom. I used seven colors of the tiniest of beads, called seed beads. I wove the beads up and down and up and down the length of the board. I stitched and looped every single one of thousands of beads together without a pattern; I knew exactly where each bead was supposed to go because the little stone man had shown me.

Sam watched me work on it every day. Every spare moment I had, I was constantly working on the belt. While she was making dinner, I was working on the belt. Every day. And after three months the belt was complete. I had finished it.

And then everything in me became afraid of what it meant because I knew it held something for me. I remembered Joseph telling me that I knew what I was to do with this belt and that it held my medicine, the truth of who I am. He told me

I was a medicine woman and I didn't know what that meant. What I did feel was that it was too big. It was too much, and I didn't want any part of it.

Sam and I were in a parking lot one evening, waiting to pick up some Chinese food and suddenly I felt tears coming up.

"What is it?" Sam asked. "What's going on?"

I told her that whatever it was that Joseph had talked to me about, the idea of being a medicine woman, and the medicine belt, that I had come to the conclusion it was more than I was willing to take on. More responsibility than I was willing to take on. The responsibility of being what he said I was felt like too much. All I could do was cry. Sam kindly suggested that I put it aside and keep living my life and keep moving forward. Sitting in the car in that moment, I made a conscious decision to not only put it aside, but to do my best to make it go away. I put the belt in a drawer in my bedroom and left it there.

So over the next months and even years, I focused all of my energy and all of my effort on growing my interior design business, riding my motorcycle, having fun, being with friends, and living in the moment, and not taking on this thing that Joseph had talked about.

There is More

I didn't go back to the Center for Peace for a long time. I continued to search for my own spiritual path to a certain degree, but I kept everything at arm's length so that I did not have to fully connect or engage with it. I was still reading books that were considered new age written by new teachers of spiritual wisdom, and I was connecting with that and resonating with that and learning more and more.

My relationship with Sam was deepening. We wanted to get married, but it was not an option. It was not legal for two women to marry. What we felt for each other was real and we didn't need the state to validate that for us. So we planned a commitment ceremony where we could share our connection and our love for each other with our friends and family in a local historical chapel with a large reception in our favorite restaurant. Having the support of our family and friends was a special feeling. We felt connected and loved. I included the medicine belt by wearing it during the ceremony. Afterwards I placed it back in a drawer. I thought there would come a time when I felt like I could use it and truly understand it. Now was not that time.

Although I was ignoring what Joseph had said to me, and ignoring my own medicine and medicine belt, I was continuing on my spiritual journey. It was comfortable being in a place of semi-awareness on this spiritual path, a partial awakening where I did not have to take on any responsibility for it or for myself. I was quite comfortable in that for a few years. But I noticed that there was something that began to gnaw at me and at my consciousness. Something kept saying to me, "Robbie, there is so much more and you are doing a disservice to yourself by not opening this door and finding out what this 'more' is. This is something important and you have an opportunity."

As this feeling of 'there is more' began to grow, I realized that I was becoming more and more dissatisfied with my life as it was. I was becoming less and less happy in my work life. The huge amounts of money that I was earning, and the things that I was acquiring as a result of this work – new cars, spa trips, vacations to places like Mexico – were bringing me less and less satisfaction. The feeling that there was something more kept growing.

I started taking some baby steps into what this 'more' might look and feel like and I kept moving forward. Sam and I decided to look for a church, for lack of a better word, in the Charlotte area, where we could connect with other like-minded people and cultivate our spiritual lives in as many ways as possible. Neither one of us really felt drawn to the traditional churches that we had known as children. While the church that I grew up in gave me a beautiful foundation, it was no longer my path. I was more interested in what I would call spirituality rather than a structured Christian faith.

During our research we kept hearing about a place called the Spiritual Living Center in Charlotte. When we looked it up online, we were drawn to it but at the beginning I was a little put off because I didn't understand the dynamics of what it was all about. The website described it as a religious science church, so immediately I started thinking about what I had heard and what those terms meant to me, like Christian Science or scientology, and so I wasn't sure. Even so, from reading the website it sounded open and forward thinking. We decided to give it a try and not let the wording or the titles or the labels get in our way. We wanted to experience it for ourselves.

When we went to the Spiritual Living Center for the first time we found a suite of rooms in a business park. Besides offices for the staff, there was a meeting room and classrooms for children's gatherings. I was immediately struck by how welcoming it was from the moment we walked into the lobby and everyone was happy to see us, even though they didn't know us. No-one shied away from us because we were a same-sex couple.

There was a lovely little book store filled with metaphysical, new age, new spirituality and new thought books. I recognized some of the authors that I had been reading for some time. I spent a lot of time on that first day, before and after the service, perusing the book store.

We went in and we found our seats for the start of the service and then someone went forward to do a reading, and I could tell from the familiarity around this that it was something that was done at the start of every service. The reading named and honored all the different religions and spiritual paths and practices, including Buddhism, Sufism, Hindi, Wicca, and Christianity, and when they honored Native American spirituality I thought that this was a place I was going to be comfortable. At that time the church was seeking out new ministers, and at the end of the service the president of the board stood up and spoke to the gathering. She explained that in their search for a new minister they had found two people who were part of the church but not yet ministers, but they wanted the congregation to consider bringing both of them on as ministers.

That was the first time that I saw Renée Leboa and Christy Snow. They were brought up to the front and introduced to everyone. One of the first things they did was sing a duet together, and I felt so at home. There was something about Renée that just drew me in. She was vivacious and outgoing. Her personality was big and a bit naughty. She was someone that I wanted to get to know. Christy was also powerful, a little bit more reserved, but she had a childlike grin and she laughed a lot at Renée – not in a way to put her down, but because she was really funny, and a bit like a spiritual comedian. There was a flow of energy between them that I enjoyed.

Sam and I decided then and there that we could be a part of the community and share in what was being created there. The next Sunday there was a vote for the community to decide whether or not to have Renée and Christy as the new ministers. We didn't vote because we were new, but the outcome was almost unanimous for Renée and Christy to become the permanent ministers of the church. I was pleased because I was going to get a chance to get to know Renée.

Sam and I quickly became involved with the Church. We became close friends with Renée and Christy and spent time with them both at the service as well as privately. We had dinners together and got to know each other and enjoyed each other's company. It was fascinating to me to be around two other people who were on a strong and powerful path that was different from mine and yet was not the Christian path that I had grown up with. It was really wonderful to be around two spiritual leaders who brought in something completely different from what I was used to.

Christy and Renée wanted to do new and exciting things with the Spiritual Living Center. They wanted to bring drum circles in, and so Sam and I not only got involved but there were even times Sam and I were asked to lead them. Many different events, workshops and happenings were offered. It broadened our exposure to different spiritual paths.

One day Christy let us know that she was bringing in a man who would teach us how to make our own Native American frame drum, a hand drum. I was so excited about this. Sam and I both decided that we wanted to make our own drums, even though Sam already had the drum that she got before I made the medicine belt. We signed up almost immediately.

Making the drum came so easily to me. I made an elk-skin drum with a strong, powerful sound. During the making of that drum, something in me really connected with, and understood it; I realized that what I was doing was much more than making a musical instrument. I was making a medicine tool, a spiritual tool that would have its own life. I knew it would teach me, and that I could learn so much from having this drum and being with it.

I found this to be true. The drum was powerful in my life and I used it many, many times, not only in drum circles but also in many of the other ceremonies that we did. I sat with it when I built a fire, and I used it at sweat lodges. I used it in so many different ways. The drum became a part of everything I was doing with ceremony and on my own spiritual path.

One of the other experiences I had through the Spiritual Living Center that I felt deeply was the connection I had with Renée. It was as if we had known each other all of our lives, and yet I knew nothing about her. She had just arrived from California, but our connection felt so strong. We didn't see each other that often and we didn't spend that much time together, but every time we were together, we could feel that connection. We felt so at ease and so at home with each other. She felt like a friend that I had since childhood and somebody that knew me, my history, even though she didn't. I believe that she felt the same way about me. It was wonderful to forge a friendship like that. In fact, I felt even closer to her than to some of the friends that I'd had since childhood.

Munay

My relationship with Sam grew in strong and beautiful ways. Spiritually we both felt that the two of us had something to offer a larger community. At that time we decided to build and create our own home, and as the planning for this our new home unfolded, the rooms and living areas that we designed were larger than the average dwelling. It was starting to look more and more like a community gathering space — a place for people to get together.

We knew we needed to be on acreage, and we found ten acres of land about a half hour outside of Charlotte. That distance was both an easy and convenient daily commute for me to get to work and it was close enough for people living in Charlotte to reach easily. It was also far enough out of town to offer privacy and it had enough land where we could grow our own spiritually-based community.

We named it Munay (moon-eye), which means 'heart of the tribe,' which is what we wanted it to be. We wanted Munay to be the place that we could open up for others to come and explore their own spiritual path along with us, a place where we could all grow and flourish. It became our priority. It also became a powerful glue that held me and Sam together.

It took almost a year to build the house, and in that time my commitment with Sam to a spiritual path continued to strengthen. There was no denying that this commitment was headed down the Red Road, the 'Red Road' being the teachings of the indigenous people of North America.

The land was heavily wooded with some trees you couldn't put your arms around completely. It was in the Piedmont area of North Carolina, several hours from the mountains, but this area felt like being on a mountain. The driveway was a quarter of a mile, and it almost felt like it was going straight up except for the winding curves that went back and forth to make the slope of the land easier to drive up and down.

Munay, the home that we designed and built, sat right on the top of the highest peak on our land. It was absolutely beautiful. Sam was born in the south west and she was in love with the Spanish mission style of architecture, reminiscent of where she spent her early years. I had never been out there, so I was intrigued. We decided to build our home to have that look. To design a house that looked like that in North Carolina seemed odd to some. Some of the construction workers even referred to it as "the Alamo house," and others referred to it as "the Taco Bell house."

Our dream home had everything that we wanted. In my interior design business, I had started to explore a concept that was considered to be a bit radical in the construction world, but was becoming popular – the idea of green building: building to work with the ecology, rather than to be a burden on it, and to save energy. We brought these ideas into the construction of Munay to do all that we could do to be kind and gentle on the earth, even though we were building what was considered a large home. We used unconventional ways to keep it green and friendly to the earth and to the land.

The house was large with big sweeping rooms. The main floor, the entrance, the kitchen, the dining room and living room and even the desk area felt like one wide open area that could accommodate many people. We had stained concrete floors that were heated by radiant heat through water. We had twenty-two foot high ceilings and passive solar heating that used the sun to heat the floor to keep the house warm in winter. The power bill for our almost four-thousand square-foot home, including the apartment over the garage, was less than a hundred and fifty dollars per month. At that time it was unheard of to have such a low bill.

The house was everything I had ever wanted in a home. We put so many personal touches into it that made it truly ours, such as embedding stones in the floor in spiral shapes while the concrete was being set. Munay was a creative expression of who we were and of our intention to welcome the community into a sacred space and into our lives.

Sam and I decided to build a sweat lodge on our land. She would learn the ways of being a lodge leader and how to hold that ceremony. I remembered how at home and at peace I felt in that first sweat lodge and how William Charles' work with the fire had struck me in such a deep way. I knew I wanted to see what that connection was, and so I decided I would learn how to be a fire keeper.

As our plans developed and our understanding grew, Sam and I sought out ways to learn more. Sam had already participated in many more ceremonies than I had and so she already had clarity on many things. I realized how little I knew and how much there was to learn. I renewed my reading and I continued to pay attention. I felt like a novice, a baby, and at the same time I felt drawn to know more. There were times when Joseph's words popped up for me: "You are not to have a teacher. All you have to do is remember."

Whenever I was around someone who was working with the fire and any time I was around someone holding ceremony, I paid attention and I asked questions. I helped and I watched. And I helped and I watched. And I watched some more, and I asked more questions. And I helped some more. I did this in an effort to soak up the teaching and to open myself up to remember more.

Since we had already been involved with the drum circle at the Spiritual living Center, it seemed like a natural move to invite people to bring their own drums and hold drum circles at Munay. We began to combine drum circles with sweat lodges and invited people to come to either or both. We started with the drum circle and then held the sweat lodge. We found that, more times than not, people came and participated in both.

As part of our learning, Sam and I attended other events and ceremonies in various places. We went back to the Center for Peace, where we were welcomed by Jeanne and Perry Robinson, to attend different workshops and events. We felt a powerful and deep connection between Munay and what had already been created at the Center for Peace.

Munay was part of a bigger, larger community. We interacted in a wonderful way with both the community of the Spiritual Living Center and the community of the Center for Peace. We enjoyed not only bringing people from these different centers into Munay to teach and create, but we also enjoyed going to their spiritual centers to learn, to help whenever we could, and to be a part of those communities, too.

Christy and Renée came out and shared some of their teachings. We also asked medicine people and shamans from different traditions to come in and be a part of Munay, to share their knowledge and their understanding, and to work with the spiritual community. We had met a Peruvian shaman at the Spiritual Living Center, who came out to do some teaching about energy and the chakras and also to teach us about the medicine wheel and shamanic journeying. Along with the Peruvian Shaman, we were offering quite a variety of other teachings at Munay. Jeanne Robinson came to Munay to teach and do readings for people, and we learned from her how to Journey. Perry came to teach Huna Shamanism. At that point Sam and I were not teaching; we were leading sweat lodges, and I was beginning to work with the Medicine Wheel.

Many people came to these events and workshops and felt connected with Munay and each other. People were willing to come and help clear the land, to create a path in the woods and to build a new sweat lodge. Others were willing to cook meals and serve food, and others were willing to welcome people as they showed up. I had never been part of anything like this.

Once we were ready, we began to offer monthly sweat lodges. Sam was the lodge leader and I worked with the fire. I felt such a strong connection to the fire, and soon some other people really wanted to work with the fire, too, so I started sharing what I knew with them. Sam really wanted me to be in the lodge with her as she led them so it was good to have others who felt so strongly about the fire as well.

Sam and I both felt blessed. I believe she and I came together to create and hold the space for the community of Munay to gather and flourish. And for a few years, it did flourish, and it was beautiful, and the people who came into my life during those years were an incredible blessing to me.

Building the Medicine Wheel

One of the teachings that we brought to Munay that I felt most connected to was the teaching of the medicine wheel. I was fascinated with the first lessons I had about it from the Peruvian shaman; he even used bones from monks in places where there would be stones. However, while I understood what he was sharing and teaching about the medicine wheel from his tradition, and I understood the connection to the medicine of the wheel, I didn't really connect with the specific Peruvian teachings. What he taught was not in alignment with the teachings that I was learning about the directions and the energies from North American teachings.

I will always be grateful to him for that introduction because it opened the door for me to explore on a much deeper level. One of the things he suggested was that I create my own personal medicine wheel and put it in a place on Munay that was only for me, a place no one else knew about or went to. I could go in private for my own prayers and for my own connection to the wheel and work with it. It was a great piece of advice, and I decided to follow it. To do so I needed to understand more about the wheel that I would create.

I found that my soul connected more and more to the teachings of the eastern seaboard Native Americans. As I read and I dug deeper and I learned more, I realized that was the way I wanted to create my own medicine wheel and work with these energies. The way I understood it, my own wheel would have thirty six stones.

I chose a spot for my medicine wheel that was special to me. It was down the hill and beyond the sweat lodge behind a huge tree that had a fork in it. We called that the grandmother tree because from its perch slightly uphill that tree overlooked and stood guardian over the sweat lodge area. I went to the other side of the grandmother tree where I knew she would keep me protected and safe, where I could sit and be quiet with my own prayers. I cleared the land and raked the leaves, and I got down to the beautiful deep rich black earth that was underneath. Then I walked the land at Munay to find the stones — each one no bigger than an apple.

It was not a big medicine wheel — it was maybe three or four feet in diameter. It was large enough for me to sit in front of. To place the stones, I gathered them all up in a pile. Then I picked up each stone and asked where it was to be placed on the medicine wheel. Would it represent the east stone, or would it represent the winged creatures, or would it represent the two-leggeds, or would it represent the ancestors? Once all thirty six stones were placed, I had my own medicine wheel, my own sacred space where I could pray and meditate.

It became my own private little haven, a sanctuary in the woods where I went to pray and to seek guidance. I went there to ask Creator – Great Spirit, God – for answers to questions or uncertainty. Sometimes in my prayers I asked for clarity and for guidance. I always got what I asked for. I always got the answers, the information, or the insight and understanding I needed to move forward. I spent time praying and learning and teaching myself and remembering about the medicine wheel and how it works. It spoke to me on a deep level. The teachings are so deep and so profound I could spend a lifetime trying to understand them: the work around the medicine wheel, the connection to all that is, to all of creation, the life lessons that come, the understanding of where we are at any given time as we move around and around the wheel of life. I felt connected to it, and after working with it for about six months, I wanted to open it up and offer it to other people.

There was a natural clearing near the sweat lodge. I asked Creator and mother earth if this was a space where I could do ceremony and bring and build a medicine wheel for the people. It was clear that this was a good thing. I raked and cleared out the sticks and twigs and then blessed the area with cornmeal and tobacco.

I was guided by intuition to create a medicine wheel that was much larger than my personal one. It was to be about thirty feet across, with thirty six stones, each representing something specific. After I understood what I was to do, I researched and found that this was the way the Medicine Wheel was created by some of the tribes in the Northeast. It was a little overwhelming to see that I "knew" how to create this wheel.

I needed much larger stones to make a medicine wheel of this size and it took me a while to find and gather all of the stones that wanted to be part of the circle. Some came from right there at Munay, and others I collected over time from other places.

Once the stones were collected, it was time to build the medicine wheel, a huge undertaking that may have been a little bit crazy, but Sam and several other people came to help me. Each stone was big and heavy, about double the size of a watermelon, and so the tough part was moving all the stones, which were actually small boulders. The best thing I could think to do was to create a chute down the mountain from the top where the house was, down to the bottom of the hill where the sweat lodge and the new medicine wheel was going to be.

There was a lot of laughter, and I believe there were even some of us who tumbled down the hill with the stones from time to time. Once we got them all down to the bottom of the hill, then we picked each one up and walked it over to the land I had blessed with the cornmeal and tobacco. Once all the stones were brought to the entrance, they were left there for me to place because I would be working with the medicine wheel. I had to use guidance from Spirit and listen to the stones as the ancestors they are to know what energy they would hold at which point on the medicine wheel.

It took me a good part of the day to create the wheel, to get the direction exactly right and to get each stone nestled exactly right into its place. When it was finished and complete, I could feel what had been created. I could feel the wheel connect not only with the earth below it but with the sky up above and all the trees around it and with the creek that was right there nearby. I could feel this wheel connect and become a living breathing entity all unto itself as it became as much a part of the woods as any animal or tree. It was an entity. A teacher.

The medicine wheel was one of the many blessings that came from being at Munay, and some extraordinary people showed up when I opened up this ceremony to others. The first time that Carolyn and Woody came to a ceremony, it was pitch dark out in the woods and the medicine wheel was lit by candle light, so I couldn't see people's faces well. That night Woody spoke about the moon and being connected to it. I had never really thought about that before; she gave me the gift of recognizing the moon as its own being, that it has an effect on me and on the earth. I felt great gratitude for Carolyn and Woody showing up and sharing their own thoughts.

After that Carolyn and Woody came to other medicine wheel ceremonies, and they soon became a part of the community at Munay. They started to volunteer and to help with all the wonderful things that were happening out there.

One day Carolyn asked if she could help with the fire. She said she felt more connected to the fire than with the medicine wheel, and so Carolyn and Jennifer became the fire keepers together. Jennifer and I shared our knowledge with Carolyn and she shared with us and we each became each other's teachers. What a beautiful time that was to be so open to learning, and to the newness of it all.

Once the medicine wheel was there, it called a whole different group of people to come to Munay. Many people worked with this medicine wheel on their own or in ceremony. People left offerings on different stones for the wheel and so it became an altar for the people. Everything that was ever placed there stayed there. Even after I left, it all went back to Mother Earth.

The People of Munay

Many people came and went. Some came to one or two ceremonies and others came to every single offering that was given at Munay.

We knew Jennifer from the Spiritual Living Center, and when we started doing sweat lodges, she was drawn to what we were doing and wanted to know more. She started to come out regularly and soon she told us that she had a deep connection with the fire and asked if she could be a fire keeper. She was the first person to step up in such a strong and giving way to work with the fire. Jennifer was quiet and unassuming and held her personality tightly in check until she got to know you. I came to realize that she wasn't shy. She just preferred to watch and pay attention to what was going on around her before she spoke. Many times when she did speak it was funny, and right on point. She had a wickedly witty sense of humor.

Working with Jennifer and seeing her relationship with the fire was powerful. She is the first person I ever heard call the fire 'grandmother', which I thought was quite unusual. I had heard other people talk about fire in different ways and that the fire was masculine and that fire could be destructive. But Jennifer saw the fire as a grandmother. I thought about it and it made sense, knowing Jennifer the way that I did and the intimate relationship she had with this fire. It was beautiful and perfect for her.

I was grateful for Jennifer. She felt strongly that the area out in the woods around the sweat lodge was her responsibility and she would show up early and take all the tools that she needed down the winding path that went from Munay, across the creek and up into the small clearing where the sweat lodge was. She worked so hard to make sure that all the people who came had a clear path and a clear way to get to the lodge.

Two other women came, Jamie and Alison. Alison showed up in such a strong way to help host and welcome people in. She helped to create a loving, welcoming, and nurturing environment. Alison was connected to what I would call the hearth and home. She not only welcomed people in and took charge of that but she also made sure that the food was prepared and put out in a good way. She was more than our hostess; we called her our kitchen angel. She took care of the kitchen, and she made sure people were nourished, not only through the food but also through her giving heart.

Jamie was also connected to the fire and felt strongly that she wanted to work with it, and so she joined Jennifer and Carolyn as a fire keeper. Jamie has a beautiful, big, boisterous, loving, laughing, personality. She is friendly and approachable and has open arms for everyone. It was a blessing to see Jamie begin to flourish and step into being a fire keeper, and to hold that responsibility, much in the same way as Jennifer did. The three of them formed a powerful team. There was deep strength in what they did and clarity in their connection to the fire, each of them as individuals and together as a team.

Having a strong team on the fire allowed me to be in the sweat lodge with Sam as she led the ceremony. Soon I began to lead lodges as well. At first it was just occasionally. When I poured water onto the stones and held the space for the ceremony, it was something I felt so deeply and I remembered it and it moved me.

Another person who started showing up to Munay was Bob, or Big Bob, as we called him. He was a giant of a man and strong as a tree. He was six foot seven. What a gentle giant this man was. He would crawl into our sweat lodge and offer the most beautiful prayers. He came and helped, along with many others, to clear the space around the lodge, rake up leaves, stack wood and build things. Whatever we needed, he was always ready to give a helping hand, and he always offered a joke or a smile.

Neece and her father, Arnie, showed up on their motor cycles to come to sweat lodges and they helped build two of the lodges. Arnie, having been a pilot and somewhat of an engineer, always seemed to have a better idea of how we could do things, but he was also good about holding his tongue and letting us figure it out for ourselves. He was quick to help us dig ditches and stack stones. Neece was always there. She was a tiny woman, but she packed a powerful punch. She would lift and tote and move and do and walk up and down the hill from the lodge to the house in a beautiful, purposeful way.

The community was coming together, and these core people held the space as much as Sam and I did; in fact, they were Munay. They would welcome any new people that came in. At any given time we could have between twenty and forty people present for a workshop or for a teaching.

However, as Munay grew and the community became stronger, my relationship with Sam became more strained. That personal connection we had felt so strongly in the beginning was dwindling and pulling apart. Our connection became more and more about the community, and less and less about each other.

I didn't really understand why things between us had become so difficult. I found that I was afraid to share with her about my own fears or frustrations. I was never quite sure how she would react. There were times when I felt loved and supported and other times when I felt completely misunderstood. But our commitment to the community and to the path was strong and so we stayed together.

Otter Woman Standing

Jeanne Robinson taught me how to do a shamanic journey. It's one of the most basic yet powerful ways that a medicine person can travel into the other realms and other dimensions of time and lifetimes to retrieve information from Spirit, from animal guides, from guardian angels and all these helpful sources.

This was not something that came easily to me. It was hard for me to put my analytical mind aside and just go into it, to allow it to happen because there is not a way to be in complete control. When we do a shamanic journey, we are both in control and not in control. I practiced and practiced and did it over and over again, and it took a long time. Learning to do this was similar to learning to play the piano in that pretty much anyone can sit down at a piano and play chopsticks and make music. There are people who will practice and practice and eventually play Beethoven. And some people fall somewhere in between and play beautiful music – maybe not Beethoven, but still beautiful. And some people just give up. They have the chopsticks experience and then no more.

It's the same way with learning to shamanic journey. It takes a lot of practice. Once you understand the technique, then you have to practice. You have to move beyond the level of playing chopsticks and move into the part that is richer and fuller.

I was stuck in playing chopsticks for a long time. I would do the shamanic journeys, and I would get little flashes of information, just little bits and pieces. I always questioned it, I would ask, "Did that really happen? Did I really see an animal? Or was that just something that I made up?"

I asked Jeanne once, "How do I know whether what I am seeing and what I am experiencing when I am on a shamanic journey is just my own imagination or if I am truly having this experience?"

She just grinned at me and said, "Truly, what is the difference? It all comes from Spirit." That wasn't the answer I was looking for, but it was the truth. Our imagination comes from Spirit, and in that imagining we can get information, messages and clarity from Spirit. And in the journeying, in meeting our spirit guides, in having those experiences we can get such profound clarity and such clear information about our worlds and our lives. So I guess Jeanne Robinson was right. What is the difference when the information that comes is useful and usually right and can bring clarity?

I decided not to question where it came from or to wonder whether it was me or God creating it. Instead, I just did it. After working with Jeanne for a while and practicing and doing this on my own, I began having some exciting experiences. Now, some people that I know would have the Cecil B. De Mille experience of journeying; they would come back and talk about a whole big movie scene that played out in front of them, and they would be able to recall a plethora of details. Well, not everybody gets to that place quickly and not everybody reaches that place at all.

I tried so hard to get it right and to follow all the "rules" until finally I remembered that Joseph had told me that to learn about my medicine belt I was to do a shamanic journey. When I didn't know what I was doing it came much easier. I finally let go of the rules and just let the Drum take me on the journey.

It took a long time before I experienced it on such a deep level. I didn't experience a shamanic journey as a movie, as seeing something in front of me. I experienced it in a different reality. I learned how to move into alternate realities. In a journey it is called non-ordinary reality. What I learned is that when I am there, it is my spirit that has travelled and my body stays where it is. It is as real to me as any experience in this world. I can touch it and I can taste it and I can feel it as if I were standing in the room or in the place or on the lakeside or next to the tree.

I learned to journey to gain clarity for myself, to gain information, and to get answers to questions about my own path, and I was able to do this for other people. I could go to non-ordinary places and meet their spirit guides or animal guides and gain information and bring it back for them. And while I may not have understood the information I was bringing back, it made perfect sense to them, and that was all that mattered. I was simply the messenger.

I did get into the habit of journeying for myself for my own information. There was a place in an alternate reality that I often went to that was on a prairie. There was a pond with trees on the far side of it and most of the time I would meet my totem animal, an otter. I would ask questions or for guidance about my path and where I was headed and gain insights on what I needed to know.

On one of those journeys I met up with my otter, who was, as usual, playful and fun-loving, and ran around and played around my feet as I walked through and around the prairie. I could feel the grasses of the prairie and I could see the wind blowing on them. As usual, I came to a beautiful pond with a few trees on the other side. While a few other animals had gathered around this pond, my otter was the most prominent.

I sat in the tall grasses near the edge of the pond while the otter ran around, jumped into the water and played. Otter usually sat and talked with me and gave me great wisdom. But on this particular journey, she didn't say anything to me. It was wonderful to watch her twisting and turning and floating on her back. She dove deep and came up with a shell. She ran up to me and played around me and then went back into the water.

I was just enjoying being there, feeling the playfulness and the joy of it all. I thought, 'Okay, this is the only information I

am going to get today. This is just about letting go and
enjoying life.' So I sat and watched the otter as she swam
around. She ducked around some more, and then she started
swimming towards me. The way she came out of the water
riveted my attention.

She walked slowly instead of running around as she had
been on this whole journey. She walked deliberately towards
me, never losing eye contact with me, and as she came up out
of the water and into the shallows she stood up on her hind
legs. As she did she grew and stood and turned into the most
beautiful woman. She had long flowing curly hair, and she
wore a white leather dress. All the while she never lost eye
contact with me. I could still see my otter in her eyes. As she
walked towards me, my journey came to an end, and I came
back to this reality.

When I was back, I thought about what I had seen and I
thought about the message and the clarity because so many
times in a journey the information and the messages are not
given in words. Sometimes they are given in scenes playing
out in front of us and sometimes the message is in which
animal shows up.

I thought about the playfulness and the enjoyment and the
beauty and the grace of this otter as she swam and played
and ran around. I thought about the intensity of the otter as
she shifted into the most beautiful graceful woman and the
intensity of her eyes and her eye contact with me. I still didn't
quite understand it all, but I felt like the message was that
there are times to be playful and times to be focused and
intense. I was okay with that much information.

A few weeks later, I was on another journey, once again
with a similar question about my path and where I was headed
and what I could expect. I found myself in that familiar place
on the prairie again, next to the pond. This time geese flew
over, and a little fox was hiding in the tall grass. Once again

otter was running around my legs and playing as I walked to the pond edge.

I sat next to the pond in tall grasses, watched the clouds, and soaked up the beautiful scene as otter playfully dove into the water and started swimming again. I realized I had seen this scene before. I recognized what was playing out in front of me. Otter was rolling, playing, and diving and then running out to me and back into the water. After a while otter slowly swam towards me, and again, as she came out of the water this time, she intently focused her eyes on mine. As she got just to the water's edge, she stood, and again she shifted into this beautiful woman, the same woman I had seen before in the same white dress. The woman took a few more steps toward me and reached out her hand to me. Right before our fingertips met, my journey ended once again.

I didn't understand why it had been cut short. I had almost gotten the information that I needed, the last key piece. And so I decided to journey again a few days later with the intention of getting the last piece of information. What was it that otter and this woman were trying to tell me? What was the message? I couldn't piece it all together.

So I went on another journey, and once again as I returned to my familiar place, otter greeted me eagerly. She played and danced around at my feet as I went to the pond. This time I knew to sit down and wait. Otter walked a few circles around me and then she dove into the water. She dove down into the bottom, and she swam, flipped over on her back, and played with a shell and a stone that she had. She swam around some more, and then I realized she was coming to me again.

I waited, and this time I asked, "Tell me! Tell me what it is that I need to know." She came up out of the water, again completely focused on my eyes, and once again she stood up and turned into a beautiful woman. I stood up quickly, never losing eye contact, and I stepped forward to meet her. She took a few steps towards me, and just as our fingertips touched, I felt a shock, a jolt, as if lightning shot through my whole body. Looking into my eyes, she said, quietly and clearly, "You are Otter Woman Standing."

What's in a Name?

Well, I have to be honest and say, I was totally and completely and confused by the whole thing. I mean... really, what kind of name was that? Otter Woman Standing, really? It just sounded so odd and it didn't really make much sense. I think it was the 'standing' part that threw me for a loop. I have heard all kinds of spirit names that people receive; usually they are beautiful and graceful and so descriptive. And what I was given was Otter Woman Standing!

I had heard these other wonderful, beautiful names. Joseph would even gift people with their spirit or medicine names. I was so tempted to write to him and ask him to give me a new name. I didn't want this one. I didn't know what it meant. I didn't really like it. Otter Woman Standing?

Part of the confusing thing to me was that the journey and the gift of it was so beautiful. The playfulness and the intensity. The woman standing up. It was so beautiful. The scene was incredible. But I didn't understand it. I certainly didn't feel that I could embody what I felt when that lightning went through me. I didn't feel worthy, and I didn't feel ready.

I knew better than to question the gift that I had been given and as much as I wanted to ask Joseph if he would give me a new medicine name I knew better. So I just let it go. I didn't tell anyone. I didn't speak of it. I just kept going. I kept doing my thing. I kept working, staying busy, creating, journeying, and learning. I certainly didn't ask anyone about it. I didn't ask Jeanne or Perry Robinson. It just seemed so odd. How could I ask? So, I just filed that away. I put it away as another experience, and I recognized that that is who I am. I didn't have to know what that meant, and I didn't have to know who I was. It was a gift that was given to me, and it was possible that it was meant just for me. So I held onto it and stayed quiet about it.

I chalked it up to another experience and hoped that one day I would understand what it meant to be Otter Woman Standing.

Recognizing and Remembering

Sam and I absolutely loved going to pow wows. It was a way to stay connected to what felt like the roots and core of what I was learning and understanding without taking that big step into the spiritual path. We would go to pow wows as often and as many times as we could. We would spend entire weekends at the pow wows, getting to know the dancers and connecting with them.

The pow wows are competition dancing. There's no formal way to learn these dances. The dances are taught from family member to family member in a tradition inherited through the generations. The pow wow dancing which happens in and of itself is a spiritual event. The regalia, the colors, the shawls, the feathers, and the fans are spectacular, and the athleticism displayed is awe-inspiring. They always had vendors who sold different craft-related items. And food, wonderful fry bread!

Once, at the Charlotte pow wow, we were walking around from vendor to vendor, which was one of my favorite things to do, and talking to the crafts people about what they did and how they did it. One vendor had books, and as I was thumbing through one of the books on Native American crafts, I opened up to a page somewhere in the middle. I was blown away when I saw a picture of a loom just like the one I had asked Sam to create for me when I made my medicine belt. I showed Sam the picture and she said, "Oh my God! How did you know that's what you needed to make your belt?"

I said I didn't know. I had no idea. I immediately bought that book so that I could take it home and read it. What I discovered was that what I had seen and what I had been given in the vision by my teacher was the old way of crafting a medicine belt, or a wampum belt, which were, and still are, a way of communicating personal and family history. These belts are sacred and may hold the teachings of the people.

I had no idea that what I had been given to create was something that already existed. I could not put words to the feeling that I had. It was like a question that I had – that I didn't know I had – was answered. It confirmed for me that what I did was real and made sense, and that it came from somewhere. I thought about what Joseph told me – that all I had to do was remember. Could this be what he was talking about? If I just followed what I felt, what I just somehow knew, was that the remembering he was talking about? That's what it felt like. How could Joseph know that I would hold memories like that? That I would know what to do? That I would remember how to make a medicine belt?

And yet he was right. I remembered.

I also found I had a knack for making what we call medicine tools, healing tools that different people use in different ways. Things like feather fans, necklaces, medicine bags, and chokers came easily to me, just like making the medicine belt had. I felt I had done it before, but I had never really worked with many of the materials, such as leather or certain kinds of beads, or especially raw hides for drum making. However, once I was taught to make my first hand drum, a frame drum – a drum that you hold in your hand and play with a drum stick – it was just so easy to keep making them.

I made drums and other items for other people who needed them. It felt like such a blessing to create them. There were times when I looked around in a ceremony and saw several drums or feather fans I had made and other things that I had given to people. It felt so rewarding.

I kept learning. Being a drum maker touched my heart in a way I could not explain. I could connect to not only myself and Spirit, but I could connect to other people through the drum.

Joseph taught us that there is healing in the vibration of sound that comes from drums and rattles. It also comes from our own voices, and our chanting can create healing not only for ourselves and for others but for the entire planet. The focused attention and the vibration of sound can bring about healing.

I began to hold workshops to teach people how to make their own drums, and at times we had gatherings of sometimes up to twelve or sixteen people making drums. It was beautiful and empowering to have people make their own drums to use on their own spiritual path, whether it was for healing work they were doing with others or just for themselves to play during their journeys, meditations and their connections into their spirits and spirit guides.

I learned that there is something deeply empowering about making your own drum and then to connect with it for the two weeks that it takes for the new drum to dry and cure and become its own being. Each drum has its own voice and speaks in a different way. There is no way to predict the sound that a drum will make. It was uplifting for me to be a part of such magic.

C'mon, Dog Soldier!

Sam and I started going to other ceremonies at places like the Center for Peace to learn more and expand our experience. We received an invitation to another ceremony that was to take place closer to home, at Watersong, in Graham, North Carolina, on the land and home of Cheryl and David Braswell.

The ceremony was called the For The One Dance. I thought the name was odd. It sounded kooky, but I had a strong feeling that it was something I had to be part of. You know that voice that speaks to you from deep inside you? That's what I felt. I knew it was something that I had to do.

I knew little about this ceremony except that, unlike the Long Dance, it was three days and that the visionary for this ceremony was Jeanne White Eagle and she, together with her husband, John Pehrson, had led this dance in many different places. I was curious to know what it would look and feel like. I had a huge expectation about meeting Jeanne and getting to know her and hearing about her vision first hand. What did it mean to have a vision, anyway?

Sam and I were invited to be dog soldiers which I understood to be some kind of helper, and I knew I could offer myself up to help and do whatever was asked of me. I did wonder why helpers would be called 'soldiers' in a peace dance. I was in a place of self-discovery with ceremonies. I was excited and scared at the same time. Would I say the right thing? Would I do the right thing? Would I cross a line that I shouldn't cross? How should I be? I had many fears leading up to the weekend. But I knew I had to be there.

When it was close to the time to leave, I thought about what I should pack. What would I need? I understood that it would involve keeping the fire going and a lot of physical work, so I packed work gloves. I had made a feather fan. I didn't know how to use it in this ceremony, but I was so proud of it and so I decided to take it with me. I knew that somehow I would need it and use it. I also packed tobacco, sage and cornmeal because these were things that I knew I would need for ceremony. We packed up the car with our tent and camping gear and drove the few hours to Watersong.

Driving down the little gravel road to Watersong was quite a treat. Little farms dotted either side of the road, and the North Carolina landscape was beautiful. As we rounded a corner, we came out of the woods into an open area. There was an inviting pond on the left side of the road. I saw a heron in it and thought that was a really good sign. Heron medicine is about self-reflection, and I seemed to be doing more and more of that.

We drove around the pond and saw the Peace Sound Chamber and just beyond it was the arbor. When we parked we went to look at the chamber and saw that it was constructed a little differently from the one at the Center for Peace, which was made of wood. This one had a beautiful mound of earth, probably from the excavation to build it, pushed back on one side so it was as if the earth was coming up and wrapping its arms around one side of the Chamber. It was made from stucco, and inside it had a concrete floor. It felt and looked different from the other one, but as soon as we stepped inside the chamber, I could feel that it was a place to hold Joseph's vision for creating peace for the world through chanting and singing. It felt familiar.

We later found out that all sound chambers are constructed out of different materials and built in unique and specific ways. They are all oval, never perfectly round. There is always a hole in the center of the floor that connects down to mother earth.

They are all partly underground, so some of them can be like kivas where they are completely buried in the ground and people go in through the roof and climb down into the chamber. Others are bermed into the side of a mountain, like the one at the Center for Peace.

The arbor was absolutely beautiful. When we got there, we were told, "There's some space over there for you to pitch your tent. Once you get your tent set up, go and see Candy Barbee. You'll find her over there. She's your Alpha Dog and she'll tell you everything you need to know."

I thought, 'Okay, Alpha Dog? What the heck is this? What are they talking about?' I was feeling a bit overwhelmed and out of place. I'm just not the type of person who will ask a lot of questions; I act like I know what I am doing until I fall on my ass, and then someone will come along and tell me what to do differently.

We unpacked the car, and a tall man with blonde hair and huge smiling blue eyes approached us and introduced himself as John Pehrson, Jeanne White Eagle's husband. He made us feel at ease.

"I have some news," said John, "Jeanne is in the hospital and she won't be here. She is okay. And she is disappointed that she won't meet the two of you, but she sends her love."

He didn't say much more than that, and although we were concerned about Jeanne we believed John's words that she was okay. That was the first time that we heard that someone besides Jeanne White Eagle would chief this dance, and it was the first time that Cheryl stepped up to chief a dance.

As we were setting up our camp, I noticed the woman setting up next to us. She was petite with long straight blonde hair half way down her back, wearing a beautiful ankle length skirt. She exuded a sense of strength and focus and she scared the bejeepers out of me. I kept watching her because I felt sure she knew exactly what she was doing.

She smudged where her tent was going be and then sprinkled tobacco and cornmeal around the area and I thought, 'Ohhh, I've already mucked this one up because we just pitched the tent.' She looked at the sun, and which direction was which way, and the door, and I thought, 'I am really in over my head. I don't even know how to set up my tent.'

I realized a ceremony of this magnitude was different from of all the workshops and events we had been to before. I knew this was a time to learn, but at the same time, I felt like I should already have known all these things. She came out of her tent carrying a beautiful drum and took it with her in the direction of the arbor. She walked with purpose, but it looked as though she was floating, with her skirt flowing around her and with shoulders back and her head perfectly straight. I thought, 'Okay, I got a long way, a really long way, to go.'

Once we had our tent set up, Sam and I headed over to find Candy Barbee. On the way there I wondered about her name and what an Alpha Dog was. I wondered what kind of craziness I had found myself in.

We went over to a group of people sitting together and introduced ourselves, saying that we were dog soldiers and we were supposed to find Candy Barbee. A huge lovable wonderful energy force of a woman jumped up and ran towards us. She was wearing a sweatshirt with long sleeves and a crazy hat that was like a beret with pins and feathers stuck on it. And she was wearing boots! I thought, 'It's ninety degrees out here and she's wearing long sleeves and boots?' She had the biggest smile on her face and dimples, and her hair was kind of tangled up in her hat. She gave us each a hug and it was the biggest momma bear hug I had ever had. She said, "I'm Candy! I'm so happy you're here. C'mon, and sit down with us."

Candy's smile and her energy and her welcome just overflowed with love and acceptance. She didn't care that we hadn't set our tent up right or that we had never done this before. She just sat us down and started talking to us about what it meant to be a dog soldier.

Candy began, "The term 'dog soldier' came from the Cheyenne people. The dog soldiers (they were sometimes referred to as the dog men) were the most elite of the warriors in the tribe who had earned their place to stay with the tribe to protect them, both when the other warriors were away as well as when they were at home. The dog soldiers lived just outside of the tribe. They hunted for the elderly who couldn't hunt. They fed the people who needed to be fed. They brought robes and skins to people when it was cold. The dog soldiers were the ones who cared for the people who were either not strong enough or did not have someone else of their own to help care for them. In the tribe no one wanted for anything. The dog soldiers did their job in such a way that didn't expect thanks or gratitude. There was nothing they wanted in return. It was a complete giving of their efforts and their energy to the tribe."

Candy described everything with such clarity and in such a beautiful way that even to this day, when I explain the role of dog soldiers to anyone I use the same words that Candy used that day. I understood what it meant and the things I'd read before coming to the Dance – about being a dog soldier, about making sure that everything outside of the dance arbor happened in a way that was proper and didn't disrupt the flow of the ceremony – fell into place. It started to make sense; dog soldiers are the guardians outside of the dance arbor.

She also told us that there were certain protocols to follow to help hold the sacred energy of the ceremony. Some had to do with how we should do things and others had to do with how we interacted with the dancers. Once the dance started, we were to be quiet around the arbor. She showed us which cornmeal lines we should not cross at all and which ones we could cross but that we should sweep them shut with a wave of a hand afterwards to reconnect the line that we had broken by passing over it. If we went into the arbor, we were to go in on the left side and walk around the perimeter, next to the poles. She said that this was to help hold the container of the dance.

"Don't speak to the dancers, and don't look them in the eye," Candy said. "If you do, you could take them out of their process. When they come out of the arbor to go to the sweat lodge or to the bathroom, they will have a white sheet covering them which is to protect them and keep them in their process. Don't touch them, but show them and guide them where to go. Make sure they don't fall or trip on anything."

Candy told us that the dog soldiers had the privilege of carrying dancers when they went into a place of surrender. She showed us how six or seven people work together to silently and loving to pick up and carry a dancer on their white sheets. I didn't fully understand what it meant when a dancer went 'down' or 'into surrender'. It was not something that happened in the long dance and there were no dog soldiers, so I was in completely foreign territory with this, but I paid attention to what she was saying.

While there was a sense of excitement from all the people around, at the same time there was deep love and concern for Jeanne White Eagle. I didn't know at the time that the situation with her health was grave and there was some question about whether or not her life would continue. We came together, and the crew and the dancers prayed for Jeanne and her healing.

What the dancers experienced during that weekend are not my stories to tell so I won't share any of those things. What I can tell you is what I experienced coming into the ceremonial space of the dance, and what I thought. I was feeling open and ready to step into the experience.

There was a sweat lodge for the crew and then another one for the dancers before the Dance actually began. It was an opportunity to set our intentions as the crew and for the dancers to begin their ceremony. After the crew finished our lodge, Sam and I were asked to stand outside the lodge for the dancers. It was very quiet outside the lodge and I could sense something shifting inside the lodge. I couldn't hear the actual prayers, only muffled voices. But somehow in that muffled sound I recognized a connection to these dancers, these people who came to dance for peace and for their own healing. It was like I understood what each one was experiencing and I knew there was such a strong connection to these people I had never met.

Once the lodge for the dancers was complete, The Chiefs intuitively placed each dancer in the Arbor where they would sleep, and rest in between dance rounds.

On Friday night, the sun was just setting, which in the summer was around eight o'clock. The chiefs signaled to the drummers to start drumming, and the dancers started moving in different ways to the center pole and back. Some danced, some walked, but they all went back and forth. I looked into the arbor and I thought, "This is bullshit. This is crazy. What are these people doing? And what am I doing standing here?"

I took a step back, and it was almost as if I had to distance myself from what I was witnessing. It wasn't making any sense to me. I don't know what I expected, but it was not what was happening in the arbor. Looking back on it, I believe it was fear that came up in me, but in that moment all I could think was 'bullshit.' Sam seemed to be engaged and okay with what was happening. I wondered whether maybe it was just me, so I took a deep breath, sat there and closed my eyes and listened to the drum and to the singing and chanting around me.

As much as I wanted to and as hard as I tried, I couldn't connect. It was as if my bullshit meter was in full roar. I didn't know what to do with it, so I kept saying to myself, "Just stay with it. Just be with it."

After about an hour, the dance chiefs called for the end of the dance for the day. The dancers all went back and settled into their sleeping spaces. Candy came with a list of things that we needed to do as dog soldiers and I was so grateful for that because I was able to get busy and get my mind off all the stuff I was feeling. I kept thinking, 'I don't belong here. I don't know what's going on here.' Even so, I also believed I could stay with it for now. I thought, 'I can do what Candy is asking me to do now. I can lower the tarps around the arbor to protect the dancers and she's asking us to bring extra blankets for dancers. These things I can do. And I did.

The crew went to dinner, and we gathered for our first meal together as those who were serving the dancers. We stood in a circle and held hands. The chiefs thanked us for being there and for doing our work and told us how we were off to a good start and that the dancers were ready and eager and willing. When I heard that, I thought, "This is just crazy!" but I decided I could stay with it just a little bit longer. I told myself that if I wanted to leave the next day, then I would leave.

We had dinner and went to bed. I was so grateful to be able to go and get into the tent, close it up and to be alone with my thoughts and with my fears and judgments because, boy, were the judgments coming up! Judgments about everything, like, 'You know there's Candy and she seems to be right on, and how can she be in the middle of all of all of this stuff. She seemed kind of normal to me. What is she doing here?'

I thought about the woman who was in the tent next to me, with her quiet resolve and dedication. I kept asking myself, "What is this? What am I feeling?" I couldn't get it, and I tossed and turned all night and then I had to get up at five a.m. to help with firewood. The dancers were going to have another sweat lodge in the morning, and it was my job to get up early to help with that.

The next day I got up and thought I could do the work that Candy asked me to do. I brought wood to help the fire keepers; I did what I needed to do to help the kitchen crew to prepare for breakfast. I watched the dancers as they woke and slowly started moving around in their sleeping spaces. Some put their sheets over their heads to change their clothes and others wrapped it around themselves to go to the bathroom. It was my job to escort them to the bathroom the way Candy had taught us the day before – without looking them in the eye, without speaking to them and without touching them, honoring their space but keeping them safe. I knew I could do that. I could make sure the dancers didn't trip or step in a hole. I was mindful and watchful.

One by one the dancers came out, and Sam and I escorted them to the bathroom and back. I felt my connection to the dancers begin to grow. It started to make a little bit of sense to me again, and I was grateful for that.

The rest of the crew slowly started showing up, and the drum team came. In daylight I could see them. I recognized the beautiful woman from the campsite next to us, the one who seemed so connected and so spiritual. Candy saw me watching her and leaned over and whispered in my ear "Her name is Teresa Hutson, she is the drum chief for this dance and she is also an amazing fire keeper."

'No wonder she is so focused and so connected and not distracted by any of these outside things that are pulling me over and over again,' I thought.

Once the dancers were in place and the drummers were ready, the dance began. The drummers started beating the drum, and the dancers began to move. I felt that sensation in the pit of my stomach again; it felt and looked crazy. I stood back and watched, disconnected. The dancers were so focused on what they were doing on their own individual path, their own movement, their own dance, and their connection to the tree at the center. I watched, and I watched, and I kept thinking, 'I don't understand this.'

I noticed that one of the dancers was looking at me. She made eye contact with me, and so I looked down immediately. I thought I had done something really wrong. When I looked back into the arbor, this dancer was continuing on her path, but she was still watching me with a little smile on her face. I found that I connected with her and I started watching her specifically. She was about five foot one or two, and she had beautiful long, white hair. I could tell that once her hair was a beautiful dark brown, probably almost black. I recognized she was Native American and that she was seeing something in me that I wasn't ready to see in myself.

She kept looking at me and smiling at me, and once in a while she would give me this little nod. She wore a long dress and I could see her feet sticking out with each step, kicking the front of her skirt as she took a step. As she danced I was drawn in and I found myself engaged more. By midday on Saturday, the second day of the dance, I found myself stepping forward more. This particular dancer had started focusing on her own dance. She wasn't looking at me anymore but I was pulled in. I suddenly started to feel what those dancers were going through when they went into the sweat lodge.

I could feel they were building something within themselves, within each other, and within the arbor. One of the dancers starting moving faster and faster, going back and forth, and then it became a run. Suddenly this dancer just collapsed in complete beauty onto the ground, in complete surrender to Creator, the vision, the dance, to Spirit, to all that was happening. As the dancer fell down, the chiefs gave the drum chief a signal, and the drums stopped. Then there was just a light boom-boom, boom-boom, like a heartbeat. I stood there, probably with my mouth hanging open, just frozen, watching.

I realized someone was poking me. It was Candy and she said, "C'mon, c'mon, dog soldier, it's time to move!"

I stood in line with the other dog soldiers with a sheet that was already folded the way that we had learned about so that when we unfolded it next to the dancer it would be easy to get them onto it to carry them back to their sleeping place. We waited for the signal from the moon mother who was working with the dancer that the time was right for us to step inside the arbor, into the beautiful energy that had built up into the thing they had been creating, which I had felt so disconnected from. Now I had to step into it and I had to fully engage with it. There was no way to avoid it.

Candy's teaching about what to do filled my mind. "Honor the dancer and their space. Don't speak to them. They may be in vision and be holding onto that moment. If you must touch a dancer for some reason, make your touch as light as a feather. Move the dancer lightly and gently roll them onto the sheet."

We bent down around the dancer and did what Candy had taught us to do, and working together we got the dancer ready to be carried. Each of us took an edge of the sheet and kept eye contact with each other so that we could all lift the dancer at the same time. In that moment I felt a connection to that dancer. I could feel the dancer's sense of release and relief in the moment of being lifted. I could feel the dancer just breathe into it. I realized the dancer had completely surrendered into the dance and into being carried. I realized that it was something that most of us don't do in our lives. We are so busy — busy doing and judging and stepping back — that we don't allow ourselves to be carried. This dancer had allowed that to happen.

We slowly carried the dancer back to the sleeping space and laid the dancer down with great care and then walked away. Our job was done in just those few moments. That is when I understood what it means to carry a dancer. I knew that dancer would be cared for after we left. We all walked in single file around the perimeter of the arbor, looking down and not looking at the dancers in other places. There was another dog soldier with sage waiting to smudge us, to clear and cleanse us, when we came out of the arbor.

I felt overwhelmed by what I had witnessed. It was beauty and perfection, and at the same time it was messy and real. It was as if the dancer had ripped through all of the bullshit and reached the other side of it, and stepped into alignment with Creator. I was able to witness that and be a little part of it. The chiefs gave a signal to the drum chief and she hit the drum once so that the dancers knew it was time to start again. They got up and stood, ready to dance, but the dancer that we had just taken to her place was still lying down in her space. The drum started again and the dancers started going back and forth again. Now I found myself wanting to step into the arbor instead of stepping back from it.

I looked up and the dancer who had made eye contact with me before was looking at me again. This time she had a beautiful smile on her face, and she was nodding, and I could hear her say, "Now you know." She hadn't moved her lips, but I heard her clearly. From that moment on, I knew this was where I needed to be and this would be a part of my life. I knew that I would do whatever I could to be a part of it, to contribute, to help with it, to just feel it. I knew that is what I needed to do.

Needless to say I didn't leave the dance as I had planned the night before. I stayed and I watched as one by one the dancers moved into their place of surrender, into that place of such perfection. It was chaotic, it was beautiful, and it was tear-jerking. It was joyful, it was angry, it was creative, and it was spontaneous.

It was a powerful weekend and a big lesson for me about community and what happens when community comes together. At this dance there were people from all over the world, including Israel, Jamaica, Germany and England, as well as many of the different states around the country. This community was much larger, broader, and more global than I ever thought and realized. These people who had never met before came together to do this healing work, and to remember that there is no separation – that we are all one, and that we dance for the one.

After the dance we had a feast to celebrate the ceremony and a short while later we gathered in the Sound Chamber for a time of sharing, a sacred time for all the crew and dancers to come together to integrate the experience. It was an opportunity for each of us, if we desired, to talk about our experience and what we learned and gained. We were waiting for the sharing to start, and I saw the dancer who spoke to me without using words coming towards me. She was beaming with the mischievous look of a child who was up to something.

She came up to me and said, "I saw you." I thought she was calling me out for making eye contact while she danced.

"Yes, I know. I'm so sorry, but I couldn't help but watch you," I said.

She smiled even bigger, took my hand, and said, "I am Sammye Jo, and I think we are going to be good friends!"

Decision to Dance

After the For The One Dance, I knew my life would never be the same. I knew I could never walk away from it. I was so deeply moved by what I saw, experienced, and felt. There was no denying it, and I was beginning to understand more of what Joseph said in that first meeting with him. It was starting to fall into place. Although it was incredibly scary, I decided to keep stepping forward.

Next, I went to the For The One Dance in Tennessee, and this time Sam danced. I went to that ceremony thinking I was going to be of service as a dog soldier again, but I soon realized that having my partner in the arbor shifted everything for me, and it was more emotional than I could ever have imagined. Watching her move through and let go of her issues and fears brought up my own insecurity.

What if she changed? What if she came out of the dance and no longer loved me or her whole life was different? I knew that it was selfish of me to focus on how it could impact my life. I could see that. But that was the reality of what I was feeling. I moved through my fear, doing the best that I could to support not only Sam but all of the dancers.

It was a great gift to be a part of that particular dance. Candy was the alpha dog again. I got to learn so much from her. Between all the work and tasks that needed to be done, we were able to spend some time together, and we had the opportunity to really talk and get to know each other. She was practical and down to earth, and even skeptical at times. She was not at all in that floaty head space that I thought people who did this kind of stuff were. She showed me that it was possible to do this spiritual work and still stay grounded.

It was at that dance that I knew that I had to dance; I had to put myself into the arbor and into the hands of Spirit. I had to be in a place where I could let go of all the fears that were coming up for me. I had to allow myself to let go of my issues and my fears. I had to let go of whatever it was that I was holding onto so that I could remember the truth of myself and of my being. I had to remember the truth that I am not separate from any other piece of creation – that I am not separate from God.

As I watched the dancers dance, I knew that I would step into the arbor as a dancer. I knew that as much as my life had changed up to this point, it was going to change even more.

Stress

Life felt a little crazy. I felt like I was living a double life, almost like a secret agent. I had my successful interior design business and for sixty hours a week I would wear the hat of the boss. I was the owner of a business, and I had employees that needed my help and advice. I had taxes and bills to pay and day-to-day decisions to make. Day in and day out.

At the end of the week, I went home to Munay, and there would be plans for a new ceremony or a new teacher to share more with the community. Jeanne White Eagle, who had recovered from her illness, and her husband, John, were among those who came to lead workshops. Sam and I led fire ceremonies, medicine circle ceremonies, and sweat lodges. We opened our doors to the people we were meeting through the For The One Dance. Then the weekend would be over, and I would put on my interior design hat again and go back to work.

I felt split in half. On the one hand, I had a magical, mystical, and powerful life immersed in ceremony and the traditions of the Red Path, and on the other hand I was focused on building my business, creating money and income and all the things that went along with interior design – the architecture and expensive furniture. I felt like I was being pulled in a million different directions. I wanted to learn so much, and yet I had so many obligations. There was not enough time and the more split my attention became, the more stressed I became. It showed up for me in physical ways.

I had struggled with my weight for years. It went up and down, and at that time it was at its worst. I realized that I dealt with stress by binging and eating in ways that were not good for me. I made choices that were not only not helping, but that led me down a path of self-destruction. Food somehow seemed to ease my stress and made me feel better, but it was always temporary. Soon after a binge eating session, I would feel the guilt and shame of my actions, and then the only way to ease that was to eat again. It became a vicious cycle of self-destruction. I did a great job of keeping this secret. Sam had no idea about my eating other than the fact that I was mysteriously gaining weight.

It was only when I was really unhealthy that I started to recognize it and knew I had to make some changes. If I was going to stick around on this planet, if I was going to stay alive, I had to make serious changes and alter the way I was treating my body. I had to get better rest, I had to take care of myself, and I had to eat better.

In the midst of all this strain and lack of time, my relationship with Sam continued to deteriorate. Keeping secrets about my eating made it easier to justify not talking to her about any of my feelings. I kept thinking there was no way she could understand the shame I felt, and if she knew, then she would be ashamed to be with me. It all just became too much. I became completely overwhelmed.

Despite the stress that I was experiencing, I could be fully present in a ceremony. I could focus fully on the energy of a fire for hours, but the minute the ceremony was over, all the stresses came back. All of the fear around my relationship and the concerns and worries about the business came back. Eventually I weighed two hundred and fifty pounds. I no longer recognized myself when I looked in the mirror. I no longer felt a connection to the person who was looking back at me.

My Dance

As I started preparing for my dance, I discovered it was much more than just making the decision to dance. I knew the decision would be life-altering, but I didn't really know how. From the moment when I decided to dance, people told me my life would change. How do I prepare for that? What should I do to prepare for that? I had no idea.

I tried meditating, but I had never been good at it. Sitting by myself in quiet contemplation was not something that came easily for me and so I just didn't do it. I did pray. I prayed a lot, but my prayers went something like, "Oh God, what have I gotten myself into?" I didn't know what I was praying for so I think I was probably just praying for mercy more than anything else.

My preparation was fear, worry, and concern for the unknown. I thought of how Sam had prepared for her dance, and all the prayers and deep spiritual work that she had done. She focused on what she would take into the arbor and the different items that would represent her and the emotional baggage that she wanted to clear. The only way I ever dealt with my fears and doubts was to plunge straight ahead. I dove in head first. I think people thought I was fearless because I did that, but the truth was, I just didn't ask for help.

When I looked forward to my dance, part of me thought, "Maybe I am doing this wrong. Maybe I should have been doing things differently." I used to be good at the 'should have' and 'could have' and I was particularly good at it when I was preparing to dance.

The truth is, at the time that I was trying to prepare for the dance, I was also busy at work, so I was a bit distracted. I was frustrated because I didn't get the time that I wanted to put into my spiritual practice and into the preparation that I wanted to do for the dance. I felt as though I was in a crazy limbo. I was sure that was exactly what would show up when I danced.

I went to Graham, North Carolina, to Watersong, where I had first been to the dance and met all these wonderful people: John Pehrson, Candy, Cheryl, and Sammye-Jo and so many others. I felt that I was going to be in good hands. Sam was going to be there to support me just as I had been there to support her. I was, at the same time, feeling both safe and completely petrified.

When we arrived at Watersong, we were welcomed by Jeanne White Eagle and John, who were the chiefs of the dance and I was so happy to see them. They would be the ones I turned to and they would hold me, protect me, take care of me, and mother and father me as I moved through the dance.

I settled in and met some of the others who would dance, including Alison who was our Munay kitchen angel. It was her first dance, too. It was wonderful and exciting to have a fellow sister in the arbor with me, and I didn't feel quite so alone. We laughed and joked, but I think the truth is she might have been just as afraid as I was to step into that arbor.

It was September, five years after 9/11, at the end of an incredibly hot summer, and we were in the middle of a heat wave. It was so hot that the county where Watersong was had put a ban on the burning of fires. Well, how were we to do a For The One ceremony – which involves fire – without fire? That in itself was interesting.

In the For The One Dance, there is a fire the in the east gate opening of the arbor where all of the energies move in and out and where everything is held. It also meant we couldn't have a sweat lodge because we couldn't have a fire to heat the stones. As all of these things had to shift and change, I watched in awe as Jeanne listened to Spirit and received guidance on how to hold everything sacred. She asked each dancer to find something sacred on the land. It could be a leaf or a stone – something from nature. She took all of the dancers to the pond near the arbor and asked us to go into the water one by one, to stand there and offer our prayers. We blew our prayers onto the sacred object that we had picked up, and then Jeanne blew her prayers onto it as well, and we released it into the water. After our prayers were released, we were dunked under the water.

I couldn't help but think how similar it was to the baptism I had in Park Road Baptist Church by Reverend Milford when I was twelve years old. I think that first baptism was as much for my parents and grandparents as it was for anyone because they wanted me to be accepted into the church. Just before I went underwater, Reverend Milford reminded me that I might want to squeeze my nose closed so that the water didn't go rushing up my nose. I did feel different afterwards, but I didn't really know why. I did know that what I had done and the commitment I had made to God in that community and in that community were pretty powerful.

This time I was in a pond, not in a formal baptism in the middle of a sanctuary. I was with this woman, Jeanne White Eagle, and both of our Cherokee heritages collided into each other that day. I felt so connected to her and John as they held me. Neither one of them reminded me to pinch my nose closed, and no water went up my nose! I was baptized in the waters of Spirit in such a different way. It was a purification ceremony. It was a releasing of those things that had been blocking me and holding me back. It was a letting go, a surrendering into this new life I was stepping into, and I felt it. I felt it so much more than the first time I had been baptized. This time I was being baptized by Mother Earth and by the waters of the mother. I was being cleansed and purified and being made ready for a most sacred ceremony. It was magical and beautiful and completely frightening all at the same time.

When I walked out of that pond with mud squishing between my toes and I started wiping my feet on the grass, I felt a connection to the earth like I had never felt before. I knew that I was part of the earth and from the earth and I knew this was my path and that when I put my feet on the earth it was precious and it was prayer and it was dancing.

I went into the arbor made new.

All of the dancers came into the arbor one by one; we found our places and settled in. I sat in my place and looked at the tree that was in the center. It was explained to me that the tree represented the source of all-that-is. It was a metaphor for God, for the Creator, for love. That tree could do anything. It could take anything. As far as I was concerned, it was God, the Creator. I felt the connection and I started to get anxious. I wanted to move my feet. I was ready to go.

Once the dancers were in and we had done the opening ceremony, acknowledging the directions, we were ready to dance. At last the drum began. The singing began. As a dancer I sang. I moved my feet on the earth and I sang. I moved on my path, straight to the tree and turned around and went straight back to my place and turned around and went straight back to the tree and turned around and went straight back to my place.

After having done that only about three times, I could clearly see my path in the grass. I could see where I had placed my feet. I could see that I was creating my path. Jeanne told me that I would dance my own path in the arbor. It was beautiful. It happened so quickly. Every time I approached the tree, I reached out and touched it, sometimes with just one finger, and sometimes with two or three fingers. I did this over and over and I sang my heart song – no words, just my own spontaneous song that came from way down deep in my heart. I felt something start to shift in me, something physical started to move inside me. The more I danced the more I felt it.

We danced into the night on Friday, and then we were given time to rest and to sleep. Early the next morning we were awakened by the sound of a flute. I could hear it as I drifted in and out of sleep; it was like the sweet songs of angels. I looked up. John was walking through the arbor, playing his flute. It was the most incredible way to wake up.

After singing the morning song to greet the sun, we prepared to dance some more. We still could not have a sweat lodge because we could not have fires, and so the drums began again. We moved and danced; each dancer danced their own path, back and forth to the tree. Some people danced, and some ran and some skipped. I trudged. I trudged and trudged and trudged; it felt like I was in muck. The woman dancing next to me was on her toes like a fairy and I wanted to be on my toes, too. All I could do was trudge. I felt more like a troll. The more I trudged the more I felt something come up in me; something inside me was rising up. It was something that needed to be released. It felt angry, powerful, strong and ugly.

I found myself moving faster and faster, running, back and forth and back and forth, and instead of touching the tree with my fingers, I pounded my hand on the tree. I felt that if I pushed that tree hard enough I might even be able to push it over and get this ugly thing out of me, whatever it was. I moved and ran and danced, and I kept pounding the tree. Just as I felt this thing come up and I felt I was on the verge of release, the drum stopped. We were told to return to our places. Oh, I couldn't believe the drum stopped, and I couldn't believe that I had to stop.

I went back to my place and sat down on the ground, my legs sticking straight out onto the path in front of me, shaking and moving and pounding on the ground. I kept moving my legs because I had to get it out.

One of the moon mothers came over to me and I said to her, "I need to get up and go to the tree." She told me to wait just a minute, and she went to speak to the chiefs. As I watched her go, that old thing in me showed up, that old feeling of shame, the feeling that I had asked for something too much and that I wasn't worthy of what I was asking. I felt that I was asking them to break protocol, to do something different and special for me.

I thought, "Who am I to ask for something special?" And so I swallowed hard. I swallowed down whatever that ugly thing was that had been coming up. I forced it back down into my belly and my legs stopped shaking. I took a few more deep breaths.

The moon mother came back over to me and she said, "If you can wait just a few more minutes, we'll start dancing again."

I said, "Sure, I can wait." I sat quietly, not breaking the rules, not asking for anything special. I sat with that thing in my belly. I looked around at the other dancers and at the moon mothers and the sun father who were working with us in the arbor. All I could think was, who was I to ask for something special, to ask to go to that tree? I took a few more deep breaths, and once again I decided that to be strong meant to not ask for help and that I needed to be stronger than this.

Jeanne and John stepped back into the east gate and asked the drummers to give us the signal to stand, and I did. And then the drum started and I started walking on my path towards the tree. I felt so tired, exhausted, defeated. And I felt angry.

I walked to the tree and I touched it with one finger, then I turned around and I walked back to my space, and I turned around and I walked back to the tree and I touched it with one finger. I danced that way for the rest of the day. Nothing else ever came up. The only thing that stayed with me was my anger and resentment.

I was angry that I had asked for something special and that I had been turned down. I was angry that I had to stay in that dance arbor. I was angry that I didn't just rush out of there and leave – get in my car and go home. I was angry that my dance had been ruined. I was angry that I wasn't understood. I was angry that nobody listened. I was angry that nobody saw what I was going through. I was just angry.

I kept dancing. I kept dancing just to prove that I could do it, that I was tough and that I could stay in there. That I was strong and that I didn't need to cry and that I didn't need to release whatever that thing was that was trying to get out. In the midst of all my anger and confusion, there were some other things going on, and if I couldn't look back and laugh a little bit at the whole experience, I don't think I would have been able to keep doing this.

We were dancing in a heat wave. It was a hundred and three degrees, and we couldn't have a fire. Things that usually happen in a dance that needed a fire had to be done in different ways, like burning sage. The smoke from sage is an ancient way to clear away negativity and heaviness. Some people refer to this as smudging. Usually hot coals from a fire are placed in the bottom of a tin bucket and then sage is placed on top of the hot coals, which ignites the sage and smoke comes out.

The crew had to figure out how to use sage on a regular basis. Every time someone came in or out of the arbor, they needed to be smudged by having the sage smoke wash all over their body. The fire ban was against open fires, but not against barbecue grills and so the best idea they could come up with was to set up a barbecue grill to have ready coals to use for the smudge buckets. They set up a bright red barbecue grill with a domed top just outside the arbor. It looked like a large red egg. It was right next to the place where I was in the arbor, and I could see it clearly.

You would think that wouldn't really be a big deal and that nobody would think anything of that, except that as a dancer I was going without food and water for three days. Seeing that barbecue with coals in it, I was like one of Pavlov's dogs. I spent that entire dance thinking that steak was going to be delivered to my space at any moment and that there was going to be arbor service, like room service. It was just insane. It was pure torture to look out from where I sat and see that barbecue grill smoking. Every time they went in and lifted the lid to get out a piece of charcoal to put into the bucket for the sage, I thought I smelled a rib eye cooking.

The other thing that was going on had to do with my white sheet. Each dancer had one and it served many purposes. It was a cloak of protection wrapped around the dancer when they left the arbor to go to the rest room, which would be the only reason for a dancer to leave the arbor in that dance. Each space in the arbor is open to the rest of the arbor. Everyone can see everyone else. There is no privacy. When someone needs privacy, like when they are going to change their clothes, they sit on their mattress and pull the white sheet over their heads like a tent. Inside the tent they have the privacy to get changed.

For most people this was an easy feat to accomplish, but not for me. I had gained so much weight and it was 103°F, and so the moment I put the sheet over my head it became a sauna. There was no bathing or getting clean in the dance, and it was so hot, the sheet just stuck to me. It stuck to my sweaty face and my sweaty arms. It felt so bad and so nasty, and I was so uncomfortable. I tried to figure out a different way to use my sheet and how to dress with my sheet, but it became a point of frustration for me.

As I looked out across the arbor at the other dancers, I saw that the dancer opposite me had a chair she could sit on. I think it was one of those chairs called an anti-gravity chair, one that kicks your feet back in the air when you sit back in it. For some crazy reason I thought I was supposed go into the arbor with some level of suffering, so I barely had a mat to sleep on and apart from a blanket and a pillow, I had no other creature comforts.

When I tried to sleep on Saturday night, all I could think about was how uncomfortable it was to change clothes underneath that sheet. And dammit, that dancer had a chair! I was so frustrated. Why did she get a chair and I didn't get a chair? How was I supposed to change my clothes under the smelly, nasty sheet?

First of all, I was going get a chair like that dancer across from me. She had her chair, and she was so comfortable and so special. I was going to have me a chair. So, I was happy with that. I lay in the arbor on Saturday night thinking, conniving and planning how I was going to solve these problems. It came to me that if I had three clothes pins I could fashion a changing room for myself using my sheet. I could do that because there was string strung from pole to pole, and I could take that and, using the sheet hanging on the string from the dancer next to me, together with my string and my sheet and the three clothes pins, I could make a changing room. I had spent the whole night designing the blue print for my sheet changing room. All I needed was the clothes pins.

I saw Jason walked by the outside of the arbor. He was a burly, mountain of a man. I yelled to him, "Psst, psst, Jason, Jason, come here."

Now, of course, the dog soldiers are not supposed to be talking to the dancers, especially from outside the arbor. I called him over anyway. He walked up to me, and he wouldn't look at me. He just stood there, looking down, without saying a word.

I said, "Jason, I need three clothes pins and a chair."

He stood there for a minute, and another minute, and then he nodded and he walked away. He never spoke to me, and he never looked me in the eye. But I was so happy because I was going to get three clothes pins and a chair.

The next morning Jason came into the arbor and he came over to me. He leaned over and asked, "Did you ask me for three hair pins?"

"No, no, no. I need clothes pins. I need three clothes pins and a chair!" I said.

"Got it."

Within two minutes, miraculously, there appeared three clothes pins and a chair. They were left there for me to do with as I wished. I stood on the chair and created my changing room using the three clothes pins. I felt quite proud of myself, and I was thrilled with my little set up.

In fact, I couldn't understand why this had not been done before and why none of the other dancers didn't also get three clothes pins so that they could make their own changing room so that none of us had to sit under those stupid, blasted hot-as-hell sheets trying to get out of a sticky, icky, sweaty t-shirt. I went into my changing room to change out of my clothes, feeling like the Queen of the Dance. I had built myself a small Taj Mahal changing room that was only about three feet by three feet, but it was perfect.

I was busy changing my clothes just as the dog solders came around the back of the arbor to raise the extra sheet that was being used as a tarp – because it was day time and it was supposed to be up during the day. There I was, in all my glory, now in my three-sided changing room, exposing myself to all of the dog soldiers and all of the crew that could see into the arbor from the outside. I was a little embarrassed but I thought, "You know what? Everyone has seen an ass at one time or another. Now they've seen mine and so now we can just get on with it."

I was so proud of the chair next to me and I was so happy to have it. I leaned on the chair. I put my elbow on the chair. I did everything except sit on it. I sat on the ground and never once put my butt on that chair.

On Sunday morning when Jeanne and John called all the dancers into the center of the arbor to gather around the tree, I was still angry but calm and I knew it was almost over. They told us that we had danced our dance and that it was beautiful and powerful. I thought, "Well, I didn't really dance. I didn't really do anything, but I am here."

They told us that the next time the drum started we were to dance our joy. I thought, 'I can do that. I can dance my joy. I can be joyful.' We went back to our own places.

As I stood waiting, Candy, who was one of the moon mothers in this dance, came and stood on one side of me and Tracey came and stood on the other side. They stood there as if to protect and take care of me, as if to hold me, and I thought, 'I don't need anybody to take care of me. I can do this by myself.'

Candy looked at me and leaned down and she said, "Do you want to go to the tree?"

All of that anger, all that I had been dancing, came out. I looked at Candy and I said, "I am not going to the tree with you. Jeanne told me to dance my joy and goddammit, I am going to dance my joy. So leave me alone."

I could tell by the look on Candy's face that I had scared the bejeebers out of her. She stepped back. Tracey stepped back. Then Candy said, "Oh, okay then, you need to dance your joy."

When the drum started, I began dancing, or rather I began trudging back and forth to that tree like the troll that I felt I was. I trudged and trudged and trudged, and try as I might, I could not bring up my joy. I stayed in my disappointment and a place of anger.

I did my best and made it to the end of my dance. I went three days without food and water, dancing back and forth and my path was worn so much that there was no more grass and I could see the earth. It had been a hundred and three degrees for three days and I danced. By the time Sunday morning arrived and after all that I had been through, all the anger and issues that had come up for me, when Candy asked me if I wanted to go to the tree, the answer was, "Oh hell no! I will be dancing my joy!"

The Beast Within

Something did change for me after I danced. I looked at my dance, my first dance, and about how difficult it was. I thought about that thing that came up in me and how easily I choked it back down, how I swallowed it back down. What did that say about my life? What did that say about how I functioned and operated in the world? That dance, as angry and upset as I was, told me everything, from being able to laugh about the clothes pins and exposing my ass to the physical torment that I felt in not being able to let go of my anger and not being able to let of my fear. I recognized that the thing that came up was fear and anger, and I choked and swallowed it back down.

I was able to start seeing other places in my life where I was doing that. I saw it at work in my reaction to something that happened. I looked at how I reacted to it and how I handled myself. Was I able to hold my own? Was I able to stand my ground? Was I able to stand up for my client or stand up for what I knew was right in any given situation? Or were there times when I choked it back down and when I didn't say anything or let out what needed to come out? I started seeing it coming up in my life more and more, and I started to see it come up in my life with Sam.

I started to see it in times when I needed to talk to her. I saw situations that I knew I should not let pass but I did. I knew I should say what I was feeling and thinking but something made me swallow it back down. I was afraid of being misunderstood, afraid of not being special enough. It was all of those fears that came up for me in the dance. I could see how it was coming up for me, and I could see how it was playing out in my life. I didn't like it, but I didn't know what to do about it.

I've always said that once you know something, you can't unknow it. Well, I knew something now. I knew something about myself that I didn't know before. I knew something about the world that I didn't know before. I knew that it was possible in the world to heal. I knew it was possible because I saw it in other dancers. I saw it with crew members. I saw it with those that showed up. I knew it and I couldn't unknow it.

There was no way for me to walk away from my spiritual life because I knew something now. There was no way for me to walk away from my own feelings, my own fears, my own anger, my own past experiences because now I knew what it was. I had faced it. It felt like a beast coming up from my belly. I knew it was there and I couldn't unknow it.

I walked around every day knowing I had that fear and anger in me. I didn't know what to do about it. Most days it just lay dormant. Most days it just lay still. Most days it was just fine. Most days I could swallow it back down enough to be okay. Most days what helped me swallow it back down was food. It helped me to hold it down, to keep it down. And so I spent a lot of time eating. I could go through my life just fine. I could go through any situation as long as I could go eat something afterwards. As long as I could do what I had to do to go calm that beast in my belly. And I did.

I continued to grow my business to create income, and I continued to thrive in my spiritual path. One important thing that happened was that I stopped hiding from who I was. I realized this when I made my medicine bag.

One day after the dance, I brought out an otter pelt that Sam had found for me at a pow wow. As I held it, I felt the connection to Otter Medicine. I kept petting it and folding it and soon I had fashioned it into a large traditional medicine bag. I stitched it up by hand and carefully placed the face of the otter on the front of the bag and the tail dangled beautifully down the back. I found some leather and quickly created a strap so I could wear the bag in the traditional way over my shoulder. I was so happy with it but as I held it I realized that something was missing.

Then I went into my drawer and pulled out my Medicine Belt. It was time. I took the belt and carefully placed it on the bag. It already felt connected. I then delicately stitched it onto the bag running from the front, down and underneath and around to the back to the top. It was a perfect fit! Now I had a sacred place to keep my cornmeal, tobacco, sage, sweetgrass and any other herbs and tools I needed for my spiritual practices.

But even with these changes, inside of me there was something missing. Or, more to the point, there was still something eating away at me from the inside. I knew it was there. I couldn't not know it now. I couldn't unknow it. In a way that dance was a gift to me. As uncomfortable as it was, as miserable and horrible as it was, it was one of my biggest spiritual awakenings, because I had to face the beast that was within me.

Playing Small

Once Munay started growing into a spiritual center, it seemed to me the relationship between me and Sam and the way we interacted with each other started shifting. It was subtle and it happened slowly, so I couldn't really put my finger on it. I realized, over a year or so, that I was stepping back and holding back in the spiritual aspects of the work that we were doing. I did that because I had a sense that it was important to Sam that she remain in the place of being the teacher in our relationship, and the one who shared things with me.

Sam and I never talked about our positions at Munay but in the beginning it was an unspoken agreement that she took the lead with many of the things we did. Although we didn't really have positions, our personal life seemed to go better if I remained more in the background.

It seemed easier for me to remain smaller and be the student. Somehow I equated making my life easier with not stepping up too much, not having people recognize me as someone who had something to offer, and not being strong in a spiritual aspect. If I remained the one who was supporting her, and if I was pretty much the side kick, then it seemed like our relationship, and how we related to each other, was smoother.

When I wanted to step up in a bigger way, I felt resentment towards Sam coming up in me. It was difficult for me to figure out how to step into a stronger place in my spiritual practices for the people of the community and not to hurt Sam in the process. I didn't really understand that dynamic. Those were conscious or unconscious choices that I made at that time that kept things easier for a while, but inside me there were unspoken resentments building up. I don't know if she felt it or if she had the same fears and resentments or other emotional responses towards me because we didn't speak about it.

I began to feel like I was holding myself back and over time I started to feel that Sam was holding me back.

Five Weeks in Africa

In the year that I had known Jeanne White Eagle, I had heard her talk about going to South Africa and all of the exciting things that go on there. The minute she told me she was going to South Africa in 2007, I knew I had to go, too. There was something in me, something in my gut, that said, "Get yourself to Africa."

Jeanne said they were planning a five week trip to South Africa and there would be four dances, back-to-back, in three different locations. It would start with a ten-day crew training gathering at Simunye Ngothando, a new dance site in Johannesburg, followed by a dance at Rustlers Valley in the Free State, and then two dances at Blue Hippo, another new dance site near Cape Town. She said there would be a lot of different people coming from many different countries.

I listened and I planned. Luckily I was in a position where I was earning enough money so it was not a big deal. I just bought my ticket. Sam originally said that she would not go. She felt the five weeks away would be too long. She believed that with all the events that were going to happen it would be a lot to organize and she did not feel particularly drawn to go. She felt it would be more important for her to stay home.

I knew I had to go, and honestly a part of me was relieved that Sam didn't want to go. For the first time in the six or seven years of my spiritual exploration – and since I met Joseph – I would venture out on my own, spiritually. Sam had always been there to guide me, to lead me, to back me up, and to explain things to me. Going to Africa on my own felt huge. This was going to be my experience and not a shared experience.

Dancing Through
Fire

That was the truth of it. I wanted to go, and I wanted to go without Sam. That's why I didn't try to persuade her otherwise when she said she didn't want to go. I didn't try to convince her to come with me. It is possible that this was hurtful to her.

I carried on making my plans. I had my ticket and I started connecting with some of the other people who were also going to Africa. I was becoming friends with some of the other people whom I had met at other ceremonies, and I sent emails to some of them. I felt they had so much to share with me and teach me. It felt like a whole new world was opening up for me.

I had to decide what to pack, just like going to any other ceremony. The difference was I was traveling six thousand miles, across the equator into the southern hemisphere and onto another continent. I had to make sure that I took everything that I needed with me. How would I know what I would need? There were going to be four dances in five weeks. That, in itself, was crazy!

Jeanne had anticipated that some people would come to one dance and then go home, and then others come for another dance, and go home. She didn't think that anyone would come from beginning to end. But I did. I bought my ticket and I was going to be there for the whole five weeks. I was not going to go for one dance and one week and then go home. I thought if I was going to Africa then by God, I was going to A-f-r-i-c-a, and I was going to stay my ass there for the whole time.

What surprised Jeanne was that there were a lot of us who felt that way. We became a traveling caravan of people from all over the world. We had people from Norway, England, Israel, Germany, Ireland, the U.S. as well as South Africans. We were like our own little traveling international community. There must have been about fifty of us altogether, sometimes more and sometimes less.

I didn't know what I should take with me. Should I pack my feather fan? I knew I should take a skirt, but should I take blue jeans? A dance shawl? What about clothes to wear if we went out for dinner? The list went on. Since there was no way to plan for it, I decided to take everything I could think of!

About ten days before I was due to leave and I was almost ready and packed, Sam changed her mind and decided that she wanted to go, too. I had a bittersweet feeling about her going with me. On the one hand, I was happy about it. Having Sam with me gave me some security and familiarity. On the other hand, I was disappointed because I really wanted an experience that was just mine. I knew she sensed that, and yet she still decided to go.

New Friends in Africa

Jeanne White Eagle told me she wanted me to meet a good friend of hers when we were in South Africa. She said, "You are going to love Susie. She is gentle and sweet and a healer and she is part of this dance. Susie will help you to understand and to know Africa."

Our first stop in South Africa was at the home of Fritz and Elba Duminy where we were to have the crew gathering and training and then the first of the four dances. People were arriving and our numbers swelled rapidly. Susie was one of the first people that I met. Jeanne was right. I immediately felt that she was a friend. Her eyes smiled. She didn't have to say anything or do anything. Her eyes were always smiling. I don't mean she had a little smile on her face which comes through in her eyes. Her eyes were full of smiles and laughter. It didn't matter what she was doing, whether she was taking me on a tour of the land or showing me where I would sleep, or fixing a meal or introducing me to other people, her eyes were always smiling.

It was so easy to be with her. It was the first time that I felt that I had known somebody before. Of course that was not possible, because Susie had spent all her life in Africa. She grew up in Zimbabwe and came to South Africa as a teenager and she had never been to America. How could I have known her before? There is no way I could have met her before, yet I had this crazy *deja vu* feeling that I knew her.

I felt so comfortable with her. We were about the same age and had a lot of similar life experiences, believe it or not, even though we came from such different places. The connection was immediate. I felt like I had found a sister. A true soul sister. I think that might be the first time I used that phrase.

I was absolutely thrilled with this new friend, who introduced me to so many people. And Jeanne was right: she was a healer. On the second day that I was there, she offered to do some healing work with me. She told me things that I didn't know about myself, and some things that I did know about myself. She moved the energy in and around and through my body. I had not experienced that, not in such a big way. I had experienced it a little bit. Even in a massage you can feel when energy is moving and something is shifting in your body. But this was different.

She didn't do it by massaging and kneading my muscles. She was doing it by barely touching me. Sometimes she wasn't touching me at all. Sometimes she was doing it by asking me questions. It was really powerful.

Susie introduced me to Afrikaans, which was her home language. I didn't know what Afrikaans was. She told me that the Afrikaners are descendants of the Dutch settlers who went to Africa. Like the pioneers in the United States, the Dutch settlers crossed the country and encountered a lot of dangers. Let's face it. If someone was going to be a pioneer in Africa and they were going to meet up with lions, elephants, and rhinos, they had better be prepared. So these Afrikaners, the Dutch pioneers who settled in South Africa, were pretty dang tough.

"It is the newest language on the planet," Susie told me, "It is a mixture of Dutch, some German, and it even has some words with English roots in them." I found it to be a beautiful language, and Susie took great delight in teaching me phrases and words that I could never quite say and then asking me to repeat them to other South Africans. It became a big game with us. Even many years later, we still play this game. It is one of the things I enjoy about going to South Africa, to get a new phrase, or be retaught an old phrase because I butchered it. It is so much fun learning words from another language and to parrot some of the phrases.

Meet the Gogos

I met Gogo Mzinyathi and Gogo Nomsimane soon after arriving in South Africa. The gogos, as they are lovingly called by so many people, are sangomas, which means healers. I understand that "gogo" means grandmother, a term of respect, in Zulu. Even the men are referred to as gogo. When a sangoma is initiated as a healer, they take on their gogo name, which usually comes from their father's father. So, if I was to become a gogo I would be called Gogo Edward, because my father's father was called Edward. This follows the belief system that someone is usually called into this healing work by an ancestor and generally the ancestor is the sangoma's father's father. Sometimes the ancestor is maternal and the gogo name would be female. In this way many women carry the names of men, and sometimes men carry the names of women.

I had heard so much about Gogo Nomsimane and Gogo Mzinyathi from many people, and I was excited to meet these two women. I had built up an image in my head of two strong and powerful, all-knowing and all-loving healers. I thought I was going to meet female versions of Ghandi. I didn't know what I should do when I meet them. Should I bow? Should I curtsy? I was a little nervous about it.

We heard the gogos were arriving, and so people came rushing out of their rooms and started clapping, and I thought, 'Wow, okay! This is huge! This is great! Yay, the gogos are arriving!' The clapping was not like applause. Instead people were clapping a double clap – one two, one two, one two. I thought if everyone else was doing it, I would do it, too, and so I also started clapping.

Dancing Through Fire

I think I expected the gogos to come riding up on blazing chariots or something. Instead they pulled up in a little beat up four-door sedan that was actually being driven by my friend Jill from Tennessee who had been in South Africa for a few weeks already studying the Sangoma traditions with the Gogos. Jill drove across the field and parked in front of us. Suddenly it was like the clown car. People piled out of the car while everyone else was still clapping, clap-clap, clap-clap, clap-clap. Jill got out of the car, laughing and full of life.

Finally, two beautiful women got out of the car. One was short, perhaps five feet two and she looked like a grandmother. She seemed shy, and she didn't look anyone in the eye much. There was such a child like quality to her. She just looked to the side the way I imagined Mother Teresa would do.

The other woman was huge and fabulous. She was about five feet ten or even taller. She was big and round and gorgeous. She reminded me of the statue of Venus. She was full of life, and she charged full on to people and hugged them and loved them. The other smaller one was behind her, and she also hugged people.

'Wow!' I thought, 'This is not what I expected.' Except for the clapping, which continued, they could have been people in America. I didn't expect to see two black women getting out of an ordinary four-door sedan, just hugging people.

There was a crowd of about twenty people around the gogos. It was a big welcoming – boisterous and noisy and a lot of fun. The longer I stood there, the more I realized that I felt their presence. I found myself backing up more and more, and I didn't know why. I backed out of the circle.

Eventually things calmed down, and the larger woman came up to me. Jill, my friend, from Tennessee was with her. Jill said, "Gogo Nomsimane, I want you to meet my friend Robbie." Gogo Nomsimane took my hands in hers and squeezed them and pulled me close to her. There couldn't have been more than three inches between our foreheads. She looked me right in the eye.

All of a sudden I couldn't hear the clapping anymore. I was so fully present with her, looking in her big, beautiful brown eyes. Her eyes were so full of love and so full of joy. She looked right into me and said, in this big beautiful booming voice, "God is great to let us meet today."

She put her head to my head, and she hugged me so hard I thought she was going to squeeze me out like a little sausage. She swung me around as she ululated, and I felt the power and beauty of really being seen. What an amazing three seconds.

Then Jill introduced me to Gogo Mzinyathi, and the smaller of the two women stepped up close to me and took my hands in hers and smiled shyly. She looked at me in a different way. She looked at me in a way that made me realize she knew who I was. In those few seconds that it took for her to look into my eyes, I felt that she knew all my secrets and everything that was deep inside me and that she knew me. She just smiled, and I smiled. Then she hugged me, and that was it. They went on to be introduced to the next person.

Wow! It was breathtaking. I could feel their connection to spirit, and I could feel it through them. What I realized in that moment is that I really can live in complete open connection to Spirit. It is not something to simply just talk about or only do when the time is right. It is not just when I am in ceremony or in church or when I have to put on that face or that façade. What they showed me is that Spirit can move through me all the time and that Creator is always there. Always.

Of the Moon and Earth

We held a tree cutting ceremony before the dance began. We went into the woods and asked a tree to give itself to the dance. Those of us who were gathered took down the tree and blessed it with corn meal and tobacco and tied red strips of cloth around it to honor its sacrifice. Then we took the tree back to the dance arbor to place it in the center.

As we prepared to take the tree in to the center of the arbor, Jeanne White Eagle asked that we each take a strand of our hair and, as we entered the arbor, place the strand of hair into the vessel of water at the entrance of the arbor. One by one we stepped to the vessel of water and placed our DNA there so that the energies of the water, the land, and the tree would recognize us. Gogo Hugh was on his knees by the vessel of water adding flowers and singing as we each stepped forward. When I reached the vessel, I leaned over and plucked a strand of hair from my head. As I placed my hand over the water, Gogo Hugh jumped to his feet and stumbled backward a few steps. He took a deep breath and said "Ah! Greetings, Earth Mother!"

Later I asked Gogo Hugh what had happened at the ceremony and he explained "The water recognized you and wanted to greet you!"

"I don't understand," I said.

"It was a powerful feeling, and it caused me to lose my breath. I needed to step back from the energy. You are an Earth Mother," he said.

In a dance the moon mother embodies unconditional love for the dancers as they move through their process, whatever they are healing. As in many indigenous cultures, for us the moon carries the feminine energy. The moon is that gentle loving energy that encompasses all of the feminine qualities. It is that nurturing and unconditional love that takes care of all of us. The moon is the grandmother that watches over us.

At the first dance in Africa I was asked to be a moon mother. Now I was really confused because Gogo Hugh had just called me Earth Mother.

I had only danced one dance at that point, and the responsibility felt huge. How was I supposed to know what a dancer would need? I thought about what I needed and about the things that came up for me and how I felt in my dance.

I thought, 'I'm going to do it. The people here believe in me. They have asked me to step up and do this and to hold unconditional love for the dancers.' Of course I would do it. It never crossed my mind not to do it. At least, not publicly. What did cross my mind was, did they make a mistake? Were they really sure about this? Have they got the right girl? I'm not sure if they've got the right girl. No one knew that I was questioning. I went through all of the fear, the self-doubt, and the uncertainty, wondering about this and that. And I still said yes.

I stepped into the arbor as a moon mother for the first time to be there for the dancers for whatever they might need, not knowing what that might be. For all I knew it could be three clothes pins and a chair. Maybe they would need a shoulder to cry on. Or maybe someone to stand in front of them to push them a little, to push them beyond their limits. Maybe I would just leave them alone. I didn't know.

I found out that Sammye Jo and Gogo Mzinyathi were going to dance. These two incredibly powerful medicine women were going to dance. How was I supposed to help them? How on earth would I be able to help them? How would I know what they need? All of my worries came up in full force. But I still said yes.

When I got ready to walk into the arbor to hold a space of love and be there for the dancers, my heart was pounding out of my chest because I didn't know what to do. There was no one to tell me what to do. I was scared for a lot of different reasons. What if I wasn't good enough? I was scared I would not do something right, and I was scared that that thing inside me would come up. What if I didn't know what to do? There was no boss I could ask what to do. I knew the chiefs trusted me, but what if they thought I would know what to do, but I didn't really know what to do? My head was spinning with all the questions that were going around in it.

The drums started, and I felt it. I took my shoes off, and I put my feet on the earth, and I felt it. I could feel their dancing through the earth. I could feel the messages coming into me through Mother Earth. I realized I was not doing this alone. I was not standing by myself. Mother Earth was here. The dancers were dancing on the earth, and Mother Earth was telling me what to do. She was my guide. She was my boss. She was my teacher. My heart was still up in my throat. I could feel my nervousness, but I trusted and I kept saying "yes."

The dance went on and on. The next day it got easier. Somehow I just knew where to go, when to stand next to a dancer, or when to move around the other side of arbor. I knew when to be quiet, when to dance with them, and when to go stand near the tree. I don't know how I knew these things except that the messages were coming from somewhere.

The only thing I could think was that the messages were coming from mother earth. The dancers were dancing on the earth, and they were touching the tree and the trees roots were going down into the earth, and the earth was taking those messages back to me. It was beautiful and scary and powerful and anchoring all at the same time.

When that dance was over, I walked away, feeling a little bit more confident. Not confident in the way of being arrogant, but confident in realizing that I was understanding how to listen. I was becoming confident that when the earth spoke to me I was learning how to listen. I was paying attention. I had never felt that before.

It made me think back to those moments in my dance before my dance started, after Jeanne had held me in the water and I put my feet onto the mother earth. Something changed then. My relationship with the earth changed. What I realized so many months later standing in Africa was that Mother Earth is Mother Earth and that her messages come from everywhere. They come from within, and I can listen.

I spent much of my five weeks in Africa without shoes on. As often as I could, I walked barefoot. We were out in nature most of the time, so it was easy. It was only when we went into town to do errands that I wore shoes. My feet started to get tougher and tougher.

While I was there I heard that the sangomas, the indigenous healers, don't wear shoes because they believe in staying connected to Mother Earth, and they wear the scars of their connection to the mother in such a beautiful way. Even I was horrified, at first, to see their feet. I was sitting on the grass with a few of the elders to chat, and I saw how hard and cracked the gogos' feet were and my first instinct was to say, "Someone, please give them a pedicure!" but the truth is, they are more connected to the earth than any of us and they listen to the mother and they feel the mother through their feet.

I was catching a tiny glimpse of what listening to Mother Earth was like by walking barefoot. But I didn't know if I could do that always. It takes dedication to always put your feet on the mother, but what a blessing that is to Mother Earth and to them in return. It has to be worth it, evidently, because the sangomas do it.

I had a deep lesson and teaching from that dance. I learned that I could hold divine feminine energy and connect to Mother Earth, and that I could be of the moon and of the earth at the same time. I could be Robbie, who I am. Not interior designer, not daughter, not sister, not partner. Just me, in the arbor with the dancers. What a blessing that was.

The Rustlers Toilet

After crew training and the For The One Dance in Midrand, we all piled into mini bus taxis, which were sixteen-seater vans, and drove about four or five hours to Rustlers Valley in the Free State. In our van we had the Gogos, Jeanne White Eagle, John, and the Norwegians, Vigdis and Eva. Sam and I were in the back.

I don't know what I had eaten or where, but whatever it was, it did not agree with my stomach. In the back of the van, there was a lot of bouncing as we drove down the road – not like the big smooth roads that I was used to. We drove hours and hours, and my stomach kept churning. I was so uncomfortable. Jeanne White Eagle sat in the front seat having a grand time, and people were singing and laughing and telling jokes. The longer we were in the van the more stressed I started feeling. All I knew was that we needed to find somewhere to stop for a bathroom break.

However, there was nowhere to stop because we were in the middle of absolutely nothing but open fields. My panic and anxiety made it worse. I was sitting with my hands on the back of the seat in front of me, clinging on for dear life. I thought, 'Dear God! When are we going to get somewhere we can stop?' I didn't know the people in the van well. I was so embarrassed that my stomach was so upset and that I had to go to the bathroom. I didn't want to yell out to the other twelve people on the bus, "We've got to stop because I have to go *right now...*"

The longer we sat there the more Sam's anxiety went up as well, and she kept saying, "I'll just tell them to stop."

"Just quit talking to me," I said.

"Look there's one tree right there in a field. You could go there," she said.

Finally, we got to some little town called Ficksburg. We needed gas, the gogos wanted Kentucky Fried Chicken, and the driver just kept circling around. I just wanted to go to a bathroom.

Eventually I shouted, "Just please stop anywhere. Just stop."

The gogos got their big buckets of chicken, and I finally found a bathroom in the gas station, or garage, as they call it in South Africa, and I was finally relieved of the anxiety and pressure. We got back into the van, but the smell of chicken did not go down well with me because my stomach was still not a hundred per cent.

It was sunset as we were getting into Rustlers Valley. There was just enough light to take in the beauty of the valley. The place we were going to stay was on the side of a mountain. We drove up a road that wound its way up, back and forth, to a building known as the Starseed, which was a perfectly round thatched structure with open sides. We all got out and said our hellos to Niyan and Leanne, who had left Johannesburg before us, and the Hare Krishna family that was going to cook for us.

It was really wonderful to see Leanne's familiar face, and when I hugged her, the first thing I said to her was, "Leanne, please can you tell me tell me where the bathrooms are?"

"Bathrooms?" she asked.

"The toilets," I said.

I was whispering quietly because that's what we do in America. We don't talk about going to the bathroom. It's a big secret. Nobody where I come from talks about going to the toilet, at least not out loud, and not in mixed company.

"Yes, the toilet. Where would I find the toilet?" I whispered.

In a loud voice she asked, "Do you have to go number one or number two?"

I put my hands on my face in total embarrassment, and at that point we had the attention of the whole room and I said, "Let's just say for now number one."

"Oh, well, okay, if you have to go number one, if you just need to pee, just go outside and pee anywhere. And if you have to go number two, there's a little toilet inside the bamboo thatch. Here, I'll show you." She took me outside to a little bamboo shelter right outside of Starseed, which is an open air room. The little stall had a bamboo wall on three sides with an open door. I went inside and saw a hole in the ground. There was no seat. There was no anything. Just a hole.

"This is where you're supposed to go," she said.

I thought, 'Well, I'm just going to let that settle for a few minutes, and let it soak in. But how am I supposed to do that?'

I turned to Leanne and asked, "Is there anywhere else, anywhere else on the property?"

"Oh, well if you go all the way down to the bottom of the hill there's a bathhouse down there." She told me it was a brick house with bathroom stalls. All I heard was 'down at the bottom of the hill' and 'a brick house'.

It was like I'd struck gold. It was away from the Starseed where everybody was, and there was privacy. We were all camping, and so right before bed Sam, Jamie and I decided to make the trek all the way down the hill to the bathroom with brick walls before we went into our tents.

We headed down the hill. Jamie had one of those headlights that attaches to your head with a headband, and Sam and I had little flashlights in our hands. We went down the undulating hill – downhill, then a few steps of flat ground, and then down the hill some more, and then another few steps of flat ground. It was kinda fun.

"Whee! Whoo," we cried out, jogging down the hill.

When we got to the bottom of the hill, there was a brick building right in front of us. It was pitch dark by then. Jamie was looking around and the beam from the flashlight on her forehead zinged all around. I was so excited; it was a real bathroom. I went in first and I went to the first stall and from the light of my little bitty flashlight it was obvious that this bathroom had not been used in a long time. I went to the next one and there was some kind of bird nest in the toilet. I thought, 'What? How can this be? There's a bird nest in the toilet!' I went to the third stall. It was clear that someone had used that toilet a long time ago even though it was not working. It was full.

I was trying to figure it all out and keep up with what I was seeing. I came running out of there, saying, "No. No. No. No! This is not going to happen. I am not going to go in the bird's nest. Or the one that has been used three months ago. It's not happening."

About that time Jamie came out. All three of us were standing there outside the brick building, and I could barely breathe; I was so traumatized by the day and not being able to go to the bathroom. Suddenly I heard something coming at me that sounded like a small helicopter. It was coming at my head, but I couldn't see. I ducked. Jamie still had the light on her head, and she was moving her head around to try to see what it was.

I can only imagine what it must have looked like from the Starseed with these panicked lights running around. The bug kept coming back. It was dive-bombing us, dzhum-dzhum-dzhum-dzhum, and then it would be gone, and then it would come back, dzhum-dzhum-dzhum-dzhum, and it would get closer.

Finally the bug went away and Sam looked at me and said, "We're going to find you a place to go to the bathroom."

I said, "Oh, no. I'm never using the toilet in Africa again. I am so traumatized. I will hold it for the next three weeks until we get home. I'm not going."

"No, no, we'll find a place," she said.

"No, no, I'm serious," I said. "I'm done looking for bathrooms in Africa. Let's just go to the tents and go to bed. I'm done."

I went to bed, extremely uncomfortable, and woke up the next morning with the sunrise. I looked down at the bottom of the hill and there were two brick buildings. I went down the hill to explore. The second building that we hadn't gone into had lovely showers and two working toilets. It was absolutely wonderful. I have never been so grateful for a bathroom in my whole life.

I decided that because these toilets were all the way down at the bottom of the hill, something had to be done with the toilets up at the Starseed. I insisted that, because we had elders there who could not use a hole in the ground, they should get some kind of plastic chair to put over the hole so that at least Pearl and Sammye-Jo didn't have to hover and squat while they relieved themselves.

They found some kind of seat apparatus. It wasn't a chair, which would have been my ideal. It was some kind of box that they put a seat on. It took about 24 hours but we solved the bathroom-toilet dilemma. We never got a door on the thatched toilet. There were two of them side-by-side, and you could come in on either side; they were separated by a thin little bamboo wall. So you had to be real friendly with your neighbor while you were sitting there.

At least we got it taken care of. At least I got over my trauma and did use the toilets in South Africa for the rest of the trip.

A Blessing from Spirit

The day before the dance started at Rustlers Valley, Gogo
Hugh asked me if I would accompany him to the dance arbor
to do a blessing on the land before the dancers arrived for the
ceremony. I was honored and thrilled that he asked me to join
him. He asked me to bring my dance shawl, my feather fan,
and whatever else I felt I needed to bring. We gathered the
things we would need and walked down to the arbor. I think it
was about a mile from where we were staying, down the
mountain and into the valley. The scenery was stunningly
beautiful. There were wildebeest, and other animals, on the
land, and also a small herd of wild horses.

Gogo Hugh wore a big straw hat to protect him from the
sun. A hat was one of the only things that I didn't pack going to
Africa. Go figure, there I was as fair skinned as I could be with
blue eyes and red hair, and I didn't pack a sunhat! We walked
down the road and when we got to the arbor, Gogo Hugh saw
that I was starting to blister and burn, so he offered me his
sunhat, which was chivalrous, and I absolutely accepted it. I
had already learned that when my skin burned in Africa, it was
not pretty.

Gogo Hugh had brought some coral trees to plant outside
the arbor. These are special trees to the sangomas because
they offer protection and healing. Our plan was to plant the
trees in the four directions around the arbor, near the shrines.
We discussed how to create the ceremony, and I realized it
was the first time that I was doing a ceremony that had not
been taught to me. I had been taught to lead a sweat lodge
and a medicine wheel ceremony. I had been taught the form of
the dance. What Gogo Hugh taught me was that I can listen to

spirit and be in the moment and create a ceremony from my heart, with my own intentions. That was new to me.

We stood at the east gate entrance to the arbor and Gogo Hugh suggested that we make a circle outside the arbor, offering our own blessings at each of the directions in whatever way we chose. He proposed that I move around the arbor to the south and he move in the opposite direction towards the north. We would pass each other in the west and meet again in the east, having each put into the ground the medicine in the four directions for protection. That sounded like a plan to me.

I was to say my own prayers, and set my own intention for protection. I would call on the energies of the land and spirit guides to come and protect the arbor and the dancers in my own way. That's what I did.

It was the first time that I created a ceremony. What a gift that was, to open up and speak from my heart without being assigned any kind of protocol or any kind of ritual or anything that had come before. It all came from me, from my spirit, because I allowed the Creator to move through me.

By the time I got to the west, and I had done my blessing in the east and moved around to the south, and Gogo Hugh, who was coming around from the north, met me in the west, I was in tears. My tears came from how overwhelmingly beautiful the process was. He smiled at me and just said, "Oh, yes, little one, little sister. What a blessing you are." And that's all he said to me.

We continued around. He moved past me and moved to the south. I moved past him and went to the north. I found myself back in the east much sooner than Gogo Hugh and as I crouched down on my knees in the east to say my last prayers I heard the horses come up over the hill.

I looked up and saw a white stallion. I remembered being told that he was called Spirit. Close to him was a mare and her foal. There were a few other horses nearby but those three seemed to be the most curious about what we were doing. The foal came almost right up to me. I sat there on my knees and I held out my hand. She stretched her neck and reached out her nose. When she was still about six inches from me, Spirit must have thought she was getting just a little bit too close because he came charging over the hill towards us and got in between me and the foal.

I pulled my hand back and put my head down so that Spirit couldn't see my face, because I was raised around horses and I knew I shouldn't make a stallion angry and I certainly should not seem like a threat.

In a crouch, with my head down all I could see were his hooves. With my hands folded in my lap I was in the least threatening posture that I could be. He stomped and moved around but stayed right in front of me. This didn't go on for long, and after maybe thirty seconds, or even maybe a minute, Spirit stretched down and took the hat I was wearing in his mouth and tried to pull it up. I reached up and grabbed it.

"Spirit, that's Gogo Hugh's! You can't have his hat!" I said, and I pulled it back down. He snorted, and I put my head back down because, again, I didn't want him to think that I was taking an aggressive posture. Once again he took the hat in his mouth and pulled up. I looked up and extended my arm and pulled the hat back down, and tucked the brim down over my face and looked down again.

Spirit stayed in front of me and came back and pulled the hat up a third time. But this time he lifted it with his nose and knocked it off my head so I couldn't pull it back down. I sat there and looked up and I was looking up at Spirit's nose and I realized how dangerously close his hooves were. If he wanted to be aggressive with me, it would not be hard.

I stayed where I was, crouched down and looking at the ground. Spirit came closer to me, leaned forward, put his nose to my forehead, and smelled me. This was familiar to me – I had felt a horse's breath on my face before. I had felt them breathe and snort and felt their wet spit on my skin. It felt so familiar and so poignant, and at the same time my heart was pounding. I didn't know where Gogo Hugh was, and I hoped he wouldn't try to scare Spirit off.

Spirit stayed there, and then he moved his lips almost as if they were quivering. It's something that horses do, and I could tell that he was touching my hair and playing with it. That was his way of checking me out, and he was feeling my energy and feeling my spirit. He was checking me out to see if I was okay. After no more than another minute, Spirit decided I wasn't a threat to him or his family, and he gave one last snort and covered my head with snot. I just laughed. It was not the first time I had been covered with horse snot. It felt wonderful.

I realized what a gift he had given me. This wild horse had come up to me at the conclusion of the ceremony that I had just created in an open heart space to provide protection for the dancers, to hold them in a sacred place and to surround the dancers with protective energy from Spirit, the Creator, and from my heart. What I was given in return was a perfect example of what I had just done.

This horse, named Spirit, of all things, had come up to me because he was protecting his family. He was taking care of his dancers, and taking care of those who depended on him. He was creating a place of safety and protection for his herd, and he was checking to make sure that I was okay and that I was not a threat. When he realized that I wasn't, he created his own ceremony – he gave me a blessing. Yes, a blessing of horse snot in my hair, but it was still a blessing nonetheless. So I had to sit there and laugh.

After Spirit and the other horses cantered off, Gogo Hugh walked over to me and said he was watching and holding his breath and that it was so beautiful. I turned around and saw Gogo Hugh's hat. Spirit had taken a chunk out of it. We both got a blessing from Spirit that day.

Praying on the Mountain

On Sunday evening after the dance at Rustlers Valley, Gogo Hugh came to me and said that Gogo Mzinyathi and Gogo Nomsimane wanted to climb the mountain at sunrise the next morning to pray, and he wondered if I would like to go with them. I couldn't believe that of all the people who were there, these amazing healers were inviting me to join them. Of course I said yes! That seemed to be my mantra – saying "yes," no matter what I was asked to do.

The Starseed, where we were camping, was fairly high up the side of the mountain, and it seemed an easy climb to the top.

I didn't sleep much that night. I kept thinking about what had happened a few days before with the stallion, Spirit, and about the dance that we had completed. We had been through what felt like a hurricane on that mountain. People had lost their tents and a lot of their belongings. It felt as though we had been there a lifetime but we had only been there about five days.

I got up early the next morning, put on a skirt, and wrapped my shawl around my waist. I brought my feather fan and my medicine bag made from an otter skin. I made sure I had cornmeal and tobacco. Then I put my medicine bag over my shoulder and went to meet the gogos.

There were six of us going to the top of the mountain: the three gogos – Gogo Hugh, Gogo Nomsimane and Gogo Mzinyathi – and me. I feel like saying 'little old me' because that's how I felt. Sam, who was now immersed in the magic of Africa, decided to come with us, too. Lucky, a young African man who had grown up in a township, also joined us. He had found a way to get to the dance, and the money had somehow been raised for him to get to Rustlers Valley because he knew he had to be there.

We met at the place where the path started. It was rocky and craggy, but I could see a clear path going up, and we started to climb. The gogos were dressed all in white, and they each carried a *shoba*, which is a stick about a foot and a half long, decorated with beads and paint, and with the tail of a wildebeest on the end. The *shoba* is used to celebrate and to clear energy; it is waved in the air to get the attention of the spirits.

At one point I looked up and Gogo Mzinyathi was already at the top with Gogo Nomsimane right behind her. Both of them were a bit older than I, and even though I was carrying a lot of weight on my body, they were carrying even more than I was. And they were barefoot! This was one of the few times that I put shoes on because I was not going to walk up a rocky mountain barefoot.

I stopped for a moment and looked down into the valley and saw the dance arbor and remembered what had happened at the dance. I looked down at the lush green of Rustlers Valley, most of which had been engulfed by fire just three months earlier. Almost all the buildings, except the Starseed and some outbuildings, had been burned and so had the grass. Now, in the spring, the burned out grass had been replaced by beautiful green growth. I felt the rhythm of Mother Earth. I looked back up and saw Gogo Nomsimane waving her *shoba* to hurry me up, saying, "Come, come, come!"

In that moment, standing on the side of that mountain, I thought, 'This is my life. This is what I am doing right now. I am not sitting in some office cubicle. I am not stuck in five o'clock traffic somewhere trying to get home or to work. I am not taking orders from somebody else or checking up on someone else. I am not answering to anybody else. This is my life. This is what I am doing right now. I am standing on the side of a mountain and a gogo is waving a *shoba* at me.'

Once I caught my breath from the realization of what my life was and how much it had changed in such a short time, I took a deep breath and headed up to the top. I thought the top of the mountain would be on the edge of a rock packed on other rocks, but as we went over the rocks at the edge, just a few feet further we came upon a grassy flat area that almost looked like a crater. It was remarkable to find a large grassy ring on top of a stone mountain. The fire had been up there, too. I could see the sooty grass with green shoots showing through. 'I could live up here,' I thought, 'I would put a house up here.'

I looked beyond where we were and saw three connected rings together just to the left; to the right there were two connected rings. Each ring was about two to three stones high in some places and in others just one stone high. These stone walls were old – the ruins of something that had been there before.

Gogo Mzinyathi told me this was the place of the ancestors, where the ancient people had lived. I stood there for a few more minutes and thought if this had been in America it would have been roped off, turned into a national park and people would have had to pay money to get up the mountain to see it. Or it would have been dug up, torn apart and re-created as a theme park. It would not have been left and honored. It would not have been sacred.

Where we were standing on that mountain was holy ground to the sangomas. It was a sacred space. I took my shawl from around my waist and wrapped it around my head so that I could honor what the gogos were doing. I understood why they covered their heads. For the gogos the ancestors still lived there.

We stepped into one of the rings, and Gogo Mzinyathi laid down a piece of cloth and placed a number of items out on it.

She was creating an altar, and it's not for me to say what was on her altar, other than that she had sacred items. When she had finished putting out her altar, she asked me if I would bless her altar in the tradition that I knew, in the Native American way.

That's when I understood why my instinct had been to bring my tobacco and cornmeal pouches. I sat at the front of her altar and took a pinch of cornmeal in my left hand and moved in a counterclockwise direction, which is for the moon and feminine energy. I sprinkled cornmeal around her altar and I asked the grandmothers to bring their blessings to it. Then I took a pinch of tobacco in my right hand and sprinkled a circle around the altar in a clockwise or sunwise direction, which is for the masculine, and I asked the grandfathers to bring their blessings and protection. Then I gave gratitude and offered a prayer.

Gogo Mzinyathi began to pray. She was praying in Zulu and I didn't understand a word. There was nothing she was saying that was reaching my cognitive awareness but I felt her words and how they moved through me. The more she prayed, the more she clapped. Clap-clap, clap-clap, clap-clap. Gogo Hugh started to clap with her, and then Gogo Nomsimane and so I started to clap, too. Clap-clap, clap-clap. The more we clapped the louder and more intense her prayers were. After a short while she stood up and lifted her hands up into the air. She was still praying, and we continued to clap. She prayed until she was completely out of breath and out of tears.

When she stopped I realized tears were pouring down my face. I didn't know what she was praying for, but I felt every word that she said just pour through my soul. When she was finished and had caught her breath, Gogo Hugh came up to me and offered a hand to help me to my feet.

"What were her prayers, Gogo?" I asked him.

"She was praying for the children of Africa. She was praying for all the children who have lost their parents to AIDS and have felt the tragedy of this disease, and for those who have, themselves, been infected. She was praying for all the people of Africa to be relieved of this disease, to be healed, to be relieved of the emotional disease. She prayed for the people who have died, and for the grandmothers and aunts and uncles who were now taking care of the children because their parents died. She was praying for anyone and everyone who had been affected in some way by AIDS."

When Gogo Hugh told me this I knew it was true. I could hear her words in Zulu echoing in my mind.

I looked around and saw that Sam had not been sitting with us. She had walked beyond the stone circles and found her way to a peak. She was standing there on a rock that looked out over the valley. It was a dangerous place. She had to leap from one rock to another over a deep crevasse. She could hear Gogo's words and she was listening. She, too, was crying.

None of us who went up that mountain came down the mountain the same. None of us felt the same. We knew something that we didn't know before. We knew this place existed, and we knew the ancestors were there, and we knew Gogo Mzinyathi had prayed to the ancestors for all the children who were affected by AIDS.

Blue Hippo

After the dance at Rustlers Valley, we all packed up in the vans again and headed for Cape Town. Up to that point of my South African adventure, I had been in the northern part of the country and now we were headed for the southernmost part of the country. We were headed to a little farm called Blue Hippo, which was a few hours inland from Cape Town, where several members of the community had gone ahead of us to prepare for the two dances that would happen there.

I was physically much better, and I was looking forward to seeing more of the landscape. It changed the further south we got. The landscape became green and more lush. The golden colors up country were gone. There were some taller trees and a lot of pine trees. It was strikingly different from the landscape that was closer to Johannesburg.

The country itself changed completely during the five weeks. I am not sure what I expected, my only experiences of Africa having been through *National Geographic* documentaries, books, and Tarzan movies. In the northern regions and around Rustlers, the trees were small and low to the ground – what we would call scrub trees. The beautiful rolling landscape, which they called the veld, was striking in its feeling of being primitive and raw. That is the best way that I can describe it.

I spent much of the drive down just soaking it up and trying to remember every detail of what I saw, how the land changed, how the sun moved across the land, how the clouds left shadows across the veld. It truly did speak to my soul, and I was so grateful in those moments to be there, even if I was on a cramped and crowded little twelve-seater bus filled with people from different countries.

When we arrived at Blue Hippo, the land was much flatter than it had been at Rustlers Valley. It was low, but in the distance there were mountains so it felt like it was down in the lower regions. A beautiful river ran through the property. Blue Hippo was a camp ground with some tipis for accommodation for those who didn't have tents. There was a primitive kitchen, a garden and compost toilets. There was a round building where we could hold gatherings and it reminded me much of a peace sound chamber although it was not built specifically for that.

People continued to arrive. We were to have two dances at Blue Hippo, an adult For The One dance and the first Youth Dance in South Africa. There were young people coming from all over the world: Germany, England, Ireland, and some Jewish and Muslim young women from Israel. These young women had already been working together for peace. There were also some South African youth coming to dance from different cultures, and the gogos brought many children from KwaZulu-Natal with them.

All of these young people were under the age of eighteen, and as they gathered we had our hands full with a large group of young people who would all be there for a week. There was still a lot of work to be done to get everything ready. The arbor had to be readied – it was built especially for this dance. At the same time, we wanted the young people to have a meaningful experience and use the opportunity to connect with each other.

There was such deep sharing that went on throughout the week before the youth dance that it warmed my heart to be there. Many of us used the opportunity to teach. Gogo Hugh spent an afternoon teaching the rhythms and movements of Zulu dancing. It was wonderful. I have to admit, I wasn't agile at the time, so I couldn't make all of those movements, especially the high kicks above my head. But it was wonderful to be there and to see it and to see the young people so enthusiastic. It was special to see young Zulus boys teaching the Germans and Israelis a part of their culture.

The young women from the Middle East cooked flat bread over the fire for us at night. Sofia, an elder from Germany, had a background in theatre costume design, and she worked with the youth to help them make their dance skirts. As she taught them to sew, she also shared with them how to express themselves through their regalia. Drumming and other things were going on, too.

Truly the young people couldn't be referred to as children. They had made the choice, just as any adult, to come and dance, to do this, to bring about peace for not just themselves but for the planet. To me, that is not a childish decision to make although sometimes I do believe that it does take a child's heart to see that it is possible. It was such a blessing to be around these young people.

In the middle of the week, some of us decided to take a few days' break in Cape Town. Marie Claire, a friend of ours from North Carolina, had only spent a few days in Africa before she decided that she was not cut out for the African bush and part of our reason to go to Cape Town was to put her on a plane so that she could go home. There were six of us that went – Sam and I, Susie and her partner Cajun, Candy, and of course Marie Claire. We thought we would take advantage of the opportunity to show her a little more of the country than just rugged and primitive Blue Hippo, and show her some sights in Cape Town.

I was so grateful for the reprieve. We had, at that point, spent almost a month with all our attention either preparing for, or being in, ceremony and to go to Cape Town and spend a few days there was almost like a vacation within a vacation. We were giddy. We were in the back of the bakkie (which is a small pick-up truck) with a canopy covering over the back, which meant we couldn't talk to the people who were in the front driving. As we drove out of Blue Hippo, we could see the mountains in the distance, and Sam and Candy (who loves Broadway musicals) started singing "The Hills are Alive" from *The Sound of Music*, and soon we all joined in. It was a raucous, festive feeling in the back of the bakkie – most likely we needed to let off a little steam. It was such good fun and a wonderful break from all the seriousness that we had been involved in.

We went to Cape Town and found a wonderful little bed and breakfast. Well, it was bed and no breakfast! We tried to find a hostel to stay in, but they were all fully booked. The place was in Oranjezicht, which is a pretty area on the bottom slope of Table Mountain, overlooking the city. It was breathtaking.

By this time it was in the second week of December, and it was summer in South Africa, with the temperatures up in the nineties – and the shops were full of Christmas decorations. It seemed so odd. I don't know why, but I did not expect to see Christmas decorations in Africa, even though I was there with people of European descent. The Christmas shopping and crowds reminded me of home. I was so grateful not to be in the hustle of bustle of it all. We had already missed Thanksgiving because it is not celebrated in South Africa; we did have a nice dinner, but the day kind of came and went without much notice or hoopla.

After we took Marie Claire to the airport, Sam and I decided to go to a game reserve where we could be taken on a tour to see some of the wild animals in their natural habitat. It was the first time I experienced anything like that. While it was a little confining to be in a truck with twenty five other people, just seeing the zebra, elephants, rhinoceroses and lions was amazing. These were animals that I had only seen in books and on film and there I was, face to face with them! It almost felt like I was seeing mythological creatures to see an elephant and a rhinoceros. I felt like I was in some other world, some other land and I was left speechless. There were no words to express the depths in my soul that these animals touched in me.

While Sam and I were on our adventure with the animals, Candy, Susie and Cajun had their own adventure off in Cape Town, seeing the city and enjoying the sights. When we all came back together, we felt fully rested and ready to go back to Blue Hippo to step back into the dance and ceremony. We had one last night before going back and we had a most amazing and wonderful meal together. I don't think I have ever laughed so hard in my life. It was just incredible. There we were, sitting half a world away with brand new friends, and I felt so at ease and so connected to them. Again I recognized the soul connections that we have to other people that sometimes can't be explained.

It's easy to meet someone for the first time and want to get to know them. That's what happens most of the time. I was finding more and more on my spiritual journey that I was meeting people I felt like I knew, as if I had a history with them, even though I had not known them before. Maybe it was because we are all on the same journey, and we were open to feeling our own connection to Spirit that we could feel our connection to each other. Maybe it was that we had experiences with each other in past lives and we were coming together again. I didn't know. What I did know was that it was real. We enjoyed it and felt it, and we celebrated it that night at dinner.

The next day we went back to Blue Hippo and prepared for the youth dance. None of us really knew what to expect with this dance, but we knew there were powerful young people who were determined, open, loving, trusting, eager, and willing and ready to step into that arbor.

Once again I was asked to be a moon mother, and I joyfully stepped into that. I wondered how it would be different with young people. Would they carry emotional baggage? Would they bring it with them or would they be clear? Would they have so much emotional baggage to let go of and process?

I realized as the dance went on that it was both. The youth dancers were both so clear and open and ready to let go of anything that they felt was holding them back. They didn't have the decades and decades of trauma, fear and sorrow that adults carry and need to release. They had only experienced these things for short periods. So, it was a joyful dance. There were a few tears and moments when they let go of whatever fear or anger came up in their lives, or their own circumstances, or their lives at home where they came from. The youth dancers let go of what they were working through easily and joyfully, and they quickly moved into a place of celebration, which made the rest of us realize what was possible, and how important it is for our young people of the world to understand how easy it is – that they don't have to experience the same things that adults do. It was such a blessing to be a part of that. It was heart- and eye-opening for all of us.

After that dance people started getting ready to return home and we took the time to say goodbye to each other. There were many of us who were leaving Blue Hippo to go to Cape Town to get on airplanes and go off in different directions. They hired a bus to come and pick us up and there must have been about 25 of us on it, headed for the airport. It was so sad. We were so quiet. We had been such a raucous, rowdy bunch for five weeks, and it was time for us to say goodbye to each other and to go in so many separate ways: to Israel, Norway, Germany, Ireland, the United States, and various parts of South Africa.

We had people from so many different places and lands coming together in those five weeks that we were our own small United Nations. We came together, and we celebrated each other. We celebrated our differences and our sameness. We celebrated that we knew each other and that we had met each other. We took all of that with us when we left – the memories, the joy, the sorrow, the blessings – and we took new open hearts back home with each and every one of us.

My whole life I felt something deep inside me pulling me to Africa. I never could put a name to it, or get any understanding of what that was or what it meant. It wasn't anything in particular that I could put my hands on. But I knew why I had been called when I saw the first sunset in Africa, and when I saw the mountains and the gogos and the people. The only thing I can say is there is a primal energy, a deep down feeling that I am not sure you can understand if you have not put your feet on the land there. The movies, the pictures and the photos just don't do justice to what it feels like to put your feet on that continent.

When I came back home after that first trip to Africa, I knew I had been changed. It was clear that I was no longer the same person I was before. I was no longer an interior designer building a company and being business-focused and money-oriented, doing the spiritual work on the side, hidden away on the weekends when I could fit it in.

I didn't talk to my clients about what I was doing, not about Africa, and not about my spiritual practices. I lived in Charlotte, North Carolina, which is in the Bible belt of America. Some people call it the buckle of the Bible belt, where it gets tied up a notch. There's some truth to that. So I didn't talk about my spiritual work to people. I barely talked to my family about it and when I did, they certainly didn't understand it. After that first trip to Africa, people wanted to know what I did when I went to Africa and why did I go. The next question that came out of everybody's lips was, "Were you there on a mission trip?"

Still, to this day, I get asked, "Do you go to Africa because of missions trips?" My answer always is, truthfully, "I go for my own spiritual journey." I leave it at that and I don't give any explanation. The truth is that people make this assumption, and for a long time I let them think that I went there through a

Christian church, to witness to, and change, the spiritual path of African people, because that is how they understand it and that is how they can relate. What I can say is that this was a mission trip for my own soul, to change myself and my own spiritual path. And a successful mission, at that!

I used to joke and say I was in the spiritual closet. It was really interesting because most of my clients knew about my relationship with Sam. I was out of that closet, but I was inside the spiritual closet. I wasn't worried about being criticized for the person that I loved, or being judged for a lifestyle choice, and granted, that was not the first lifestyle choice that I ever made, that would go against "societal norms." I did have a problem letting my Christian clients and friends know what I was doing spiritually. I look back on that now and I find the choices I made in the moment fascinating. I was positive and clear in my business path and clear in my personal relationship choice, but as far as my spiritual path was concerned, there was something about it that felt taboo, out of the norm. It was a secret I didn't share. I spoke little about it with the people who worked for me. A couple of people had a better understanding about it, but they didn't truly understand it.

Most people said, "Oh, it's just a phase. She'll grow out of it." At forty-something I didn't think it was something I would grow out of.

I knew in my heart something was different, and I knew things were changing and shifting. I knew that the 60 or 70 hours I was putting into my business every week, working with my clients, creating exquisite places, being on building and constructions sites – all the work that had fulfilled me for so long, that had really created a drive in me to be better and to do more and more and more – was changing.

It was 2007, and the building industry was thriving. I was a successful interior designer. And yet I felt unfulfilled. My business was the one thing that had driven me for so long, and now it was the one thing that was draining me. I knew I had to find a way to release some of the business, some of the work, some of the stress, and step more fully into my spiritual path.

Show Up and Say YES

Jeanne White Eagle said to me, after the trip to Africa, "Robbie, just keep saying yes and show up." The way she said it made it clear how important it was for me. It sounds like such a simple thing to say to someone, but the way she said it resonated for me on a soul level. And so I did, over and over again. I went to ceremonies and I went to medicine dances and teachings, and I listened to anyone who would share. I kept showing up. I offered my help. I offered to be of service. I offered anything that I could give in return.

I dove into learning as much as I could and remembering, as Joseph had told me, and I sat at the feet of some pretty amazing people to learn the practices and medicine ways of the shamans. I felt deeply blessed that these people allowed me to watch, to witness, to understand, and to ask questions. Even though I didn't have a formal teacher, I had so many people around me who were willing to share with me and to answer my constant barrage of questions.

I learned so much. I dove deeper and deeper into the teachings of the medicine wheel, and I connected with it on such a level that I saw how different aspects of the medicine wheel showed up in every aspect of my life. No matter what I was going through, I knew where I was on the medicine wheel. I knew where I was standing – in the east, or the south or the west. I knew where any idea or project or feeling or manifestation came from. I just stuck with this and with the questions and the learning, and I put myself in front of anyone and everyone that I could learn from.

I recognized, after coming back from Africa, that I was stepping into a place where people were coming to me with questions. What does this mean? What do you think about this? I was a little flabbergasted that anyone might think that I could hold an answer or bring some level of clarity for them but I kept showing up and saying yes. For example, a friend of mine told her sister she felt I could help her find purpose and direction in her life. I sat and talked with her sister, and what I shared and what I said seemed to help in some way.

Sam and I continued to hold our monthly ceremonies, and the community at Munay was growing stronger. On one occasion we had a sweat lodge, and it happened to be one of the rare lodges that I poured. Forty people showed up. It was difficult to get twenty people into our lodge, at best, and then it was a tight fit – it could not accommodate that many people. All I could think was that all these people showed up, and there was no way to turn anyone away for ceremony. So I led two sweat lodge ceremonies back-to-back for twenty people at a time. I was in the lodge and in ceremony for six hours. The fire keepers were exhausted, and I was exhausted, but all forty people who showed up to pray in that ancient way had their opportunity to pray, to feel their connection to spirit and be part of that purification ceremony. That, also, was part of my saying "yes."

That is when I realized that my "yes" was not just a "yes" to the person I was going to help, or to the teacher I was learning from, or to the ceremony that I was going to attend. My "yes" was to Spirit. When I said, "Yes, Creator, I will lead this ceremony, I will lead this lodge" that's where my commitment was.

I kept showing up and I kept saying yes. When I realized that my "yes" to Spirit was a "yes" to myself, everything shifted again. My perspective changed. I knew that if forty people or no people came to a sweat lodge, I would go into that lodge. I would take the stones in and offer prayers to the Creator, to the directions, for the people, because that was showing up and saying "yes." That was the commitment that I made to Spirit.

I am not sure if Jeanne White Eagle knew what she created that day, or the door that she opened, when she said, "Just show up and say yes," but I think that she did. I think she knew that I would eventually get it, and I did.

Fears, Resentments and Anger

I spent the next year following Jeanne White Eagle's advice and listening – listening to my elders, to the teachings that were being offered, and paying attention. I found my heart opening in such a meaningful way. I felt I had found my true calling. I kept trying to figure out how this fit into running a million-dollar-a-year business. I couldn't make those puzzle pieces fit together.

The more I stepped into the medicine path, deeper into the shamanic world, and the more that opened up to me, the more I started resenting being pulled away from it, having to focus my attention on the business, having to worry about payroll, taxes, and deliveries to clients. All of those things seemed so unimportant. Yet those were the things that kept Munay going, that paid the bills and the mortgage, and enabled all the other things to happen. How could I have resentment for something that made it possible for me to do the spiritual practices that I was doing?

I found myself going around and around with this. I was sitting at a desk in my office day after day, feeling more and more pulled, wishing that I wasn't sitting at my desk, wishing that I was sitting out in the woods with my medicine wheel, wishing that I was working one-on-one with someone to help clear energies, to help counsel them and to be with them and bring them closer to their connection to Creator.

Yet there I was, sitting in my office, making those mundane (what felt like unimportant) decisions, day in and day out. It was such a difficult place to be. The more I resented one aspect of my life, the harder it was to stay rooted in the other. How could I stay rooted in my spiritual practice when I resented what brought me there, what allowed and afforded me the opportunity to be there?

In the midst of all of that, my relationship with Sam became more strained. It felt like it was reaching a breaking point. I don't know that Sam felt the strain in the same way that I did. I can only suspect. We spent so much time focused on who would be the next teacher we would bring in for the community and so much time letting the community know about the next sweat lodge, ceremony, or work day event. We no longer took vacations together. Everything we did was for the community. If we did go out of town together, we were focused on something to do with Munay or another ceremony.

We did have some incredible trips at that time, and some wonderful journeys. We went to the Gathering of Nations pow wow, that year, and it was magnificent. It stirred my soul to see the regalia, the dancing, the connection, the faces, the beauty, the children, the elders. It was beautiful. But we were there as vendors, to sell our drums and our wares. As much as I enjoyed seeing the people and being a part of it, it still was work.

As much as I could be there for other people, I struggled immensely to balance my own feelings. I struggled with saying the words to Sam that would let her know that I was hurting. I struggled to find the words to tell her that I was feeling pulled apart and pulled away. I was scared.

My past came back to haunt me, my fears of being abandoned, of being alone. I was afraid of being hurt and that I would say something that would hurt her feelings or would make her feel differently about me. Instead of being an open, honest, caring, and loving partner, and sharing my innermost thoughts with her, I kept silent.

Just as my resentments towards my business built up, my resentments towards Sam built up as well. In some ways I hoped she would be a mind reader and she would just get it. I hoped that she would understand how hurt and afraid I was that we were growing apart and how worried I was about so many different things. I know now how silly that was, but that is the truth of where I was.

I won't speak to her experience, what she was going through, or what she felt. That is her story. I can only speak to what my feelings were. All I can say is that my fears, my anger, my resentment, became a third party in the relationship and I didn't want to deal with that third party at all. My anger, fear and resentment stayed bottled and bundled up and I swallowed it all down and added that to the beast in my belly, and that's what fed that beast. The only thing that would quiet that beast was more food.

So I ate. I ate when I felt stressed. I ate when I felt the fear come up. And I ate when I felt the anger come up. Somehow, even if only for a moment, the food would quiet the beast. It would soothe the anger and calm those fears. And then I could carry on. I could keep going to the office just a little longer. I could hang on long enough to go down the path to the medicine wheel or the sweat lodge and build a fire. It was a vicious cycle. It was a sad place to be. I didn't share this with any of my friends, or any of the community.

I know now that the community would have lovingly embraced me and helped me work through so many of those fears and resentments. But I didn't share it with the Munay community because I had it in my head that somehow because Munay was my community, that I had created it, that I could not let anyone see me be weak. If I was weak, why would they trust me? How could they come to me or trust me to lead a ceremony? How could they trust me to be that for them if I was so tortured and so weak and so hurt? That created one more fear: that I would be found out – somebody would discover that I was not as strong as I pretended to be.

And so again, I stuffed it all down.

Collapse

I did not study business or economics in college, and I never followed news or read business journals. Quite honestly, I ran my business instinctively, with my own ideas of how I wanted a business to be run. I had people in place who knew a lot of these things. I had a business manager who ran the day-to-day aspect of the business. That left me free to focus on creating new business, including marketing through newspaper articles and working with different magazines for our work to be featured. I was good at that.

My work as an interior designer led me to become a public figure in the social circles of Charlotte where people sought out the most popular, best, and most prominent service providers – designers, doctors and lawyers. I was on the top of that list, and I was featured in a lot of magazines. I did not do an in-depth market analysis about the business of my business. I guess you could say I was a 'fly by the seat of my pants' kind of girl. I was doing quite well, bringing in over a million bucks a year and supporting quite a few people through the business.

The attack of 9/11 was a huge hit to all business economically, but I had managed to keep things going. Over the following years I had downsized the business and the number of employees to match the economy and by this time my business was much smaller. I had fewer clients and fewer employees, but it was still good for those days. My income had been reduced to half of what it was before, but my overhead was much lower. Even though it was nowhere near what it had been pre-9/11, we had plenty of business.

Collapse

In the fall of 2008, I heard the beginnings of chatter, among people involved in new home construction, architects and other interior designers, about mortgage failure, business closure and banking failure. These were terms that, quite honestly, I didn't understand. Later I heard concerns and comments from builders, bankers and mortgage lenders that things were not steady and might go awry. I didn't pay much attention to that. I kept doing my own thing. I heard the concerns for about eight months to a year but my phone was still ringing and I was still busy. Business was good.

After some time I heard panic in people's voices. A few clients called me and said they were putting their project on hold until it was clear what was happening with the economy. I had never, in all my years in business, had someone put a project on hold after they had made the decision to move forward. It was scary.

Nevertheless, I kept plugging along, doing my thing, completely immersed in working fifty to sixty hours a week and doing all of my spiritual practices over the weekends.

Suddenly it seemed as though the plug had been pulled. My phone stopped ringing. I realized I had gone a whole week without a new client calling me. I had not experienced that in about twenty years, not since I first started my business. That was when I started paying attention and recognized the signals that came in. Builders and architects called me to find out if I had any new business coming in. The most frightening part was that the answer was 'no' – there was nothing new coming in.

The rug was pulled out from under bankers and lenders when the mortgage crisis hit, and it trickled down. Builders who had been reputable for decades lost their businesses and got out as fast as they could. They could not get loans for the materials to build new houses. They tried to sell their spec houses, but there were too many houses on the market. It trickled down to the framers, the bricklayers, masons, tilers, roofers, landscapers, and the interior designers. It trickled down to my business.

It felt as though everything happened so fast and yet I knew it had happened over months. Maybe I was in denial. The way that it happened in the banking world seemed hidden – insidious. The impact on those who were on the front lines was devastating. Some of us in the industry watched people lose their houses; we saw others who couldn't get loans and others who couldn't pay their loans. We watched as the value of people's homes dropped faster than they could breathe.

It reached a point where I had no new business coming in and no new clients. I was able to sustain the business for a little while, but I started letting some of my staff go. I brought down my overheads even more by moving into smaller premises. My business kept being peeled away, day by day, moment by moment. It felt like an excruciatingly long and painful process to watch my business collapse, but it actually only took a few months.

I was stunned, but I was still optimistic. I kept thinking it would shift and that someone would do something. I thought the bankers or even the president would do something. I didn't understand the economics – the business of the business. I couldn't understand how we could go from building so many multi-million dollar houses to saying there was no money.

Then came the day when I had to let the last of my staff go. I closed down the place where I was doing business, and I took a desk and a phone to Munay. The rest I put into storage. I was still optimistic that as quickly as it was pulled out from under me, one day I would need another showroom and another base of operations. I arranged for my office manager to work from home, and I worked from Munay.

Day after day I sat at my desk. The phone would ring, and it would be a builder or an architect asking if I had any jobs. I called the magazines that had featured my business so prominently over the years to talk to them about writing an article about what was happening. They told me they were closing down the magazine. There were no more advertisers for their beautiful home magazines, no more builders, no more interior designers. In a matter of months, an entire industry in our area shut down. There were a few people still doing a small amount of work – just a few remodeling jobs that were going on. Some, like me, were clinging to hope. I hoped that an old client would call me to buy some new drapery or to refurbish something that I had done years ago. I kept my business phone number, I kept my website, and I kept my email address. I sat in my office every day hoping for business that never came.

Day after day I found ways to keep myself busy. Some of it involved Munay and keeping the community going, but for the most part I kept reaching out and trying to find ways to make heads or tails of what felt like complete devastation. I held on. My office manager and I had our computers connected but she had gone from working sixty hours a week to working a couple of half days a week. I didn't have the income to pay her anymore.

It turned out that, along with business management and economics, I also did not understand good money management. Even though my company brought in millions of dollars, I had nothing put away, no savings for a rainy day. I had no plans for retirement. Everything I had was kept in the day-to-day aspects of the business, to pay people, the mortgage and salaries. It paid for the mortgage at Munay and it paid for what Sam and I had created.

Munay was a million dollar home sitting on ten acres of land. At that time the mortgage alone was 4,500 dollars a month. I sat in an upstairs room in that million dollar house, and the phone didn't ring.

Baby Steps

One day, in the middle of a conversation, someone said something to me, in an off-hand way that hit me completely sideways. She said, "Robbie, you think about and act around food the same way that an alcoholic thinks and acts around alcohol, and you might want to take a look at that."

I had a physical reaction to her comment. Her words pissed me off. I didn't care that she was a psychologist. I didn't care that she was well trained in what she did. I thought she was wrong. I think I even turned red looking at her.

And there was that beast. The beast reared its ugly head with all of my anger, all of my sorrow, my sadness, resentments, fears – all of it came up in that moment when she spoke about food and talked about it in a way that made me think I had to change something about it.

I didn't like it at all. I sat there and I listened to her tell me that there were twelve step programs for people like me and that I could go through life with a different relationship to food.

I thought, 'Why would I want a different relationship with food? I really like it! It serves a great purpose for me. It keeps that beast down. It keeps all of that anger down. It keeps that suffering down. And I can choke that beast down with some Ben & Jerry's ice cream faster than you can think about it. It has served me well.'

I knew if I could eat, then I wouldn't have to feel, and I thought she had told me that I couldn't eat. If I didn't eat, that meant I would always have to feel the beast and I would have to face it. I had been doing a darn fine job of keeping that beast quiet.

After that conversation with her, and probably after a few cheeseburgers and French fries, I calmed down, and I thought a little bit more about what she had said. I sat in my office at home, with nothing else to do, and I went online. I looked up these so-called twelve step programs that she had mentioned for people like me and I read a little bit about them.

After reading for a while, I switched over to a different website and did something different. Then I forgot about it and went on with my life. I went on with dealing with things by stuffing everything down and holding onto my feelings.

A few weeks later I remembered her words again, probably just after I had eaten the better part of a pizza, and I went back onto the websites and read a little bit more. I read what some of the people were saying about what it felt like to be a compulsive overeater and what it felt like to be a food addict. I thought, 'Food addict? Is there such a thing? How can you be addicted to food? How can you have an addiction to something that you have to have?' It seemed insane to me.

I did my own little dance with the websites for about another month, looking and then walking away. Finally one of the websites had a list of questions to answer. At the top was the note, "If you answer yes to three or more of these questions, then you might have a problem." I thought, 'Okay, let's just take this little test because I just can't imagine in any way, shape or form that I could be a food addict like these people are talking about or that psychologist seemed to think.'

It was a list of fifteen questions. I told myself I was going to answer honestly. I was not going to pick and choose. No one else was going to see it. I didn't have to put on my strong Robbie face. I didn't have to be the strong one or the good one or the wise one. I could just be me.

I answered the first question 'yes.' I answered the second question 'yes' and I kept going down the list. It may have been around the eighth question that I answered 'no' for the first time. Of the fifteen questions, I answered 'yes' to all but two of the questions. I had been honest, and I got scared that maybe there was something wrong with me, that somehow I was broken. All my fear came up. I was terrified that I would have to give up food and the way I eat and how I eat and how much I eat.

I was scared because I would have to give up the one thing that I felt I had control over, the one thing that wasn't spiraling out of control. I would have to give up the one thing that I could do. The thought not only scared me, it pissed me off, so I closed the website.

I continued my dance with the website for another few weeks. On and off. Reading and closing down, reading and closing down, until finally I clicked on the page that said, "Find a meeting." I had thought long and hard about it. I knew people in my life who were actively working twelve-step programs for other things, whether it was alcohol or drugs. I knew it was working in their lives but I still couldn't figure out how food could fit into that. How did it work?

I decided I would just go to an Overeaters Anonymous meeting to sit there and see. I found a meeting time that worked with my schedule, which basically consisted of walking from my living room to my office at home, sitting there, and doing nothing all day. I drove to where the meeting was to be held and sat in the parking lot.

I looked down; my hands were shaking. I had done so many things in my life. I had traveled to Africa. I had been in sweat lodges and in medicine dances. I had gone for days without food and water. Yet, there I sat in the parking lot of a Lutheran church, shaking with fear about going into a meeting with a group of people who had food problems.

I called Renée who had been sober through AA for years and very open with the members of the Spiritual Living Center about how she overcame her addictions. I told her how afraid I was and that none of it made any sense to me.

She said, "Oh, honey. It doesn't have to make sense to you when you're sitting in the parking lot. You just need to get yourself into that meeting and talk to people. And if you don't want to talk to people, just sit in the back. You don't have to do a thing. Just sit there and listen. Just get yourself into the room."

"Yes. Yes. I can do that," I said. I thanked her and I thought about just sitting at the back. That was something I could do.

I pulled myself together and walked into the church where I saw a little typed sign on the door sign that said "OA Meeting Room 201." On that door I saw another little typed sign that said "OA Meeting Inside." I took a deep breath and I remembered Renée saying, "You don't have to say anything. You can sit at the back and listen. Just get yourself into that room."

I opened the door, and I stepped in. I was in the room. I looked around and saw a table with chairs around it. I expected the chairs to be in rows, auditorium style. Even if there were only three or four rows I would still be able to sit at the back row because even three rows back was better than sitting in the front. Now, the worst thing of all: I had to go in and sit at a table, face to face with people. There were three or four women sitting in the room. I couldn't turn around and run because that would be admitting to those three or four women that I was weak. So I sat down at the table.

An older woman with short grey hair, who looked like she could have been anybody's grandmother, reached out, put her hand on mine and said, "I'm glad you're here. Welcome." I smiled and nodded. I thought, 'I can still sit here and be quiet. They can't make me say anything. They can't make me do anything. I'm just going to sit here.'

No one else arrived. It was just a few of us, sitting around a small table in a small room.

They started off with a reading of the twelve steps, after which they read an extract from a book that was one person's experience with food addiction and compulsive over-eating. The story was about a woman who was so afraid to feel her anger, sorrow and sadness, and she was afraid to let anyone else see it or help her feel it, that she ate and she ate and she ate. The story spoke about the woman feeling ashamed about her eating, but even though she felt shame, she kept eating. Although her stomach hurt, she still took another bite.

I cried and wondered, 'How does this woman know this is my story? How did they know this is what I go through every day?'

The grandmotherly woman reached over and said, "It's okay. You are not different in here."

I cried even more because I had felt so different and so ashamed. At two hundred and forty pounds, I wore my shame and my addiction on my body. I wore my guilt and my blame and my anger and my resentment on my body. In one hour in that room, I realized that the beast that I thought I was keeping down within my belly was actually showing up on my body and that beast was showing up as armor. It was showing up as padding to keep the world away and to keep my feelings from getting out.

In that hour I realized I was just like the woman in the story, and I wanted to be different. I wanted to learn how to feel. I needed to learn how to feel and to understand my feelings. I needed to know how to be with the beast and how to be okay with the beast. I wanted to learn how to tame the beast without food.

At the end of the meeting, the woman who had touched my hand before reached out to me one last time to take my hand, and said, "I hope you'll come back." I didn't say a word.

I did go back. I went back every week. I learned. And I paid attention. I learned through my fears and anxieties. Week after week I went back and sat in that room with those four women, and I learned how to be okay with my fear and my shame and with who I was. I learned how to make decisions that were in my own best interest and that were for my own good.

I learned how to be.

Grandmothers of the Web Dance

Even though I was growing a community with Sam, I always felt that the Center for Peace in Tennessee was my spiritual home. That may sound a little bit crazy but that was where this door had opened and where it all started for me. That's where I had my first sweat lodge and my first dance. It was where I was first introduced to any of these teachings. That is why I went back, again and again.

Every chance I got, I returned to the Center for Peace, where Jeanne and Perry Robinson and William Charles were. So many other people had rooted and found their spiritual home there. Candy was there, and Jeanne White Eagle and John were often there, too. I attended many dances there – the Corn Harvest Dance, which Candy chiefed and the meditative Drum Dance, created by Joseph Rael, as well as many others. But one dance stands out because of the great gift I received.

I danced the Women's Web of Life dance only once, in May 2009. I had never thought much about doing what was called "women's work" just focusing my energy only on women or just being around women. Maybe I was always just too attracted to men to only be around women. I can laugh about it now. For some reason I felt compelled to dance this dance.

The chiefs of this dance were Cheryl Rose and Jeanne Robinson, two women I admired more than I have words to say. Their incredible gifts through this medicine work, their knowledge and their integrity, is more than I can describe. I knew with them leading this dance that I would be emotionally, physically and spiritually safe.

Dancing Through
Fire

Two of the moon mothers were Sammye Jo and Margarita Davita. Over the years Sammye had not only become my friend and my teacher but she was like my sister. We were close and I trusted her with everything. Margarita was a long time community member at the Center for Peace, and she was the partner of William Charles, who was the fire keeper at my first sweat lodge. Margarita and I were just getting to know each other at this point but I had been with her at many dances, and I had once been her moon mother when she danced. We had developed a relationship of trust and friendship and so I felt safe having her as a moon mother at this dance.

This dance was the first time that Candy and I danced together in a medicine dance. Most of this dance was a blur to me. I had been having migraines since my late twenties and now, in my early forties, I had about six to ten migraines every month.

I had gone through all kinds of examinations and medications and everything you can possibly imagine to stop them but nothing seemed to work except for one pharmaceutical medication that was prescribed by a doctor. There were some side effects to that medication that made me feel uncomfortable but it was worth it to end the pain. What I had found over the years of doing the shamanic practices of pouring lodges, of being in dances, was that every time I stepped into doing this spiritual work I would get a migraine. I didn't really understand it and nobody could explain it to me.

I wasn't surprised when the dance started that I got a migraine. Yet when I danced this dance, it felt different. As I danced, the pain grew worse and worse. I realized that the migraine was not going to stop, so I didn't let it stop me. I'm not sure what I looked like to people on the outside of the dance arbor, I am not sure what the women saw when they looked at me, what the chiefs saw or what Sammye-Jo saw. I don't know what Margarita saw, but she came to me and said,

"If we can't stop your pain, then you're going to have to come out of the dance."

I must have been very pale; they could see that I was suffering. The pain was intense, but it wasn't worse than any of the other migraines I had ever had. However, something was different physically, so I told her I would take my medication, and I did. The pain slowly subsided, but a few hours later it came back.

Sammye Jo told me that she was able to see what was happening and what was going on energetically and why I was in so much pain. She said there were two spirits that were with me that were trying to give me information, and they were trying so desperately to give me information so fast and so quickly that it was too much for me to take in. It was too much for my body to handle, and therefore, it created the migraine. It released the flow of blood going through my brain to the extent that all of my blood vessels expanded, and I thought my head was just going to burst right off of my shoulders.

Sammye Jo asked if she could help and I said, "Yes, please." She took me out the back side of the arbor, which at the time I thought was strange, and she started speaking in a language that I had never heard. Sammye-Jo is Chippewa and Cree. I don't know if she was speaking in one of her own languages. I don't think she was. I quickly realized she was speaking to these spirits. The more she spoke to them, the more her voice rose in anger, and I realized she was really getting mad.

The angrier she got, the clearer I became. I realized all of a sudden that these two spirits were my grandmothers. Not my immediate grandmothers, but my great-great-grandmothers, one on either side. My maternal and my paternal great-great-grandmothers. These were the two women who carried my Native American lineage.

My mothers' great grandmother was Muscogee Creek, and my father's great grandmother was Cherokee, and these were the two spirits that were coming through. It was the first time that I ever recognized something like this. I started crying and I said to Sammy-Jo, "Please, please, please quit yelling at them. They're my grandmothers. You have to quit yelling at them."

When she realized that, Sammye Jo calmed down and carried on speaking to them in the same language but in a much softer and gentler way. She had a whole conversation with my grandmothers. I couldn't hear what my grandmothers were saying back to her, but she was clearly having a conversation with these spirits, these beautiful energies who I see now as my guardian angels, my guardian spirit guides.

She asked them to slow down and not give me the information and messages in a way that was detrimental to my health. The headache slowly dissipated when I went back into the dance arbor. I knew I could finish dancing what would turn out to be one of the most important dances of my life.

Vision of the Fire Dance

During a medicine dance, the dancers dance while the drums play. There are breaks that are sometimes just a few minutes, and sometimes longer. During the breaks, the crew has their meals. Joseph says that the rest times are as important as the times when the dancer is dancing. When the dancers are dancing, they are in the process of discovering themselves, and when they rest they integrate what they have processed. It connects the spirit to the body.

We were on a break during the Women's Web of Life dance, and I sat in the arbor with my eyes closed and reflected back to what had happened with Sammye Jo. My head was hurting just a little bit but not nearly as much as before. I kept thinking about these grandmothers. I kept thinking about my father and my father's mother, and her mother. I thought about my mother and her mother's mother. That's who was there with me. It felt so powerful and so safe, but at the same time I was confused. What was it that they were trying to tell me? I didn't get the message clearly. I was in too much pain.

An elder who was playing the drum came up to where I was sitting and crouched down on her knees in front of me. I looked up and saw that it was Patti McFee. I had not been around her much and didn't know her well, although I knew she had been part of the community for a while. In fact, I was a little intimidated by her because she knew a whole lot about a whole lot of things so I paid attention when she talked to others, but I didn't really engage with her much. She was holding a box that was about six inches deep and about two feet long and one foot wide. She lifted the lid and pulled out the most beautiful dance shawl I had ever seen and laid it across my lap. It took my breath away.

"Robbie, I dreamed that you were to dance with the fire shawl," she said.

I was in such a daze that I didn't really understand. "What? I'm supposed to what? You dreamed this?"

"The spirits told me that yes, you are to dance with this fire shawl," she said. She opened up the shawl and showed it to me. Then she left it with me and walked away.

The lovely red shawl was magnificent with stitching in all the colors of the fire: yellow, orange, red and purple. There was blue stitching at the bottom of the shawl that looked like flames coming up. The ribboned fringe on this shawl was stunning, also in the colors of flames. It must have weighed ten pounds. I thought, 'I am so tired! How am I going to dance with this?'

I was honored, and at the same time I was petrified. I didn't know what it meant. I sat there in silence. Candy, who was also dancing, leaned over and said, "You better hold on because that fire shawl is going to turn your world upside down. That is powerful medicine!"

As her words echoed in my head I thought, 'Well, my whole world has already been turned upside down, so what else can come?'

When the drum started and it was time to dance, I draped the shawl around my shoulders. I could feel its weight as I moved and stepped. The fringe moved and swayed with me. I realized the shawl was actually dancing with me. It became part of my dance. As I moved, it moved. It quickly felt as though it was part of my body and connected to me. When I held my arms out, the shawl draped over my arms and the fringe below felt like wings.

I felt as if I could fly around the arbor. In fact, I did! I ran with my arms out and I just flew and I thought of myself as a beautiful owl. I pulled the shawl up from my shoulders and

over my head and then I pulled it around in front of me. I
closed it down around my face and I went close to the fire that
was in the middle of the arbor. I stood there with the fire,
looking down through the bottom of the shawl. With the shawl
covering my face, I could look down and see the fire near my
feet and I could see the fringe of the shawl, which started to
dance with the flames. I stood there, just swaying back and
forth.

In an instant I was transported to another place. I was in
another dance arbor. I looked around but didn't recognize
where I was. I didn't recognize any of the people. I heard a
whisper in my ear that said, "You're safe and we have
something to show you."

As I looked around at the dancers in this dance arbor, I
realized they were the ancient ones. They were the ancestors.
They were the oldest of the ancestors. As Joseph would say,
they were the ones who came before the before the before.
They were the ones who came before everything. They were
strong and steady and fearless. I felt they knew everything.
Not just everything about me, but the truth of everything. They
were still connected to the Source of life in all of us. They had
not forgotten who they were. They had no illusion that they
were separate from the Creator. They knew. I had never felt
such a moment of clarity and peace as I did when I was there
with ancestors. I knew I was safe.

They told me that it was time to dance with the fires again.
They said that for too long we, as people, had abandoned the
fire – the fires of all the directions and the fire of Spirit that was
creating all-that-is. In our abandonment of the fire, we could no
longer feel it and we could not feel the flames and the gifts.
We had forgotten that we couldn't feel it. We had forgotten
who we are and why we are.

They showed me the Fire Dance. They showed me the
medicine of the Fire Dance. They showed me the form of the
Fire Dance, and they showed me the magic of the Fire Dance,

and they told me it is time we realized that we are the ancestors and that what we do right now will change the planet. They said that what we do right now can change everything and that this dance will help the people remember who they are and how powerful they are. They will remember what they are capable of.

One by one, the five ancestors reached into the fire that was burning in that arbor and pulled out a coal from that fire and they blew their breath of life into those coals and they presented me with the coals. One by one each one of the ancestors placed a coal from the fire into my heart and gave me the gift of the five fires to bring back to the people, to hold the vision and to hold the truth of it. They gave me the gift of the Fire Dance. They gave me the blessing of the Fire Dance.

In an instant I was back at the Women's Web of Life dance. I still had the shawl pulled up over my head and the drums had stopped. Sammye Jo and Margarita were standing on each side of me, holding me up and helping to steady me. They turned me around and slowly walked me back to my place in the arbor and helped me to sit down. I took the fire shawl off and I folded it up and I put it back in the box that Patti had left.

We danced for another day, but I don't remember much of the dance after that. I was trying to hold on to that vision, to that gift and I was trying to understand what it all meant.

Sun Moon Fire

What I knew about visions was that they were powerful, life changing, and came like some kind of lightning bolt. I couldn't reconcile in my brain that what had happened to me when I was dancing with the fire shawl in the Women's Web of Life dance was some kind of vision.

I knew what I felt and what I witnessed. I knew I was no longer in the Women's Web of Life arbor and that I spent a few days in that other place. But after the Women's Web of Life dance, I tried to discount it. Who was I to be given something like that? I let it go as some kind of weird dream. I gave my attention to my business and the community, and I tried my best to hold together my relationship with Sam. I carried on juggling my work life and my community life.

However, I felt that there was something at my core level that was different. I had experienced changes through being on this path. I felt different after my first sweat lodge, my first dance, and my first trip to Africa. This was different from different. I didn't really know what that meant, but I sure felt it at the center of my being.

I tried to keep going on with my life. I kept moving. I kept showing up and saying yes. And then the dreams started coming. I dreamed of fire. Not the big, destructive, burning-everything fire that engulfs houses and forests. My dreams of fire were different. Night after night I dreamed of dancing with the beloved in the fire. I saw the fire in front of me, with flames that were five, six, or seven feet high. When I stepped closer, I could feel the fire reaching out to me with a gentle hand. It was the hand of someone who loved me and I reached my hand out to greet it. And as I did the flames wrapped around my fingers and gently lifted and pulled me into the bigger flame. I stepped in, and as I did I was no longer on the earth. I was two or three feet above the earth, inside the flame. I moved and danced inside the flames.

I'd had recurring dreams as a child and they were usually scary. This was not scary. It was beautiful. When I woke up in the middle of the night after a dream, I felt that something was missing. I wasn't in the flame anymore, and I would wake up with this longing that I couldn't explain.

I thought if I was busier finding interior design work and doing my spiritual practices, then I could distract myself and make myself tired enough to sleep through the night. I spent months doing that, and it didn't help. Night after night I had the same dream.

Sam never knew that I was awake night after night. I did not tell her about my experience in the Women's Web of Life dance, and I didn't tell her about the dreams either. I did not tell anyone. The Elders teach us to not speak of our visions for a period of time, some say three months. I believe a vision is like a seed and it takes time for that seed to become fully rooted and for it to be ready to be exposed to the world. We must make peace with it and nurture it and come to our own understanding of it before we speak to another about it. Once we tell our vision to another, it is no longer ours. It belongs to the world, and the world will try to interpret it in its own way. We must fully have that vision planted with our soul so that it will not be altered or trimmed by the world.

I knew the dreams were a message for me, and I knew I needed to do something. There was another dance coming up at the Center for Peace. It was the Sun Moon Dance which is four days long; it is a big commitment. When a dancer commits to dancing, they commit to dancing it four times. It is a visionary dance. It is where dancers go seeking a vision, much like a vision quest.

I knew that the dreams were telling me that I should work with the fires at that dance. Not as a moon mother, this time. Not somewhere else. This time I needed to be with the fire. I wrote to the chiefs, Steve and Nan Citty. They had been chiefs of this dance for years, since Joseph had passed the Sun Moon dance over to Steve. Steve asked John Pehrson to chief this dance with him and together they led this ceremony for a few years. When John became the chief of the Star Dance, Steve asked Nan to step into that role with him.

I knew they would be able to see how much it meant to me to work with the fire. At first the answer was "No, we have a fire keeper, but we do want you to come to the dance. Maybe we will have you serve this dance as a moon mother." I wrote back and said, "I will serve the dance in any way that I can best serve Spirit, and the dancers, and the two of you as chiefs." But again, I asked them to consider putting me on the fire. I didn't tell Steve and Nan about the dreams. I just kept asking.

As the dance drew near, most of the people who were coming to the dance to serve knew what they were going to do; whether they were going to be in the kitchen to help feed the people, or on the drum, or inside the arbor or outside the arbor as a dog soldier. Steve and Nan had not yet made a decision. I knew with all my heart that I wanted to be with the fire. If I could work with the fire, in that big ceremony, and I could connect with the fire from my dreams, the dreams would stop and I would have fulfilled what the fire was asking of me.

Two days before the dance, Steve wrote to me and said, "We're still not sure so when you pack to come to Tennessee, pack the things you will need if you are going to be a moon mother and pack the things you will need if you are going to keep fire and we'll just see how it goes."

That was so unusual. Usually the chiefs are clear about where each crew member is to be, how their energy will be used and how they can best serve the dance and the dancers. It was confusing to me to not be clear, but I trusted that Steve and Nan knew what was best and I knew that as much as I wanted to work on the fire, I had to be there, and if they needed me to be a moon mother, then that is what I would do. I would be there to serve the dance. I would say yes and show up and do whatever they asked me to do.

When I arrived Steve said to me, "Robbie, we need you on the fire. Would you go up and help Marcus with the sweat lodge fire for the dancers? He's our other fire keeper." I was ecstatic and so relieved. As much as I love being a moon mother and as much as I love working directly with the dancers, this was the first time in a dance ceremony that I was going to work with the fire. I was sure that working with the fire would answer any obligation that the fire was asking of me.

Marcus had worked with the fire for the Sun Moon dance for years, and he had worked with these two chiefs for so many years that he could practically read their minds. He knew what they needed and when they needed it. I was learning from one of the best fire keepers that there was. I was deeply grateful for that.

Sam was dancing that dance, and while I wanted to give her as much attention and support as I could, my first obligation was to the fire and to work with the fire for all of the dancers. I needed to be with the fire, and stay focused on it, and this proved to be difficult. I felt torn, and many times I struggled with my place, but I knew the fire was where I needed to be. I had to focus my energy. I could not step away from it, and I could not do it differently from the way that I was doing it. The fire was calling. I had to answer that call.

Endings and Beginnings

After the Sun Moon Dance, Sam and I struggled with the reality of where our relationship was. Neither of us could remain silent any longer. We had both been silent for so long that breaking the silence was very difficult. Once we did it was like the flood gates had opened. All of the fears, resentment and anger that we had been holding onto for our own individual reasons came rushing out. It flooded our space and the relationship. It flooded our lives.

Once it started coming, it was clear there was no damming it back up, or holding it back anymore. It became clear to me that the relationship, the partnership and my role in it couldn't exist anymore. Not as it was. It became clear that there was no way to repair it. There was no way to change it or fix it. There was no way to make it better by taking away all the anger and resentment, by cleaning up that flood and stopping it. There it was, all of it, in front of us, spoken and unspoken. It was there.

One of the most difficult things I have ever done in my life was to speak the words out loud to end the relationship, the partnership, and to walk away. With all of the flood waters and everything that had been between us, and what had not been cleared or resolved, there was no way to stay in it. There was no way that we could navigate through those waters and keep the community. There was just no way to do that. I knew that my decision to end the relationship with Sam would most likely end the community of Munay, and everything we had created around it, as well.

Not only did I have to find the strength within me to end an eight-year relationship but also to walk away from our spiritual community. I felt so responsible for the community, to all of the people. I felt responsible for their happiness, and for what they had worked towards creating. It was not just the physical things like bridges and paths, or ceremonial spaces, like the sweat lodge and medicine wheel. It was also the love and the connection that was created between each of us. I knew I was walking away from that.

I knew I was possibly breaking a trust and a bond. I really hoped to the depths of my soul that it wouldn't break the community. Still I had to take the chance. I could not stay in the relationship. It had to be done.

I had to be able to leave in such a way that I felt like I was holding onto my integrity and my honor, and the only way I knew how to do that was to stay silent about it all and to just leave.

The decisions that I made in those moments were based on the fear of being judged, the fear that members of the community would feel they had to pick sides or decide that one of us, either Sam or I, was right or wrong. The only way I knew how to do that was to not say or share anything with anyone about my decision, not about why I made it, and not about the details of the relationship. I also didn't share anything with anyone about my fears or my anger or my resentment. I continued to hold them in.

I didn't speak to Alison, who was my closest and dearest friend in the community at the time. I didn't seek out her counsel or comfort. I stayed quiet. I didn't talk to Jamie, or Big Bob, or to anybody. I thought I was being strong, showing strength, and that I was taking the high road by making decisions that would make it easy for all of these people to continue loving Sam and loving me. What I learned in the months and years after that is that friendship and community is a two-way street. I couldn't ask the people in the community to trust me with their fear, anger, grief and sorrow, and then not trust them with my own.

That's really what it boiled down to. I didn't trust anyone else to hold those things for me. To help me, support me, and be with me in those times of grief and sorrow and loss – loss not only of the relationship but also of the community. Not trusting others to be there for me pulled me further and further away from those that I loved the most.

Leaving Munay and Sam and the community made me feel as if I had left that life completely behind. I wasn't sure what that meant for me with my spiritual path. I found a little house in an old neighborhood in Charlotte, and interestingly enough, when I told the man who owned the house and had grown up there my name he said he knew someone by the name of Ed Warren years ago and asked if I was related to him. That was my father.

He remembered my father from when he was twelve years old, and my father had made such an impression on him. He told me that my father took a chance on him when he was a young boy, took him under his wing, and taught him in the boys groups through the church. It was so wonderful to sit on the front steps of that house and talk to him and listen to him talk about my father and see my father through his eyes.

What I realized when I was sitting on those steps was that not only was Spirit moving through this man, Spirit was moving through my father, leading me to exactly where I needed to be. I couldn't afford the rent for this house, but he told me because of my father he would lower the rent and he would make it possible for me to live there. He waived the deposit and let me move in and start over. What a gift!

However, I still had bills and obligations that I had to pay at Munay. Sam and I decided to put Munay on the market to sell it. That was one more blow to the community and all of the people who had been there so often and felt that Munay was part of their home. It was also a signal that the break was permanent and really happening.

The housing market was dropping, and we ended up upside down on the mortgage at Munay. Even though Munay had been valued at a million dollars, that number kept dropping, almost by the day, and eventually it ended up below the actual mortgage amount. This was called an 'under-water' mortgage. Sam was still living there, taking care of the animals we had, and taking care of the things around the house and showing it every time a potential buyer came by. We were desperate to sell it. We had to get out from under it because we were in danger of foreclosure.

I had never experienced anything like that. I had always been able to earn what I needed to earn. I had never experienced being upside-down on a mortgage, or late on payments. While there was part of me that felt panicked about it all, there was a larger part of me that felt at peace, that it would all work out as it should. I kept remembering my landlord sitting on the steps and how Spirit opened the way for me to be able to do that.

Over the next few months as we continued to try to sell Munay and I tried to generate business, the community was slowly falling apart. I didn't have the income coming in anymore. I didn't know what I was going to do. For several months in a row I didn't think I would have enough to pay the bills and the rent, to pay bills at Munay, or even to buy groceries.

I even gathered up jewelry that had been given to me over the years, even as a child by my father and later from old boyfriends. I took all the rings, necklaces, and anything I could get my hands on to the jewelry store and sold it. I was shocked at how little I got for the silver and the gold and the tiny diamond chips in small rings and necklaces.

Yet somehow I always had enough each month to pay for what I needed. Spirit saw that I got what I needed.

Letting Go

The house that Sam and I owned was not selling. The bank had given us a date of foreclosure and they were going to take the house – something I had never dreamed would happen. I may have spent some of my time in denial about what was happening, but there was nothing I could do when it did happen.

Our realtor did her best to sell the house. When we did find someone to buy the house, even though it was what was called a 'short sell', for fifty thousand less than we owed on the house, even though it was based on the tax value of the house, the bank rejected the offer. The bank chose to foreclose on the house, to take the property rather than to sell it. During those times, the banking and mortgage industry was just insane. It didn't make sense. I thought there must be something going on behind the scenes that we didn't know about. There had to be some kind of kickback for the banks to foreclose because they were foreclosing on so many people, everywhere. So many people were losing their houses.

After the house was foreclosed on, after we lost Munay, I was sad, but I still had an overwhelming feeling that things were shifting and changing. I knew that it would be okay. The way that I looked at life, at my life, was different. I loved my little home, my own little piece of the world, even if it was a rental house. I made my own decisions and decided for myself where I would go and what I would do.

Although I felt the loss of Munay and that community, at the same time I felt as though something was lifted off me. It may be hard to understand how working so hard to build a house and community with ceremonial and other healing spaces and then to lose it could feel like something good. But it did. It felt like it opened up the opportunity for me move into something new.

Even though I didn't really know what that new thing was, there had to be a letting go of the old, a letting go of the past. Sometimes we have to let go of the old. Even when it feels as though it is being ripped from our fingers, we just have to let go. No matter how much resistance I had, no matter how much I fought and tried to save that house, when it was ultimately ripped from my fingers, there was something about it that felt good.

I kept trying to move forward. I kept trying to do the things that I needed to do. I worked every day. I had mountains and mountains of bills and financial obligations that I was trying to pay off, little by little, but it was becoming more and more impossible to do. I found myself in a financial hole. I tried to pay down the monthly debt that had been created by my business and I was back to not having anything. I tried to make that work until I finally surrendered and went to a bankruptcy attorney.

The first thing she asked me was, "What took you so long to get here? The market collapsed three years ago."

"What do you mean?" I answered, "I've been trying to pay off all my debt. I've been trying to work this stuff down. I have been trying to do the right thing."

"There's only so much of the right thing that you can do," she said.

"What do you mean?" I asked.

"You've been trying and trying and you've been digging yourself further and further into a hole. You are trying to pay off the debts of a million-dollar-a-year company while you have no real income to speak of. It is impossible to do. It will never be done. While I admire what you're trying to do, it's really stupid. The numbers don't match, it doesn't work. Of anyone I know who needs to file bankruptcy, you are it," she said. "I have seen so many people with the collapse of the building industry and the housing industry. So many people come through my doors and say they want to file for bankruptcy, but they have all these assets, homes and vacation homes, retirement plans and money put away. They want to claim bankruptcy and not pay off their debtors. You have absolutely nothing and yet you are still scrounging around trying to do the right thing. You are what these laws were designed to help and protect. Not the multi-millionaires who have all these properties and money in offshore accounts that could pay off their debts. You will never dig yourself out of this hole. You cannot catch up. You cannot undo what has been done. We need to file for bankruptcy, and you need relief from this stress. Your company, your corporation is gone."

I went home that day and let it all sink in. I thought about what she said and about what I thought was right, that I had to pay these debts off and figure out a way to pay the loans that I had gotten for the company and the old lines of credit. When I looked and saw what she saw, in black and white, the amount of debt that my company owed versus what my income was now, there was no way out of it. It was insurmountable, and there was no way to reconcile it.

I had a lot of anger at myself. I thought that I should have seen it coming, and I should have gotten out when I could have. I should have done this, and I should have done that. But I was an interior designer, not a financial analyst. I didn't know how to look at what was happening on Wall Street with mortgage companies and insurance companies backing each other over and over again until it didn't have any meaning any more. Without a business degree, I didn't know what that meant for me, for my clients, or for the builders.

I was holding myself responsible to a level that just didn't make any sense. I was misdirecting my anger at myself. I had to turn to the tools that I had learned during my twelve-step program, of understanding responsibility – what I was and what I was not responsible for. What I could not be held accountable for was other people's choices. People had chosen to buy houses they could not afford, and bankers and mortgage brokers had chosen to create shady deals and unscrupulous practices to help these people get in over their heads. Still others were gambling with these people's debts. These things were not my doing.

Somehow I was holding myself accountable. All of this brought up more shame. The idea of bankruptcy to me meant that I was not good enough. If I signed those papers it meant that I had failed. I told the lawyer that I would get back to her; I needed to think about it a little bit longer.

I put it on the back burner and kept trying to pay the bills. I kept trying to move forward. I kept having the dreams. The fire was coming to me in the night. The ancestors were whispering in my ear. I felt that something was building up, and I didn't know how to pull that pressure release valve. What was it that was building up?

Faithful Journey

I received a message from Jeanne White Eagle that they were going to South Africa again. I felt that familiar pull that I needed to be there, but I did not know how I was going to get there. A round-trip ticket to South Africa was around twelve hundred dollars, and at the time I was selling jewelry to pay the power bill and maybe buy a few groceries!

Even so, I knew I had to be there, and I didn't know how to make it happen, but I also knew that I would make it happen. I knew I needed to go. I needed to look Gogo Nomsimane in the eye and feel that love and that safety. I needed to see Susie, to see her face, and to know that it would all be okay. These were the people that I loved so much who were half a world away, and I knew I had to get there. I knew I had to be a part of the ceremony, a part of the For The One Dance that was going to be in South Africa that year.

I sat and prayed about it and asked, "How is this going to happen? What seems so impossible can be possible, but how? How will this show up for me?" As I sat there and prayed and I felt my connection to the earth in Mother Africa, and I felt my longing to be there, I could feel Mother Earth move up through the earth into my body, and I could feel her pulling me there. I knew that all I had to do was ask.

The next morning I composed an email, and for the first time I poured my heart onto that page. I had never told anyone in the community, or even the broader community that I was part of, the depth of my feelings, sorrows or regrets, or of my pull to be part of this medicine dance, and of my connection to the place. I had never shared those deep feelings with anyone.

That morning I asked for help. I asked if anyone was willing to contribute any amount of money to help. I asked that if they couldn't send money, would they please send prayers to help me get there and for me to receive what I needed.

I took a big deep breath and, as scared as I was, I hit the 'send' button and sent that email out all around the world. Within a few days I started getting letters in the mail, containing deeply heartfelt words from my dearest friends and family around the world. They told me how much they believed in me and how much they wanted to support my spiritual path, and how they understood how it felt to be called by Spirit. Some people sent a dollar with their letter. Some people sent a check for ten dollars, and others for a hundred dollars.

I was blown away. I sat in my living room day after day, reading the letters of support that came in. I received letters of encouragement and understanding, and I had never felt that. I had never exposed myself emotionally in that way before and then felt the support come back to me. I had never felt worthy before. But my friends and family saw that I was worthy, and so I read those letters every day, and every day I added a little more to the pile of money towards my ticket.

When I had received about nine hundred dollars, my mother told me that I could go ahead and buy the ticket on her credit card, and she would pay the rest, which was three hundred and eleven dollars. I was blown away because I didn't think that my mother really understood what I was doing. But I knew my mother loved me and she has always supported me in every way, and this was one of them.

I took all of the cash that had been coming in and put it in my mother's hands, and she bought my ticket for me. That ticket was bought on faith, hope and love, and on the prayers of my friends and family, with the support of Spirit and my family. During the next few days, as I packed my bags and prepared to leave, a few more letters with checks and a few more single dollars arrived. By the time I left I had received an additional total of three hundred and eleven dollars. I had never been as happy in my life as I was to take that money from my friends and my community and to put that in my mother's hands and to know that the exact amount of money that I needed to pay for the ticket in full and complete had come in.

Not a penny more, not a penny less. One thousand two hundred and eleven dollars.

Just when I thought I couldn't be any more blessed, I received an email from Susie in South Africa and she said, "Robbie, there is someone who wants to sponsor you for all of your meals and lodging while you are here for the dance. They want to remain anonymous." I don't know how much money that was. It was another few hundred dollars, for sure.

What I realized in those twenty four hours before I got on the plane was that my trip to South Africa was paid in full, with the support of people who knew me and loved me. It was one of the most amazing gifts I could ever have received. Not the gift of the ticket, or the food and lodging, but the gift of the recognition that I was loved and supported and understood.

Clearing the Hollow Bone

At first, it didn't occur to me that this was my opportunity to take the time that I wanted two years earlier in 2007 when I thought I was going to Africa alone. Instead, Sam was with me for those five weeks. Having recently ended my relationship with her, I was given another opportunity to go alone, and in so doing I realized I was stepping out on my own spiritual path. Sam had been so much a part of my spiritual growth, awakening, and development and everything I had become, but now it was up to me to stand on my own two feet and walk my own path, finding my own may. That is what the trip to South Africa did for me.

Going to South Africa opened those doors. I didn't have to consider anyone else. I didn't have to behave in any special way. I could look at the choices that were in front of me and decide what I wanted. I hadn't done that in so long and I didn't realize what it meant to make those choices for myself. There were moments when I had to stop and ask, 'What is it that I really want?' I had spent so much time and energy thinking what it was that we needed and what we wanted and to keep things in our relationship going forward that I hadn't really considered what it was that I needed. That was part of the gift that I got in Africa. What did I need? What did I want? How was I going to stand on my own?

What a beautiful gift it was. I spent time with Gogo Hugh on the sacred land of his ancestors. I listened to his stories about how he visited his grandfather on this land as a child. I walked the land and felt it. Walking the land reminded me so much of the land that I had seen in the movie, Out of Africa. It brought back such vivid memories of what I held in my heart for what that part of Africa was, and what the settling of Africa was. His land showed that to me in person. He showed me his grandfather's house with beautiful green vines growing up the walls, and we walked down the path through the veld to a beautiful small river and a waterfall where we had a picnic. It was absolutely magical. What a gift it was to me to be able to make the choice to spend the day in that way.

I got time to spend with Susie and her partner Cajun. To be with the two of them on the land at Simunye, to sit on their porch, to hear their stories, to look at the chickens that they had in little traveling coops, to see how they had created a life together in that rugged environment – just to sit with my friends, no agenda, just to be – was such a gift.

I truly believe that on that trip to Africa, that first time venturing out on my own, Spirit did start to hollow me out and clear me out, and relieve me of all of the things that I had been carrying for so long. I was learning how to deal with fear, anger, sorrow and resentment rather than to eat. My weight had dropped significantly over the months that I was in the twelve-step program. I could see clearer, I could feel deeper and more authentically, without reaction. My whole way of life and being *in* life was changing.

I was, once again, asked to be a moon mother and to work with another new moon mother to prepare her to step into her role. As I devoted myself to being fully present for the medicine dance, for the chiefs, and the dancers and to do the medicine work, I felt the connection to Spirit, and I felt myself become the hollow bone for Spirit to move through. Spirit was able to work with me and mold me into something new, something different, to use me as a vessel and move through me. I could feel the breath of God blow right through me, as if I was the hollow bone whistle that dancers blow in the Sun Moon Dance.

For the first time on that trip to Africa, I began to feel the freedom of the breath of Spirit moving through me. The freedom of being a vessel for God. It showed up in the way that I was able to work with the dancers, and in the way that I was able to be fully present with my friends. I know this is continual work, to remain that hollow bone. It always has been, and it always will be.

What I realized on that trip to Africa was that all of my experiences, all of the things that had brought me to that point, were necessary. Everything that I had learned in my years with Sam, everything that I had learned from watching the teachers, and from showing up and saying "yes," from listening to Joseph, and listening to Jeanne White Eagle, from paying attention every time Perry Robinson spoke and to watching Steve Citty and Nan be with the sun moon dancers. It was all necessary.

I realized on that trip that everyone was my teacher and that the clearing of the hollow bone had begun. And it felt good.

Otter Dance

When I came back home in December 2009 after spending three weeks in Africa, I felt revived and alive. I felt spiritually fed and complete and open. I knew I could conquer the world and do anything. When I got back I was faced, once again, with a bank account that had nothing in it and with a business that was barely afloat – if you could call it a business anymore!

I had to figure out how to support myself. I knew I had to do something different. I had created my own business twenty some odd years earlier, and I had been in business for myself for my entire adult life. I had not worked for someone else, except in my early twenties.

Now I needed to be emotionally open to go and work for another company. I started applying for jobs, and I excitedly searched for jobs with companies that I had done business with in the past. Some of these companies were still, somehow, hanging on after the crash in the market and were still in business. There were a few jobs that were quite promising, and several companies seemed eager to have me with my skills, knowledge, and level of expertise in the production and design business, but while they liked the idea of having me on board, they told me, "We can't pay you what you are worth." I said I was willing to take any salary they deemed fair. I wasn't looking for the same income I was earning when my business was thriving. But it was hard for people to understand why I would make such a decision, and because they were unsure of my motivation, they never offered me a job.

I realized that one of the things that had driven me so hard to be successful in the business world was my ego. It was an ego-driven business, and I had been right on board with that. However, through the years of following this spiritual path, I began to recognize more and more that ego would not bring me happiness and fulfillment. The status and material things that I thought came along with being the best interior designer were driven by ego and were no longer as important to me.

If I could make enough money to pay the bills and to keep myself afloat, I would be happy. I didn't need to be compensated at such a high level. But those companies had not been on my spiritual journey with me, and it was hard for them to comprehend why someone who had been the owner and CEO of the largest interior design company in the Charlotte metro area would take a pay cut as well as a status cut. They kept asking me, "Why would you come and work for us when you can work for yourself?"

I tried to explain and encouraged these companies to take advantage of me, my knowledge, and my experience. I urged them to take advantage of my connections to what was left of the construction and design business and pay me a fair wage. They were suspicious, they thought there was an ulterior motive, and they were fearful. They told me that when the economy picked up I would just leave and start my own company again. They couldn't trust that I would stay.

I was going through an incredibly confusing time. I was completely willing to let go of my ego-driven, materialistic life to step into a new idea, to step into being of service and bring my expertise to another company to help them grow, but I had one rejection after another. So I faltered along with the few clients and some small jobs I still had.

I felt there was something that I needed to create. I knew something needed to be born, something that would connect me with other people who were on the same spiritual path, I didn't quite know what that was.

I had remained friends with many people from the Munay community, but we were no longer gathering and connecting on a regular basis for drum circles and sweat lodges or medicine wheels or any ceremonies. It was as if we were all scattered to the wind. I could not quite figure out how to create something that could bring it all back together. There was very little space at my new home, and I could not have an open fire in my yard, much less have a sweat lodge. There was no way I could recreate what I had before at Munay. Something new was trying to be born, trying to come about. I felt so strongly about it, but I didn't know what it was.

Then someone asked me, "Do you have a website?"

"What on earth would I have a website for?" I asked.

"So that people can know who you are and what you do."

"Oh, you mean for my interior design business?" I said.

"No, no. I mean for your spiritual work," she said.

"Work, spiritual work? I am on a spiritual path," I responded.

"Yes, yes, but you also do spiritual work," she said.

And so an idea was born. Later more people started asking me if I had a website.

Other people began to ask me if they could come to me for spiritual counseling and for help. My answer was always yes, and I turned what could have been my dining room into a space where I could sit and talk to people. I started seeing people quietly in my home, doing energetic clearing and shamanic work, and doing shamanic journeying for answers, for help.

I heard Joseph's voice, saying, "Ah, you're a medicine woman!"

I thought, 'Oh, is that what this is?'

I didn't understand how all these people were finding me. Sometimes people remembered me and said, "Oh, yes I remember you. You used to have a place out in Stanley, North Carolina. I was there a couple of years ago."

When I spoke to Sammye Jo about it, she said, "You know, people just know and they come. They seek you out and they call you. They can feel it, and they know." She told me there had to be a way for people to find me and connect with me, and I thought about the people who asked me about a website.

One night I woke up in the middle of the night with the words "Otter Dance" in my head. Well, Otter is my medicine totem. It is my power animal, ally, friend, guide and teacher. Otter medicine had played a big role in my life. But Otter Dance? What does that mean?

I rolled it around my head. I looked up the domain name, and it was available. So I bought it. Over the next few months, I started working on a website. I listened to what people had been asking me, and came up the questions I thought I should answer on the website: What is it that you do? Where have you traveled? Do you have photos? What is a Sweat Lodge? What is Otter Medicine?

I met an experienced designer, Katie Mattson, through Big Bob. She was not just a techie web designer. She was on a spiritual path, and she understood what I was looking for. Katie got me and what I was doing. I gave her the text, and she worked on it. Then she called me and told me we were ready to go live. For a moment I went into a panic, but I realized that if I didn't put myself out there, nobody would ever know.

She pushed the button, and Otter Dance was born.

Otter Dance Lodge

I tried to find a balance in my new life while my old life was falling apart and collapsing around me. I had finally gone ahead with the bankruptcy proceedings. But I was also lucky to find a position with a prominent, local re-modeling company. It felt like a blessing to work for this company every day on a nine-to-five job and be done after only forty hours a week. It gave me more free time than I had ever had before while working in my own company. I wasn't making a lot of money, but I was making enough to pay the bills. I had a new job, and I had Otter Dance. It all felt so exciting.

When people asked me, "What is Otter Dance?" I didn't really know how to answer because Otter Dance was a website, and yet it was so much more than that. It felt like a place, but it wasn't a physical place. I couldn't understand what it was. It felt important. It felt big. It felt like a community, except that there was no community. It wasn't even a virtual community with things like online chats. It was just me and a website, sharing information.

In the midst of this I kept getting strong messages from Spirit. My dreams with the fire continued on and on. Night after night I dreamed of dancing with the fire and how the fire reached out to me and took my hand so lovingly and lifted me up and spun me around, twirling and dancing. I didn't understand what that meant. I kept thinking about the Women's Web of Life dance and dancing with fire shawl. I kept thinking about what I saw. I wondered what it was that I had experienced because in that moment it felt real, but I didn't know how it could be real.

There were times when I woke up in the middle of the night and felt like I could feel the heat of the fire. I heard the ancestors whispering and saying, "Now is the time. It is time for you to give this to the people."

It was scary, not in the sense that something bad was going to happen. It was frightening because it felt so big and so important, and I still didn't understand it. I had heard people talking about visions, about Joseph and how his dances and the sound chambers came to him in a vision. Other people had had visions, but I still couldn't imagine that what I had experienced was a vision. I thought it was a dream.

I held onto it. I kept turning it around in my head. What had I seen? What did my dreams mean? What were the messages that the ancestors gave me in the Women's Web of Life dance? What was all of that?

After I had been away from Munay for about a year, I was asked to meet a group of women who were creating a community on a beautiful piece of land up near Lake Norman. We talked for hours and hours about what they were creating. They shared with me what they believed about the earth and what they held true for themselves, and it was so in alignment with what I believed to be true for myself. They invited me to build a sweat lodge there and hold ceremonies as often as I wanted to.

It was the first time since I had left Munay over a year earlier that I was being asked to step into this sacred ceremony, the same ceremony that brought me into all these teachings. I was being asked to step up, and step in, in a different way, and to make a commitment to the ceremony on my own. I remembered what Jeanne White Eagle had said to me, and so I said yes and told them I would hold a ceremony every month.

I sent out an email saying that we were building a sweat lodge, and so many wonderful people showed up to help build the lodge. Some of the people from Munay showed up in support, as well as some new people from Charlotte whom I had met in other ways.

We cleared and readied the land. Then we blessed it and built the lodge with love, prayers and blessings in the old way that I was taught from watching so many other people build lodges. Afterwards I led the lodge while Jamie kept the fire. It felt whole and complete. I felt as though I had closed a circle after leaving Munay, after starting over and venturing out on my own. This was the first lodge with Otter Dance.

Exploring all Fronts

Along with a new-found freedom in my work, I had a new freedom in my personal life. I had the freedom to explore, to date, to put myself out there and see what it was that I wanted. I knew I was neither ready nor willing to step back into any kind of serious or committed relationship. What I did want was to get out there and have fun. I had never done that before. I had spent my entire life going from monogamous relationship to monogamous relationship.

Without really exploring it, how could I know what was the best option for me? What did I want? What did I want to create? Who did I want to be with? I had bounced around from relationship to relationship, but I had never answered those questions for myself. Some relationships lasted one year, others two. The relationship with Sam was longer than any of the others. It lasted eight years.

In all of my past relationships, I had never really explored what it was I wanted or how I wanted to be in a relationship. Who did I want to be with? Who was I and what did I want and need, if anything, from someone else?

I became quite excited at the possibility of finding out. A lot of people laughed at me, but I joined several dating sites. I wrote up my profile, talking about what I was interested in, what I was not interested in (mainly *not* being in a relationship). It was fun and enticing. In the beginning I was bombarded by emails. It soon became clear that most of these men had not even read my profile. It seemed that they were just shotgunning in the dark to see who would respond.

I learned a lot about myself during that time, about discernment, and about paying attention. Through the few emails that I did return and the connections that I did make, I learned to ask a lot of questions and I paid attention in a different way from ever before. One thing I thoroughly enjoyed was first dates. I was clear; I didn't expect anyone to pay for my meals, or anything else. I was willing to sit down and have a meal, a drink or a cup of coffee with someone just to see, just out of curiosity. I found that if I really paid attention and asked a lot of questions I could learn a whole lot about a person.

I went out with a broad spectrum of people in a range of ages. I found out quickly that I had nothing in common with men my age and slightly older. Most of them were stuck in the pattern of working hard to buy their big houses so that one day they might retire. They were looking forward to slowing down towards retirement. They wanted to have grills in the back yard and watch TV in the evenings. That was not me. Me? I was ready to go back to Africa, to explore and to go to Croatia and Norway. I was ready to travel all over the world for the medicine dances and to connect with people from all over the world.

I found that men younger than me were much more interested in what I was doing and what I had to say and share. I found that fascinating. Quite frankly, I couldn't understand what they found fascinating in me at all. But they did. And they were interested. I had also, through the help of my recovery and the twelve-step program, not only developed a stronger sense of myself and how to deal with people and with my emotions, but also found myself in a new body.

It was absolutely amazing to be eighty pounds lighter at forty eight years old. It was a lot of fun to be in a new place with a new body and to have people interested in me for what I thought and for what I what I was doing – and for younger men to find me sexy!

I went on a lot of first dates, and a few second dates. I explored a lot and asked a lot of questions. When I knew that I would not want to have a second meal with a particular person, I was straight-forward and honest. I would gently tell them, "I have enjoyed our conversation, but this is not going to go anywhere. There is nothing here for either one of us and so there is no reason for us to continue. Thank you for your company and thank you for sharing a meal with me." That I could say this and walk away was new behavior for me.

I enjoyed exploring this and finding out these things about myself and I was having quite a good time doing it. At the same time that I was exploring on my personal journey, really connecting with these things about myself, connecting with my wants and desires, likes and dislikes, I was also creating a stronger spiritual foundation for myself.

Quite honestly, I didn't think I would find another life partner who was connected to the spiritual work that I did, so I didn't bother to look for that. I thought I would just have fun and enjoy this part of my life. I didn't need a life partner. I didn't need someone to be in my life. I could stand on my own on my spiritual path and move forward and enjoy life – and keep them separate.

I became good at compartmentalizing my spiritual life from my personal and business life. I enjoyed the work that I was doing in the remodeling business. It was good to be in touch with my creative side, and life felt fulfilling again. I felt like I was moving forward. At the same time, more and more people were coming to me and asking me to counsel them, asking for help. I was also going to Tennessee as often as I could to attend dances. I needed to stay connected to the dances and to the fires.

Speaking of the Vision

I got a long email from Candy, which was not unusual. Often Candy would write to me and share insights and visions, or sometimes just the weather. Candy was good about sharing what was happening in her day to day world with me. We joked about it a lot. That day her email said, "I had the craziest dream last night, and I have to tell you about it because it doesn't make sense to me and maybe it will make sense to you."

In her dream she described seeing me standing near a rather large fire. I had all kinds of things like sticks, ribbons and feathers tied in my hair in different ways and my hair itself was wild and full, curly and crazy. Much like it is in everyday life, but without the sticks tied up into it. She said I was dancing around the fire "with wild abandon" and with great intent and intention. She added that I was so focused on the fire she knew it held a powerful meaning, and even though she didn't understand it, she felt that it was really strong, and powerful.

She also saw another fire a little further away, and she saw a man feeding Hershey's Kisses to that fire. He stayed with that fire off to the side while I danced with the larger fire. At the end of her description, she asked, "Does this mean anything to you at all?"

Reading her email took my breath away. I had been dreaming these dreams for so long and now my dreams were spilling over into Candy's dreams! She was seeing the dancing with the fire and the messages. It scared me so much that all I could do in that moment was write back to her and tell her that

I had no idea what the dream meant. But I knew eventually I would have to tell someone about the vision.

I thought that being a Fire Keeper for the Sun Moon Dance would stop the dreams, but, as much as I loved working with the fire during that dance, I was wrong. The fires showed up in my dreams every night. Every night the fire and the ancestors took me back and reminded me of my experience and showed me, again, what I saw in the Women's Web of Life dance. The ancestors kept saying to me, "You now hold this. It's time to give it to the world. You are to give it to the world."

I woke up every morning with a sense of urgency and a sense of responsibility. During the experience I had given my word to the ancestors that I would bring this forward, that I would introduce this to the world again. I felt my own honor and integrity pushing me to keep my word.

I sat in my little house in North Carolina trying to figure out my life, dating, and what I wanted in a partner. I was trying to figure out how to earn a decent living. I was also trying to figure out how to be this thing that Joseph told me about – a medicine woman. At the same time people were coming to me asking for help, ceremonies and guidance, or to do journeys to meet with their spirit guides. I felt a little crazy because it felt like I was walking in both worlds. I was in the normal world trying to be everyday Robbie, and then I was stepping into a sacred and ceremonial space with the ancestors, working with people one-on-one, working with their spirit guides and stepping into the spirit realms and other dimensions. It was so confusing.

My dreams kept my head swirling. I had no idea how all of these things were connected or how to put them all together. What I did know was that after holding the vision for almost two years I couldn't hold it anymore. I had to speak it out loud. The seed of the vision that was planted by the ancestors and spirits in the Women's Web of Life dance had grown into something that could no longer be contained inside me. It had to become manifested into the world. The only way I knew how to do that was to dance what the ancestors had shown me and to dance it into the reality of this world. I wasn't sure what that meant. But that's what I knew I had to do. I had to dance the Fire Dance, and I assumed that I would do it at the Center for Peace.

I knew I needed to expose myself and my vision and ask the council at the Center for Peace for permission to dance the Fire Dance in their arbor. In order to do that I had to explain what the dance looked like, explain to them about the five fires, give them as much detail as I could about walking on the fire, and what that meant and what that would create for the dancer and the world. I had to explain what that would bring up and shift and change, not only for the dancer who walked across the fire but for everyone present.

I wrote to Perry and Jeanne Robinson, and Steve and Nan Citty, who were on the council, and told them about my vision and experience. I was scared to death. I thought, 'Who am I to write to these people who have been on this spiritual path for so long, who know and hold these truths so deeply?' I needed their permission and blessing for me to do it. I think on a deeper level I needed their understanding. I really needed their help, and I was not good at asking for help.

Instead of asking for their help, guidance, and advice, I simply asked for their permission. I wrote an email that I sent out to all the council members and when I went onto the Center for Peace website to get all of their addresses I realized that Sam had stepped up and become a council member and that she would be part of the decision-making process. I have to admit that scared me because even though I was with Sam when I had the vision I had not told her about it. Up until I wrote to the council, I had not shared it with anyone. So Sam – and all the others with whom I had been so often and whom I trusted so much – would be hearing about it for the first time through an email. That was scary to me. I rarely allowed myself to feel vulnerable with others. But I needed to put myself in their hands and ask.

I wrote the email, reread and reread it so many times that it stopped making any sense so I hit the send button and sent it out there with a prayer, asking the ancestors for a blessing. All I knew was that I needed to dance this dance. If I danced with the five fires, it would change everything. The dreams would stop. I would then know what to do with the vision. Without dancing it myself, though, how could I know? I couldn't ask anyone else to dance this dance, not if I had not done it myself. I couldn't ask anyone else to walk through the fire, not unless I had done it myself. So I had to ask permission.

Weeks went by without an answer or a response. I knew they had received it and I knew they could come together in council. I just had to be patient, and I am not patient. I know that about myself. Once I make a decision, I am inclined to push and push, and so I was resisting the urge to push them by writing to ask why they hadn't responded. I had to trust that it would be okay.

I even started building it up in my head, knowing they would come back and embrace me and hold me up and hold up this vision that I had. I knew I would be supported. This was my spiritual family. My mentors. My teachers. These were the people who had shared so much with me. I just knew in my heart that I would be completely supported.

I started planning what it would look like. Having written the letter I almost felt that I now had permission to speak of the vision and the dance. I spent some time with two of my dearest friends, Marty Jones and Teresa Hutson. I met both of them for the first time at my first For The One dance; Marty and I were dog soldiers together and Teresa was the drum chief. After that we were at many ceremonies together, and both of them were with me for those memorable five weeks in Africa.

We spent the night at Marty's house and we had a great dinner. It was a wonderful girlfriends' night out. We had a slumber party and took silly selfie pictures with our cell phones and even posted them on Facebook. We had a great time. As the night was wearing down, and we were all getting a little bit tired, I knew it was the right time to share the vision of the Fire Dance with them. I knew they would understand and that they wouldn't laugh at me. It just felt that the time was right to share it.

We sat around the table in Marty's sun room, and she burned a little sage. I told them about the vision, the medicine, the healing, the changes, and the shifts that it would bring for every person. Marty and Teresa were wonderful; they laughed with me and they cried with me. They told me that they would be there to support me when I danced this dance. They said they would help me in any way they could. They told me they felt the importance of this dance.

When I went to that very first For The One dance, I was so naïve. I was blown away by their knowledge, their understanding, and their sheer presence in spirit. Now to have them sitting around the table, giggling with me, like school girls and yet holding me up and supporting me, I felt incredibly blessed. I knew that not only were we sisters on a spiritual path, we were friends on the deepest level and no matter what happened, when I danced the Fire Dance, I would be safe, I would be supported, and I would be okay.

I kept moving forward. I had now spoken about it and written about it. The dreams were still coming, but they felt less urgent and less forced. It felt more like a relaxing into, and more of a settling into the reality of what was to come, and it felt good. The ancestors were letting me sleep better. The fires did not want to dance as much. It felt as though these beautiful fire beings and the ancestors knew that inevitable things were now set into motion. I didn't know that. But they did. The ancestors knew that once I spoke about this there was no taking it back. Once I shared it with another being, it became real. It was no longer my vision and my secret. It belonged to the world. It was still my duty to carry it, however, and they knew that. I did not know that.

Pushed out of the Nest

In November, 2010, I was in South Africa, staying in the beautiful home of my friends Jill and Debbie, preparing for another dance, thinking about the dancers and serving as a moon mother. I woke up at about three a.m. to find that a thunder and lightning storm was rocking the world. I stayed up and watched and listened to the lightning and thunder doing their dance.

When the sun came up, I decided to get up and check my emails, as I did every day. I was desperate to hear from the Center for Peace. Sure enough, there was a response in my inbox. They told me, in a most loving and kind way, that they didn't see how I could dance the Fire Dance there, given what it entailed. There were reasons why I couldn't build the five fires in the arbor, and I understood why. Their beloved pets were buried in the places where I would build the fires. Dayska, the wolf that had breathed in my ear and Red Dog, were both buried there. Of course that wouldn't make sense.

Perry and Jeanne Robinson asked if I would be willing to come and meet with them and whether I could change some of the aspects of this dance. Then I would be able to do it. They said that I would not be able to do it in the arbor, but perhaps in the meadow near the arbor. I told them that of course I would meet with them when I returned from South Africa.

I looked at the things that they asked me to change. They wanted me to eliminate the fire walk, to not hold the dance in the arbor, to change things just enough where, from my understanding, it would not be the same dance that the ancestors gave me. When I returned to the States, I set up a time that I could go and meet with Jeanne and Perry. I felt sadness around it because I felt I was being asked to make a choice between my beloved elders, mentors, and teachers and their understanding and parameters, and the vision that was given to me by the ancient ones.

I didn't know what to do or what the answer would be. I had spent my whole life being a people pleaser and trying to work within all the things that other people needed me to do so that everyone else could be happy. I had spent my whole life trying to keep the people who were important to me happy and make the right decisions and do the right thing *for them* and now was being faced with this decision in what felt like the worst of ways.

It was a four and a half hour drive from my home to the Center for Peace. I drove in silence. I asked Spirit and the spirit guides for answers to help me know what to do, to know how to be okay with this. I felt I was losing something. I felt I was making a choice between bringing the Fire Dance into reality and being at my spiritual home when I did it. If I didn't dance this dance at the Center for Peace I had no idea where I would dance it. I felt lost. It didn't even occur to me that this might not work, that I might be told 'no.'

When I sat down with Jeanne and Perry, they were so kind and loving. They asked many questions about my vision and the dance. They wanted to understand; they wanted clarity. The rest of the council had given Jeanne and Perry permission to talk with me, ask me questions, and to take my answers back to the council. As I shared with them what I was given from the ancestors and they shared with me their concerns, their questions, their issues, it became clear that the Fire Dance was not going to be birthed into reality at the Center for Peace. I was devastated.

We agreed that this was not going to be a good fit, and they told me that if I was able to see clear and commune with Spirit to get the clarity and make the changes to the dance that they needed, then I would be welcome to dance the Fire Dance at the Center for Peace. They told me how much they loved me and how much they respected me and the vision, but they felt strongly about these things. They felt strongly about not having the dance inside the arbor, about not having the fires in the places of the four directions, and me not walking across the coals.

Those were the things that set up the vision and the alchemy – the energy, the medicine, the foundation – of this dance and how it worked. I did as they asked, because I respected and honored them. I went home and I prayed and I questioned and what came back to me from the ancestors was that this was not something new. This was not something to be altered or changed. They gave me the dance because I needed it more than anybody on the planet. They gave it to me because they knew how much my soul needed it, and in that knowing and needing and healing, I carried the key to bringing it to the world, to the people.

I tried to let go of the idea of dancing this dance at the one place where I felt the safest and that I called my spiritual home. It was difficult to let go of that idea, but I did. I wrote back to Jeanne and Perry, thanking them for all their insights, guidance and advice. I told them that I would not be changing or altering what was given to me and that I had to dance the dance in the way that it was given to me. They told me that they loved me and they gave me their blessings.

Honestly, I felt like a baby bird being pushed out of the nest. I didn't know what to do or where to turn. I didn't know who to ask. After all of the things I had learned, all of the teachings, all of the traveling, all of the lessons, blessings and ceremonies, I felt pushed away. I had to figure out how to fly on my own, how to take that leap out of the nest, and how to spread my wings. I had to figure out how to be Otter Woman Standing.

Different Kinds of Love

The trip to South Africa at the end of 2010 opened an unexpected door for me. At the For The One dance, I met a man named Vaughan. We didn't speak to each other much during the weekend, but we became friends on Facebook when I got home. I was drawn to him, but he was on the other side of the world, and at that time I was still dating a lot of different people and exploring what I did and did not want in a relationship.

Gogo Hugh and I stayed in contact through email. I had only ever gone to South Africa for medicine dances, but we spoke about the possibility of me going to South Africa to teach people how to make their own frame or hand drums, which are so different from African drums. As we began making plans for this trip, Gogo Hugh enlisted Vaughan's help because he was both a drummer and drum builder.

Gogo Hugh had to step away from these plans because other opportunities came up for him to follow, and so I began to work closely with Vaughan. We exchanged some emails and then decided to have a Skype call where we could actually see each other while we spoke. The moment I saw him I felt the same connection that drew me to him when we first met at the dance some months earlier, and he felt it, too.

We were both shocked at how powerful and strong the sense of knowing was in our connection. As had happened with every relationship in my past, in fact, with every relationship I had ever been in, I quickly moved into a place of thinking, 'Maybe this could be a romantic relationship. Maybe this is something different.' I think Vaughan did, too. We were both open to exploring what it might be.

Different Kinds of
Love

We talked for hours almost every day, and often I felt I knew what he was going to say and what his thoughts and opinions were. The more I talked to Vaughan, the more my friends here said to me, "You are going to go to South Africa and you are going to fall in love and you are absolutely not going to come back!" There was a little part of me that got excited about the idea of that happening. It wasn't out of the realm of possibility. I actually had a friend from Tennessee who did that, and she had been living in Johannesburg for four years.

Vaughan and I kept communicating with each other. The feeling that this might be 'something' – a romantic relationship – escalated. I kept telling myself and my friends that I didn't know what it was. I knew I felt love for him but I didn't know what kind of love it was. I decided I would know when I got to South Africa and we saw each other.

After I arrived we just picked up our conversation and talked for hours. It felt very much like it did when we were on Skype. The conversation rambled from fun, silly and stupid things to very meaningful and deep spiritual topics.

The connection was there, and it was real, but it was not what we thought it was. Vaughan told me that he had met a woman that he was romantically interested in. Initially I was disappointed that we would not have an opportunity to explore what was between us, but I was also very happy for him.

In the next few weeks together I became increasingly grateful for the unexpected and deeply powerful lesson the experience gave me. I think that had Vaughan not started dating this woman, the lesson would not have come through. I think Vaughan and I might have jumped into a physical relationship, which it would have been a mistake.

What I learned over the next few weeks with Vaughan is that we can connect with other people in deep and profound ways, and it does not mean there is a romantic relationship. It does not mean that we have to act on it in a romantic or physical way. That was something new to me.

In the past every time I met someone I jumped into the relationship so quickly and either changed myself or adjusted my own being in order to be in that relationship, and it became unhealthy. That is why my relationships had not lasted. I spent those two weeks with Vaughan and moved past the disappointment and into a place of truly seeing that Vaughan and I really were connected in a deep and meaningful way that had nothing to do with romance or a sexual relationship or anything beyond the idea that two people really truly can connect with each other.

Our relationship grew from there. We connected in ways that I have not connected with anyone else, and this was only possible because we took romance and a sexual relationship off the table at the beginning. We were able to explore the depths of our connection in a different way, and I realized that Vaughan is part of my soul family.

An equally important gift was that I learned to practice discernment and to recognize the truth of a relationship and what it really is to me. I began to understand what it means to connect with someone and to move past an initial attraction into the deeper layers of a true soul connection.

Sacred Grove

Even though I was experiencing challenges in my life, between work and everything else that was going on, including trying to figure out how to realize my vision of the Fire Dance, I was still leading sweat lodges. After I had been holding lodges and other gatherings in the same place once a month for two years, the caretakers of that land decided to make some changes in their offerings. Their new offerings did not include space for the lodge. It was a beautiful place, but my time had reached a point of completion.

Several years earlier, when I was at Munay, some friends told me about Sacred Grove Retreat. They recommended that I go see it, yet I resisted. I did not feel the urge to go there. I didn't look it up, and I had no idea who ran it

I started looking for a new place to take the Otter Dance Lodge. One day, out of the blue, I picked up the phone and called the number on the Sacred Grove website. A cheerful, chirpy woman named Ellen Whiteside answered the phone. When I told her who I was, she said, "Oh yes, I know who you are. I have heard of you. We've never met, but I know who you are."

I asked if I could come out and see the land. Ellen said, "Sure. Come on up today!" She was so welcoming and inviting. It was an open door. I got in the car and drove the hour up to Sacred Grove.

Driving out to Sacred Grove, I felt something that I remembered feeling when I drove out of the city to Munay. The deeper I drove into the country, the more my body started to relax. The same thing happened as I headed to Sacred Grove. Driving further away from the city and the hustle and bustle and the traffic and the traffic lights, onto a two lane road, out into the beautiful country with woods and farmland... just seeing it did my soul so much good. When I found myself at Sacred Grove, I realized the hour had gone by so quickly that I hadn't even noticed.

I pulled into the driveway and saw a big fire pit area with a circle of large square boulders surrounding it. It looked like a lovely place for socializing and to sit around the fire. I was barely out of my car when a beautiful, tiny woman, barely five feet tall, with short, curly, black hair flitted across the land to me.

"Hi, I'm Ellen, and it is so good to have you here!" she said. I had to bend down to hug her.

It was so delightful. I remember thinking she was like a precious magical little elf. She invited me over to the fire circle, and we pulled up some chairs and put our feet up on the stones. We sat there in the sunlight and warmed ourselves and talked about everything and anything.

I felt like I had known Ellen all my life. I don't know why it took me so long to go out to Sacred Grove and meet her. We immediately knew that we were kindred spirits, that we were connected in some deep way. It didn't really matter how we were connected or what the connection was.

We knew we wanted to create the same things. She had a beautiful piece of land with two guest houses, a labyrinth, two fire circles, a yurt for gatherings and small cabins for people to stay in. It was just the most beautiful land I had ever seen. It felt magical. Walking through the woods between the two fire circles from one side of the property to the other, I knew immediately that there were fairies in those woods. There couldn't be anything else but fairies living in those woods. It was no wonder that Ellen was attracted to live here with her elf self.

When I told her that I was looking for a new place to pour sweat lodges, she threw her arms open wide and hugged me again and said, "Oh Robbie, it would be so wonderful to have you doing ceremony here on this land. This is sacred land. It needs ceremony. It cries out for ceremonial work to be done here. You are welcome to put your lodge anywhere on the property that you want to."

We walked around for a little while and found the perfect place to put the lodge and the fire pit that would go with the lodge. There was another wooded area right near where the lodge would be. In it were many saplings, so I knew we wouldn't have difficulty finding some that would be willing to give of themselves to build the sweat lodge there.

It felt perfect, like home – welcoming, open, and inviting. It was bright and shining. I could breathe! For the first time since I left Munay and since I had been to the Center for Peace, I felt I had found a home. I was deeply grateful that Otter Dance Lodge would continue in such a welcome and open environment.

Bardo and the Fire Dance Plans

Candy was the next person I told about the Fire Dance and about the vision. I told her about the dreams that I had been experiencing over the last couple of years. All she could do was laugh.

"Oh you did know what my dream meant! You knew exactly what it meant!" she said.

"Of course I did, but it scared the hell out of me. I wasn't going to tell you!" I said.

Candy was so supportive, just like Teresa and Marty had been. She said, "You name the place and you name the time, and I will be there. I will support you in dancing this dance." One by one I started sharing this with more people, people who were closest to me and those I believed would understand what the vision was and what I needed to do.

Of course, the first thing people would say to me is, "Oh, you're going to dance it at the Center for Peace!"

I had to say, "No, I am not going to dance there. I am going to find a new place. There's another place that's waiting." I didn't know what that meant, and I didn't even know how to find a new place.

I was still trying to maintain my own sanity, between working and exploring my own personal life. I had to discover what it meant to be a medicine woman and to be Otter Woman Standing. It was at about that time that I spoke that name out loud for the first time. In fact, I may have written it before I spoke it. I may have used it to sign an email. Or I may have posted something on Facebook. I don't remember how I used it first but I did it in a timid way. Claiming the name I had been given so long ago was part of figuring out what it meant and of spreading my wings and learning how to fly.

I knew it was time for me to stand on my own and time for me to stand up and figure out what it all meant. Quite honestly, it was an odd name. Otter Woman Standing. I had no idea what it meant. I did know what it meant from the journey, when I got it, but I didn't understand the depths of what it truly meant. It took me years to step into it fully. I was trying it on, with baby steps, on training wheels. Otter Woman Standing. This is me. This is who I am.

A few people asked questions and said, "Wow, that's weird and kind of interesting." I never spoke to anyone about how the name was given to me. I just said "Yes, that's my name." Mostly I just went by Robbie. I know quite a few people who go by their spirit name, but I couldn't get into people calling me Otter Woman Standing. It sounded so formal, so big, and so odd.

When I started talking out loud about the Fire Dance, it was really interesting how things in my life started shifting. I didn't put two and two together right away. It took a while of stepping into it and feeling it before I could really understand what was happening. I realized that the more I trusted and followed Spirit, and the more I spoke about the Fire Dance and holding the vision, things started shifting for me personally. The scary things – the foreclosure, having no work, losing my house, my partner – these events that felt like hard, difficult, negative things in my life were slowly starting to show up as things that needed to happen in order for me to move forward into the fullness of who I truly am.

It is not easy to recognize that in the moment. It is much easier to see when looking back. Things started to get a little bit easier. The pain of the break up was easing; the pain of losing the community was easing a little. My own community was starting to shift and change. Otter Dance was a virtual community of people who connected through the Internet, and it was growing as a virtual community space where people could talk, and share what they were doing and talk about ceremonies. People signed up for a monthly newsletter and at that time there were about two hundred people in the group. People who had been to America and Africa for dances, and people who had come from other countries, and went to other countries, were part of Otter Dance. It was a small, but international community. I took advantage of being able to feel community in that way.

I explored ways to use Facebook in a better way and the two spaces worked for me in different ways. What was happening on the Otter Dance page was different from what was happening on my Facebook page, where I talked about business, or interior design things. On that page I still didn't talk publicly about my spiritual life. But I did on the more private Otter Dance group page.

Even so, people I had never met were finding me through the website, the Facebook page, or the newsletter. Sometimes they found me through recommendations from other people who knew me. People were finding me. They were coming to me for medicine work, asking me to help with their own spiritual journey, asking me to find something for them. I performed funerals, and I married people. I performed legal marriage ceremonies because I had a ministerial license.

In the public sphere, people mostly knew me as an interior designer, who had lost her business and whose success had been greatly diminished and who was now working for someone else. To the outside world, I was just someone trying to hang on. But the smaller spiritual community knew me as I was.

What was happening within me was my own conflict. I had been an interior designer for so long that it had become my identity. That's who I was. If anyone asked me what I "did"– which is usually the first question when we meet somebody – I always told them I was an interior designer and that I worked with architects. I said that, even though I was barely doing that work anymore.

In fact, I was contemplating leaving the company that I worked for because my 'non-working' life with the medicine work was beginning to infringe on my 40-hour work week. On the one hand, this was deeply meaningful. On the other, I didn't know quite what to do with it. I didn't know how to charge for the work I was doing spiritually. I knew how to charge and get paid for the interior design work, so as far as I was concerned, I was still an interior designer. If someone came to me seeking guidance or help, I just asked them to make some kind of donation and whatever that donation looked like to them, that was okay.

There were times when I got home from work and there was a casserole at my doorstep. People were feeding me or bringing me candles or items that I could use if they didn't have any money. I never turned anyone away for not having any funds if they needed spiritual guidance. I found myself feeling like I had an identity crisis. Was I an interior designer who was sneaking around on the side doing all this spiritual work, or was I a medicine woman putting on a false front to the world that I was an interior designer?

I decided to take a class on self-discovery that Renée was leading, because as much as I thought I knew about it myself, I really didn't know what was going on at all. It was in that class that Renée talked about the concept of Bardo, a Tibetan word that means 'the between state'. Being neither here nor there. I just burst into tears when I realized, sitting in that class of about a dozen people, that I was in Bardo, and I had probably been there for a few years.

In that moment I couldn't see any way to get out of the Bardo place, and so I just cried. Even so, I had an understanding of where I was. I was in the in-between place because I wasn't willing to let go of one and step into the other. Honestly, I didn't know which one I would let go of and which one I would step into. I had been an interior designer, at that point, for twenty six years. I had owned my own company. I had created myself, my whole identity, around that. I struggled so much to let go of that idea that I was in Bardo.

And yet I was barely an interior designer anymore. I was going through the motions. Yes, I was being somewhat creative, but it really wasn't who I was. It was what I was doing to pay the bills, to keep a roof over my head, and to barely stay afloat. It was in that class that I realized that I had to shift something. Something needed to change, and I wasn't exactly sure how to do that.

The answer came out of the blue. A former client, who had given me substantial work before, but for whom I had not worked in well over a year, called me. I had helped her with the design and planning of a huge house, and with the construction complete she was ready to furnish it. I knew what kind of dollars that meant.

I knew that the work I could do for this one client would provide me with enough money to support myself for a couple of years. I had reduced my own overheads and expenses in such a way that I could do this work for about ten hours a week for about six months, and then be financially okay for a couple of years.

I saw this as a gift. It was my way to get out of Bardo. I had to make this change. I could make this shift. I could take this one job, furnishing an eight thousand square foot house, and I knew it would take a while to do that.

So I left the remodeling company, which was hard because they were such good people. I asked my former office manager if she would be willing to come back and work for me part time and she said would. I made a small office in my home with a desk for my office manager, who came in one day a week. I had a work table where I could do my drawings and where I could put all of the fabrics together and work on creating the design and plans for my client. I had the space that used to be the dining room to meet with my spiritual clients, the people who were coming to me for medicine work.

I now had a bridge that I could cross when I needed to. I could see my way out of Bardo. And yet, when someone asked me what I do, I still told them I was an interior designer. There was still some fear in me of being judged by other people. What was I to do? Shake their hand and say, "Hi, I am a medicine woman!" How could I do that?

That was scary to me. I kept growing the Otter Dance community and doing all of my spiritual work, and I kept staying open to what was coming to me through Spirit, through Creator. Then something did come to me, in an unexpected way.

There was another women's dance, a different dance from the one in which I had received the vision, called the Moon Dance, which was by invitation only. I had heard a few women speak of this dance, and I was deeply honored that one of the elders, Cheryl Rose, invited me to go. I had met Joan and Angie at other dances and other ceremonies at other places, and the dance was to be held on their land. Their arbor was in the woods, tucked into the rolling hills of Virginia. It was absolutely magical. While I was dancing there that weekend, I heard the land speak to me. I heard the land say, "Just ask permission to dance the Fire Dance here."

Once the Moon Dance was complete, and all the women had gone, I asked to stay another day with Joan and Angie so that I could talk to them. I told them about the Fire Dance. I spoke about the medicine of it, and the magic, the beauty and the gift of it. I told them about the fearlessness of it. I told them that I needed to dance this dance in ceremony, in a place that would welcome me and that would hold the energy of this dance.

They said they would do their own ceremony down at their arbor, and ask the land, Spirit and their ancestors. They would talk among themselves and come to a decision. I left there feeling, once again, the same way I felt when I wrote to the Center for Peace – exposed and vulnerable. I had asked for help. I had asked for what I needed.

A few weeks went by, and I received an email from Angie saying, "The land said 'Yes, come and dance your Fire Dance here. Come and birth your Fire Dance here.' After that, we don't know, but you can dance your dance here."

Oh, what a huge blessing that was. I felt so relieved to receive that embrace. Finally, it was going to happen. We decided I would dance in April. That gave me plenty of time to get myself ready, to figure out the logistics, and even to get up my courage.

I felt the excitement building in me because I was going to dance. It was going to happen. I spent the winter preparing. I talked to more and more people with whom I had been in ceremony for the past nine years – these were people I could trust to hold the space for me while I danced, to be a part of the crew. I needed five fire keepers. I needed drummers. I needed someone that I could trust to stand in the place of being a chief, without really being a chief, without having had the vision, without knowing what was coming. Someone who could hold the energy, watch over me and read the energy and know what was happening. That was a tall order.

It came so quickly and so easily. I knew exactly who to ask for everything. I knew to ask Candy if she would be the Fire keeper for the East. The east is about clearing away and releasing things that no longer serve; it is a cleansing of the soul. Candy's energy is so powerful and I knew she could commune with and hold the intention of clearing for me while I danced. I knew that she actually embodied the east medicine of the fire.

When I thought about the south fire, which holds a soothing and nurturing energy and embodies the feminine energy of unconditional love, I knew Teresa would hold that. I knew she could breathe the south fire energy of unconditional love into being.

The west fire is the call-to-action fire. It is the fire that motivates, that creates and brings manifestation, and I knew Jamie was to hold that fire. She is so strong and so powerful, and she is an incredible manifester in her own right, and so she was perfect to hold the west fire energy.

The north fire is the guardian fire. It is the fire that watches over and protects; it carries such beautiful masculine energy. I knew that Big Bob was the one to hold that fire. After I left Munay he and I kept in touch and met regularly for breakfast and to chat. He always told me that I was on a path of something big and that, no matter what, he would be there to support me. It was as if he knew something that I didn't know. I knew he was the perfect person for the north fire.

Once I knew who was to hold those four directional fires, I was able to relax a little bit. I knew everything else would fall into place. The drummers would fall into place. The fire mother would fall into place. And it was so easy.

A fire mother is much like a moon mother, but the fire mother caries the energy of the fire. The fire mother would be in the arbor with me to hold me up, to help me, to use her medicine, and I knew that would be Marty.

When I thought about who could hold all of the energy, who could see the big picture, who could understand what was happening, who could protect me in every way, and who could protect the crew in every way, I knew the only person who could hold that space for me was Sammye Jo. I knew that she was the one. She had seen through me so many times, and she knew me like nobody else knew me. Whether she realized it or not, she opened the way for that vision when she worked with my grandmothers and spoke to them in the language of the ancestors, when they were trying to get the vision to me during the Women's Web of Life dance. She was the one who opened the door, and so I knew she was the one to hold it open while I danced.

I knew the drummers would fall into place. I had asked Anni, who had made drums with me, and who had danced with me many times, and for whom I had been a moon mother while she danced, to support me this time and to be a drummer. She said yes.

All of the details fell into place during the course of that winter. It was such a blessing as people said yes to be a part of this. I still had the Spirit Fire Keeper to place, but I didn't feel any kind of urgency about it.

Everyone was getting so excited, and April seemed so far off. I knew the timing was right and that I had to be patient. I kept doing all the things that I needed to do. But things were really starting to move now.

Trai Hill

I had reached a point where I was a little bored with my exploration of dating. I was more focused on my spiritual life, although I was still dating here and there. I had pretty much resigned myself to the fact that I was probably not going to find anyone who was on the same spiritual path that I was, or who would even remotely understand it. So, if I was going to date, it was going to be just for the fun of dating. I had also given up on finding a deep and meaningful relationship and thought I would continue to keep my romantic and my spiritual lives separate. I was okay with that. I didn't need to engage in a deep, long-term relationship.

I spent a lot of time with Renée and at the Spiritual Living Center in Charlotte. It was the only place I had ever been that acknowledged all of the spiritual paths. I had found that the teachings of the Science of the Mind were the same as the old traditions, the wisdom that had been coming from the elders and passed down from the ancestors. It was just put into a new, scientific form, using new and different words. But it was the same old teachings. What I found more and more since 9/11 is that all of the world's religions truly do teach the same thing, and they all do lead to the Creator, the Source of love and the All-that-is. It does not matter what path anyone chooses because everyone gets to that same place.

I so enjoyed my time there on Sundays. There was no other place for me to be spiritually fed. I sat in the sound booth with Renée's partner, Becky, who ran the lights and made sure the music was right. Renée gave her talks and shared her wisdom and the choir sang. Becky was a barrel of laughs, and we had so much fun sitting up in the sound booth.

One Sunday, when I had been going back to the Center almost every Sunday for about two years, I was sitting up in the sound booth with Becky watching people arrive. As usual, I had left my cup of tea outside in the lobby because I knew that if I brought it up to the booth there was a high probability that I would knock it over and short-circuit some expensive equipment.

We had a really good view up there, and although we were visible to the people below – people could wave at us – we were behind glass and no one could hear us talking. That morning the service was beginning, and I saw a latecomer enter. He was about six feet tall with short, almost black, hair. He had chiseled good looks and dimples when he smiled at people. There was a casual air about him that caught my eye. He looked comfortable with himself. I nudged Becky, and I said to her, "Wow, who is that?"

"Oh, Robbie, that's Trai," Becky said.

"You say 'Trai' like I should know who he is," I said.

"Sure, he's been coming here for a few years."

I looked at her as though she was crazy and I asked, "How is it that I have not seen that man, who has all of the hairs on my arms standing on end, in two years?" I could feel everything in me light up when I saw him. I did not know how we could both have attended the same church for two years and not seen each other. There were less than a couple of hundred people going to the Spiritual Living Center at that point. It was easy to see anyone and everyone who came in, especially from my vantage point in the sound booth with Becky every week.

I thought, 'Isn't that interesting? How did he slip below my radar?'

The service went on and I think Renée was in the middle of singing one of the beautiful songs that she always sings when I noticed that same man stand up and walk out to the lobby.

I thought, 'Okay, I'll go see what this is all about.'

I walked out of the sound booth, down the stairs and into the lobby, and went to get my tea – which I thought was a good excuse. He was standing close to where I had left my tea, near a little kitchen area to the side of the lobby.

"Hi, how are you?" I asked.

"I'm groovy, how are you?" he asked. I giggled a little bit because I hadn't heard anyone use the word 'groovy' out loud, and I thought that was kind of funny and endearing all at the same time. Just as I reached for my tea, he reached for a cup of coffee and somehow everything collided and my tea spilled all over the counter and all over the floor.

I walked around to where I could get paper towels, and he pulled a handful of paper towels off of the roll, which he handed to me, and said "Here you go." He stepped over and around me as I knelt down to clean up the spilled tea.

"See you later," he said as he walked away.

I felt like a complete bumbling idiot as I was down on my knees, cleaning up the mess that I had made, and questioning a whole lot. Did this guy not realize that I had come out here specifically to maybe have a conversation with him? Did he not realize that I was just slightly interested to know a little bit more about him? And then I thought, 'Ah, maybe he is gay. That's it.' And so I dismissed it. I cleaned up my mess and went back up into the sound booth thinking that he was either not interested, or he was gay. That was just a collision of tea all over the floor, and I wasn't really interested in having any more mishaps like that.

Over the next few weeks, I didn't see him again. I didn't see him come in or out of the church on Sunday mornings. I didn't really pay that much attention. Actually, I didn't even think about it again.

A little while after the tea incident, there was a silent auction at the Center to raise money for a project that the church was supporting. There was art work and many different items, and some people were offering gift certificates for auction. I wasn't particularly interested in any of it and I didn't really have extra money to spend.

After the service I was standing in the lobby talking to Renée and some other members of the community. Chatting to her after the service was one of the few moments we had to just connect for a short while. In her boisterous way, Renée stepped over on my left side and quickly bumped me with her hip. Then she gave me a shove and pushed me about a foot and a half. I looked up at her to ask, "What?" when she stepped right up beside me again and bumped me again and pushed me another foot and a half. Then she did it again, but that time she pushed me a couple of feet. I realized she was trying to drive me somewhere.

She pushed and shoved me about twenty feet across the room, until she had pushed me right in front of Trai. Renée stood right in front of the two of us and said, "Trai Hill, furniture maker, meet Robbie Warren, interior designer." She put her hands together and said, "Well, my work here is done." And she walked away.

And I thought, 'Well, isn't that interesting. Here he is again.' Next to him was a beautiful table, so I asked him, "Did you make that?"

He grinned and said, "Yes, I am a furniture maker."

"That is absolutely beautiful," I said.

"You're an interior designer," he said.

"Yes. I am an interior designer."

At that point I was still in a place in my life where I wasn't really sure what I was. Do I go around telling people I'm a medicine woman? No! I was still identifying myself to the world as an interior designer.

We chatted for about a minute about nothing important and then I think someone came up and asked him about the table. Or someone came up and hugged me hello. Before you know it, we were off in other directions and not really talking to each other.

When I got home that afternoon, after lunch, and I checked my Facebook page, I noticed I had a friend request – from Trai Hill. With a big grin on my face, I accepted.

First Date

I started getting greetings from Trai every morning on Facebook. Just, "Hello. How was your day?" or "Hi, hope you have a great day." I was interested. I had so many friends on Facebook, and he had maybe fifty. I was intrigued by that. He seemed to keep to himself quite a bit.

He was intelligent and curious and asked a lot of questions, and his greetings opened the door for messages and exchanges over coffee each morning. He was on a spiritual path, even though he wasn't quite sure what, exactly, that was. He was searching and open and fearless in his approach. We chatted just a little on Facebook here and there. I would see him on Sundays and say hello at the church. This went on for a while.

It was Father's Day and Renée had asked me if I would do an individual blessing for all the fathers. Of course, I agreed. I messaged Trai and asked him if he was going to be there on that Sunday and he said no, he didn't think he would be. I said I was disappointed because I was going to be doing a Father's Day blessing, and I was looking forward to including him in that blessing – he has three beautiful children.

I was absolutely delighted when I looked up on Sunday morning and saw him arrive at church. In fact, I think I even felt a few butterflies in my stomach, which I had not felt before.

During the service the fathers came up across the stage one by one, and I gave each one of them a blessing. I spoke to each man as the warrior of their family, to offer a blessing and to honor them for who they are to their children, their family and to the community. Trai was somewhere in the middle. I think that was the first time that we had really had an opportunity to have a moment with each other and it was in front of a couple of hundred people. We looked into each other's eyes, and I gave him a blessing. He smiled at me. His smile was endearing and strong, sweet and powerful, all at the same time.

After the service different people wanted to come up and speak to me, to thank me and share whatever insights they got. That's what usually happens after something like that. I was still up on the platform and a woman was speaking to me from her heart about whatever had come up for her during the blessing. I noticed over her shoulder that Trai was standing there, waiting his turn to speak to me, and I got anxious. I did my best to keep my attention focused on the woman in front of me who was sharing, but I could not help but see him over her shoulder, and my attention kept getting pulled away. I knew I couldn't give her my full attention. I knew it wasn't fair, and I wanted to be able to listen to her, so I turned slightly so that he was not in my vision anymore. Then I was able to give my full attention to the woman.

People around us moved, and my peripheral view shifted, and once again he was back, in my line of vision. It was so distracting, and I thought, "Ohhh, Robbie, you are in so much trouble here!" The woman finished sharing, hugged me and left. Trai came up and hugged me, just a quick hug and a pat. He thanked me for the blessing. We started talking, and honestly, I don't remember what we talked about. I think he asked me about the blessing and what I thought a warrior was. Then I saw that someone else, standing off to his side, and I started to feel that same pressure; there were more people who wanted to speak to me. Yet I wanted to tell them all to go away, because I wanted to give all my attention to Trai. He stepped to the side and said, "I'll wait."

I spoke to the next and the next and the next person, and more people came up to greet me. I turned to Trai and said, "I don't believe that we will be able to finish this conversation here and now, but I believe there is more to be said. Can we get together later?"

He looked at me and said, "Sure."

"Great," I said. "How about you meet me this afternoon?" I gave him the name of a local restaurant that I went to often, where I felt comfortable, safe and secure. It was a beautiful June afternoon. The sun was out, it was nice and hot, and I knew it would be pleasant to sit outside and have a meal and continue our conversation. He said he would see me there later, and he left.

I finished my conversations with everyone who wanted to come and chat. Then I went home. I got ready for my meeting with Trai that afternoon. I felt those butterflies again as I thought about what I should wear. That's when I realized that this felt like a date. I had feelings about this. This was not just some guy that I was meeting to have a conversation. I planned what I would wear carefully (as we do) and made sure I got there a few minutes early so that I could have some iced tea and have a few minutes to relax before he arrived.

I sat outside under the shade of a tree at a table. I looked up and saw him park his car about half a block down the street. When he got out of the car, he was wearing a pair of khaki cargo shorts, and what looked like a Hawaiian shirt. He was also wearing a pair of Crocs that were a swirl of neon green and yellow. I could see him coming down the street because of those shoes.

Crocs are, to me, the ugliest shoes on the planet. I giggled and thought, 'He has no idea this is a date, because surely he would not be wearing those Crocs if he thought that it was!' I just laughed and felt at ease, because if he didn't think it was a date, then it wasn't, right? Isn't that how it goes? We both had to be in agreement that it was a date in order for it to be a date.

I took a deep breath and relaxed. He sat down. I think we ordered a beer and dinner. We were there for a couple of hours. We ate, and we talked, and it was absolutely wonderful. I couldn't tell you anything that we talked about, but there was not a moment that we were not talking. I found I could share with him so freely about my spiritual path, and could share with him my experiences of past relationships, about the last few years of dating so many different people.

He shared with me freely and easily about his fourteen-year marriage that had just ended not too long before, and his confusion around it. I found we were telling each other the things that most people only share after knowing each other for a long time. Even though we had only said hello a few times on Facebook, and had a few brief encounters at church, suddenly I felt as though I knew this man. I wanted to know him better.

This was different from all the other experiences that I had, through dating sites and introductions from friends. The thought ran through my head, 'I am in trouble here. I am in emotional and relationship trouble here, because this man shows up with these crazy ugly silly Crocs, and I am still here and still considering a second date.'

The restaurant was in a neighborhood where people did a lot of walking. There were shops and other restaurants and places to see, so after we finished eating we walked around and did a little exploring and went into a few shops.

We had been together for about four hours, and it was dark by the time we found ourselves back at the restaurant, standing near his car.

"My car is parked over there," I said.

"I don't know if I am ready for the evening to end yet," he replied. "I feel that there's more to say."

I looked at him and smiled and said, "My home is not far from here. And I have a pool. If you'd like to come back to my house, we can sit in the back yard and dangle our feet in the pool and cool off a little bit and continue with our conversation."

"I think I would like that," he said.

There we were at nine o'clock at night, heading back to my house, and I thought, 'I really must be crazy to invite this man back to my house'. I figured he thought he was going to get lucky because, let's face it, that's what most men would think if you invite them back to your home on a first date. But then I remembered the crocs on his feet, and I figured he didn't think this was a date. At that point I thought I was off the hook.

We went through my house and out the back door and sat in the corner of the pool, me on one side and him on the other, dangling our feet in the pool with our knees at right angles to each other. We spoke about ideas and insights and feelings. Every once in a while, his foot would brush up against mine and flashes and lights would go off in my head and I thought, 'Is he trying to play footsie with me? Is this a come-on? Is he trying to flirt with me? What's happening?'

He didn't miss a beat with his conversation, and the conversation was so fascinating. I loved the way he thought about things. I loved the way he would take an idea and turn it inside out and look at it from all angles before he could let it go.

In the middle of all these deep philosophical ideas and spiritual concepts, he kept brushing his foot against mine in the water. I thought, 'Okay, I am not going to move my foot away.' I was getting so distracted by the fact that I thought he was playing footsie with me that I started to lose track of what he was saying. And what he was saying was so interesting that I started losing track of the fact that I thought he was playing footsie with me.

It must have been close to midnight when we finally decided to call it a night. I walked him to the door. Our feet were still wet from having been in the pool and they were pruned. We went through the side door to where his car was parked. I stood at the door, and he stood just outside the door. He turned back around to say goodnight and what I fully expected to be a goodnight kiss was, instead, the most beautiful embrace.

It was not one of those silly little pat-on-the-back kind of hugs. He wrapped his arms fully around me. It was a deep and meaningful embrace. I hugged him back fully. I put my arms fully around him, and I felt the depth of him and the idea of him. I felt the fullness of who he is in the world.

When we pulled back away from each other, he looked me in the eyes and said, "I have had a remarkable time tonight. Goodnight." And he left.

He left me standing there, and I knew in that moment that I was done. I couldn't date anyone else. I knew in that moment that I had to take my profiles off the dating sites. If a friend said to me, "Hey, there's this great guy I want you to meet." I would have to say "no."

That was it. I was done.

Freedom in Love

The relationship with Trai developed so easily and felt so genuine. We had both been through difficult relationships and been in a place in past relationships where we knew we didn't want to find ourselves again. We knew what we did want, and we both knew what we didn't want.

From the beginning we were clear with each other about these things. It was empowering for me to say to Trai, "I will always tell you what I am feeling, even if I think you don't want to hear it and even when it will scare me to tell you these things."

He made the agreement to do the same thing.

We agreed that we would trust each other. We decided to deal with whatever came up in the relationship in that moment, and if it was a deal breaker, then it was just a deal breaker. We would be okay with that. We would rather know the truth than to hold things in, to withhold from each other, and to stay silent.

We had both been silent in previous relationships. Not by force, but by choice. Now we were choosing to not be silent. We would share our feelings. We would share our thoughts. We would share those things that came up that made us feel vulnerable, or less than, even the things that came up that might be so scary that we might think that the other might never understand. We agreed we would share all of these things. And we did.

What we both discovered in this process was that the more we shared, the more we trusted. The more we shared about the true depths of our feelings, our fears, our concerns, and the things that made us angry, the easier it became to do.

What was also remarkable was that those things that felt so intense in the first few months we were able to laugh about later because once we got it out there, it wasn't so scary anymore. Once one of us shared whatever that intimate fear was with the other, and we found out that the whole world didn't fall apart, and nobody's head exploded off their shoulders, and that it was just okay, and that there was no judgment, once we got past that point, then we realized that it could just be funny.

I have never experienced a relationship that was so open and so honest, where I could reach into the depths of what I was feeling and still have the ability to laugh. This relationship allowed me to laugh at myself and to laugh at him. It allowed me to lighten up. It was such a gift. We spent those first few months sharing our lives with each other, and we made it safe to talk about not just our intimate feelings but also our spiritual path, life, our upbringing, and our parents.

The more we did that, the more connected we felt, the easier it got. We quickly became partners. We joked around in the beginning. I didn't want to call him my boyfriend because at 48 years old I was too old for a boyfriend. It felt silly and stupid, but he kind of liked it. He is nine years younger than I am, which may not sound like a lot, but if you think about it, we can be in two different decades a lot of the time.

He was okay with being called a boyfriend. I said no, how about 'partner.' He said that sounded so business-like. I explained to him that in many of the countries that I had traveled to people refer to their life partners as their partners. I said that it is only in the USA that we refer to partners only in the context of same-sex partners. That helped him feel more comfortable with it, but then he said, "How about if I call you my companion?" to which I replied, "Oh no! That sounds way too much like Lassie! Companion sounds like, you know, a young man who is taking care of the old lady. You know, pushing her around in the wheelchair."

Maybe that was just my perception because the age difference felt so prominent.

Even though I had been dating men even younger than Trai for the better part of a year and a half before he and I got together, I knew I wasn't going to be in a relationship with them, so it didn't matter that I was 48 and dating a 28-year-old or a 30-year-old man. Somehow it mattered now. I couldn't make sense of that, but it did. So, 'companion' was out, even though he thought it was a good choice. We spent some time bantering back and forth what we would call each other. I said, "There is no way you can call me your girlfriend. I am too old to be a girlfriend. And I am too old to have a boyfriend. I am just going to call you my partner until we come up with something else."

He was okay with that. We do laugh about it. Even now I still I call him my partner.

Over those first few months, I realized that I wanted him to be happy. I wanted him to learn and grow in whatever path he chose, for work, or his spiritual path, or whatever personal path he chose. I wanted to see him grow and shine. I wanted to hold him up and support him in whatever way, so that he could experience life fully. I wanted for him what he wanted for himself.

For the first time I truly felt that I had someone in my life who wanted that for me as well. This was the first time that I felt my partner truly as a partner. My partner wanted to see me shine, and loved to see me succeed, to see me happy. It wasn't in that sick, co-dependent way. I didn't want to see him happy so that I could be happy. I wanted to see him happy so that he could be happy.

I was responsible for my own path and my own happiness, and he was responsible for his. But I could want for him those same things that he wanted. And he could want for me the things that I wanted. We connected in that way, and we moved into our relationship, holding each other up, absolutely loving each other. This was something new to me – complete honesty, vulnerability, fearless courage, support and encouragement.

In the past I had let my fears, anger and resentment get in the way. The things that had come up from my childhood got in the way of my own happiness. It was like I had spent all of this time with all of these other people in the past creating my own downfalls and pitfalls and the demise of my own relationships because I just didn't get it.

I can't tell you why it clicked in this relationship. But it did. And it made sense. Maybe it is because I spent some years on my own after the relationship with Sam, or maybe that I spent some time not trying to be in a relationship and just having fun. Maybe it was because I spent time asking Spirit, "Where am I to go? What am I to do? How am I to focus my life?" I spent time realizing that I didn't need anyone else to be complete. I felt great. I felt whole or as whole as I could feel. You know, there are always questions that come up, question marks, lessons to learn and new teachings, but I did not feel like I needed someone to be with me in order to move through my life. I didn't feel like I needed someone to lean on or to support me in order for me to learn these things. That was new.

I was finally standing on my own. I was beginning to embody the name that I had been given. Otter Woman Standing. It made sense in this relationship and in the way that we related to each other.

There was freedom in that. Freedom in the commitment. Freedom in the connection, Freedom in the partnership and in the love. It is a freedom that makes all the difference.

Purpose is Welcome

Early on, when we were dating, I asked Trai if he would help me with something. It wasn't something major. It might have been something like to clean out the gutters or take the trash to the street. He turned to me, looked me straight in the eye, and said, "Of course. Purpose is always welcome."

That went right through me. When he said that, he spoke to what it feels like to be in service to Spirit, to the people, and he didn't even know he was speaking to that. At the time he didn't know that being in service was something that his spirit connected to in such a meaningful way.

There were a couple of people that I dated for a few months, thinking that there might be something there, but I never once invited them to any of the ceremonies or spiritual practices in my inner circle. I invited Trai Hill from day one. It was so easy to share the spiritual side of my life in my relationship with Trai. I didn't worry that he might think I was crazy or that the experiences that I had had were made up or not real. Some of the things that I had been through didn't even seem real to me, as though they couldn't ever have happened. For someone who had never been exposed, in depth, to the shamanic world and the world of Spirit, he was open to listening.

If he thought I was crazy at first, he'd say, "That sounds a little wacky." But he stayed open, and he listened. I told him about the medicine dances and invited him to come to a sweat lodge. I just kept including him. He was eager to understand and see what it was all about. He was honest enough to ask me not to have any expectations about what he might or might not feel about any of it. He said he had to be on his own path and that it was important to him. At the same time he wanted to understand and know more about what I was doing and what my life was about.

He came to a sweat lodge, and afterwards he told me he was much more drawn to the fire. After that he came to the lodges, but he sat outside with Jamie, who kept the fire at almost all the lodges that I held since leaving Munay. There was a beautiful partnership in the relationship that Jamie and I had created around the ceremony and working together. Much of our communication was unspoken and like a dance in itself.

When Trai came to the lodges, he would watch Jamie and pay attention to her connection to, and communion with, the fire. Every once in a while he would ask some questions. Jamie, of course, was giving, and she would share with him anything that he asked. Otherwise she kept busy with the work that was in front of her. This went on for a few months. Trai never asked Jamie to teach him. All he did was watch.

We had a sweat lodge planned during February of 2012, one of our coldest months in North Carolina. Jamie was sick but she was still planning to come and keep the fire. But we were expecting rain, sleet and snow. There was no way that I would ask her to stand outside for between four and six hours in that weather. Half of that time the rest of us would be inside the lodge where it was warm and cozy. She agreed that she needed to stay at home and take care of herself.

I called one of the other fire keepers that often filled in when Jamie couldn't make it, and she was not available. I called another and she wasn't available either. And nor was anyone else.

Then Trai said, "I believe I can do what you need me to do and what I don't know, you can tell me."

I really didn't know what to do other than to take a chance. I knew he had been watching Jamie, but I didn't really know how much attention he had been paying to her. We didn't really talk about it that much, and he didn't ask a lot of questions. I agreed. For me to keep the fire and lead the lodge at the same time was possible, but it would be extremely difficult, even under the best conditions. The weather forecast, with sleet and snow, meant that it would have left the people in the lodge exposed for too long during the time that the lodge door was open for me to crawl in and out.

The best thing to do seemed to be to trust Trai, to trust that he did know what to do and that what he didn't know I could tell him in the moment. I expected to have an intense teaching situation, but I quickly found that he really had been paying attention and had asked Jamie enough questions.

He didn't always know why something was done in a particular way, and so he asked me questions about 'why', but not 'how'. Why do I use cornmeal first, and then the tobacco? Why do I move counter clockwise with the cornmeal and clockwise when I am making a circle with the tobacco?

We had about fifteen people for the lodge that day which made it pretty full, and they were cold. Trai was quick to bring in the stones so that the lodge would heat up quickly, and soon we were warm and comfortable inside the lodge. When he closed the doors on the lodge so that we could say our prayers, I knew Trai was out there in the snow and the sleet. We could hear the sleet hitting the top of the lodge. When Trai bent down to open the door at the end of the round, I could see that the hoodie of his jacket was full of snow. As he bent down it came tumbling out and hit him in the back of the head and dumped down just outside the lodge. I had to giggle just a little bit as he shook it off and I saw that he was fine.

He did everything with such strength and reverence – even the things that he didn't fully understand. He had reverence for the ceremony. It was really quite amazing to watch him step into holding the space. He may not really have understood what some things meant, but after that lodge he did understand how to hold the space to allow others to say their prayers, to have their ceremony, to have their tears and laughter and sing their songs. He knew what it meant to hold the container and use his strength to create a safe space. He did it with such humility and curiosity, and such an open heart. I was deeply grateful for his willingness.

After that lodge he sat with Jamie more often when she was tending the fire. She shared more with him and he asked more questions. He learned more and more, and he deepened his connection to the fire. He still didn't understand why, but he told me he didn't have to understand why. Part of his spiritual belief was that there are things in this world that we can't always see, but we can feel them. And he felt the connection. He understood what it means to be in service.

In March 2012, I invited him to come to a dance and I thought, "Boy, this is really taking a chance!" I tried to explain to him what happens at a dance but it's almost next to impossible for anybody who has never experienced something like this to understand.

"I don't have to understand it," he said. "I am going to go. I want to see what it is about because it is important to you. I want to feel it, and I want to step into it."

Like me, the first time I went to a dance at the Center for Peace in Tennessee, he went to serve the dance as a dog soldier. I was a moon mother in that dance. I was inside the arbor and he was outside. Even though I could not see him, because I was focused on the dancers, the chiefs, and medicine and energy of the dance, I could feel his strength on the outside of the arbor. During the breaks, and in between, I got to reconnect with him. He told me that he could feel what was happening.

At the end of the three days, the dance was over, and it was time for the feast, the time for sharing and the giveaway. It was always a beautiful time for us to come together in community and share with each other and connect before leaving to go home.

After we got in the car to drive back to Charlotte, Trai said to me, "I can see that something changed in the dancers. Many of them didn't even look the same as they did when they went into the arbor on Friday. I could see they were lighter and that something had shifted and healed, that something was opened. I could see all of that. I don't understand it at all. But I don't have to understand it to be in service to it. I can serve it because I see what it does. I see the medicine of it, the energy, and the result of it. So while I might not understand exactly what you are doing in the arbor as a moon mother or what the chiefs are doing, I don't have to. I know that I can be in service to it."

What a powerful revelation that was for him, and it was so beautiful for me. It was one more confirmation of who he truly is. It reminded me of the things that I had forgotten, of what it felt like the first time I went to a dance, of seeing the dancers change for the first time, of seeing them shift. I was re-experiencing these things through him, and for me it was magical. It was an affirmation of all of the work that I had done over the years and of all of the learning that I had gained.

Birthplace for the Fire Dance

While Trai was soaking up everything that he could soak up and learning and connecting, I found that all my friends absolutely loved him. He and Candy quickly bonded like brothers. They laughed together and loved each other. It was great to have a partner who connected so much with my spiritual family in such a strong way.

Things seemed to be moving forward, and I was getting closer and closer to the time that I was to dance the Fire Dance. I explained to Trai about the Fire Dance and the vision, and while he didn't truly understand the gravity of it all, I think he did get the essence of what it was. He knew there wasn't anything for him to do other than to just support me and let me move forward and do what I needed to do.

Joan and Angie had a wonderful community up in Virginia that I wanted to get to know more. I knew I was going to be dancing the Fire Dance there within a month. We had set a date and we were moving forward quickly. I went back to them in early spring, when it was starting to warm up a little, to help rebuild their sweat lodge for the spring and summer season. It had been many months since I had seen them in person and almost six months since we had spoken on the phone about having the Fire Dance there. I loved being on their land with them, being in ceremony and building the sweat lodge. Being in their community and reconnecting with Joan and Angie was a lovely escape.

Just before I got there, Joan had broken her ankle. She had six more weeks of healing to do. When she was in the house, she kept the weight off her foot by sitting in an office chair so that she could roll around the house easily. While we were out in the field building the lodge and collecting the saplings from the creek bed and doing the things that needed to be done, she did all the work that could be done from a seated position. She sat propped up and cleared the little branches and leaves off the saplings.

We spoke once in a while about the Fire Dance that was coming up, and I mentioned to them that I had the crew almost fully intact. I realized, from the look on their faces when I said that, that they were a bit surprised.

After we got their lodge built and sat down and were able to talk a little bit more, I realized that I had not clearly communicated my expectations and what I saw for the Fire Dance, and they had not communicated with me what they thought and what they expected would happen. While I was putting together a crew of twelve to fourteen people, they thought it would be just me. Evidently we had different ideas about what was going to happen, and we needed to sit down and talk about it.

We knew it was not good timing to try to talk about it then and there, and so we decided to hold the thought in our minds and hearts. We kept our attention focused on finishing the lodge and doing that ceremony and waited until there was time for us to sit and talk.

I had a feeling in my gut that something was about to shift, but I wasn't quite sure why, and I wasn't sure what to do about it. During the lodge I prayed, I asked, and I stayed open. I stood in front of the fire at the end of the ceremony, and I felt the fire speak to me. There was a Fire Being in it that I had met before. I heard it speak loudly and clearly. It said, "The land said 'yes.' That means it gave its permission. This land and this arbor gave its permission. It did not give a command, and it did not give a mandate. It just said 'yes'."

I wasn't really sure what that meant, but the words were clear. I went to bed that night with the words "the land said yes, it did not give a command" ringing in my ears. Joan and

Angie went to bed, too. When we woke up in the morning to sit and talk, I could tell it was weighing heavily on their minds.

Joan started talking, sharing her concerns about her broken foot and being able to manage to feed twelve to fourteen people while I was in the dance arbor. They had a small house, and where would everyone sleep? It was okay if everyone wanted to sleep in tents outside, but the crew still needed to be fed three meals a day for three days. She said it felt like too much for her to take on, but because the land said 'yes' she didn't know what to do.

That is when I understood what the fire was saying, and that the message wasn't for me, it was for Joan and Angie. What they were struggling with was that because they had asked permission of their land for me to dance the Fire Dance there, and they got a clear and resounding "yes" from the land, they interpreted that, as did I, that I must dance there, that I was mandated, that I was commanded.

Joan was worried that if she said "no," then she was going against that to which land had said "yes." She was worried and concerned that she wouldn't be able to hold up her end of the bargain and that it would not be in her own best interests. She wondered how she could do this.

I told her what the fire had told me. I explained that a "yes" was simply giving permission and that the land trusted them as the caretakers to make the best decision. It was not a command, and it was not a mandate that "yes, the Fire Dance *must* be there and they *must* let me dance there."

We all looked at each other, and we almost burst out laughing. There was a collective sigh of relief, even from me. These were my friends, and I didn't want them to suffer or feel they had to do something that was going to push them beyond their physical limits. I didn't want them to feel that they had to do something. Clearly we had misunderstood. A yes was simply a yes. It was permission and "I trust you to do what's best."

Over coffee that morning, just as easy as that, we decided that it was not best for me to dance the Fire Dance on their land. The timing wasn't right. It wasn't to be. Even though I was disappointed, it still felt okay.

In just a few months it would be the three year anniversary since I had been given the vision. I felt that if I had held it this long, I could hold it a little bit longer and everything would fall into place. As I drove back from Virginia, feeling much at peace and at ease with the decision, I realized I was going to pass right by Sacred Grove, the land where Ellen lived, where I had been holding sweat lodges for the past year. It was a place where I felt at home and welcomed.

I sent Ellen a text message and asked if I could stop by and just talk to her for a minute. With her usual enthusiasm she said, "Of course, come on by!" It took me a few more hours to get there, and as I was driving I knew I was going to talk to her about the Fire Dance. I didn't know what I was going to say, and I didn't think I was going to ask her anything about it. There was no dance arbor at Sacred Grove and I didn't think there was enough space to build one. Ellen had never been to a dance. But for some reason I was being guided to go to Sacred Grove.

Ellen and I sat by the fire pit and talked for hours. I told her about the vision and about the dance. I told her about all the other dances. She said, "What you are describing is what I have always dreamed for Sacred Grove. I have always wanted this place to be an international spiritual community where people come from all over the world to drum, to dance, to heal themselves, to reconnect with the earth. That's what I am here for."

And so I asked her, "Ellen, can I dance the Fire Dance here on your land? Can I birth the Fire Dance into reality here on your land?"

She didn't even take a breath. She said "Yes."

Birthplace for the Fire Dance

We decided to walk the land and see where it could happen and where there was space for it to be. Sacred Grove is beautiful – not just the land, but everything about it. There is a thirty-foot diameter yurt where we held gatherings and drum circles. Off to the side of the yurt is a labyrinth and to the other side of the yurt is a big fire pit where we held bonfires and drumming and other events. Behind the yurt, between the labyrinth and the fire pit, was an open area.

Ellen and I walked into that field, and as we did we saw that there were four trees on one side. I said, "Ellen, do you have a compass?" She said that she didn't, so I said, "Let me pull up the app on my phone."

I stood in the middle of the field and saw that those four trees stood exactly east from the center of the open space. I dropped to my knees and sat there.

"What is it?" Ellen asked.

"Ellen, this land is just waiting for a dance arbor. These trees are the sentinels. They hold the space for the east gate, the place where we go in and out of the arbor. They are already there, and they hold the space," I told her.

She looked at me and said, "Okay." She had never seen a dance arbor, so she couldn't picture it, and she couldn't understand what I was saying, but she trusted me.

I walked around the area and paced it off and I realized that the space between the trees in the east, the tree line in the west, the labyrinth in the south and the fire circle in the north, was exactly the size of a dance arbor. It was as if all of these things had been holding that space sacred, waiting for the dance arbor to show up. It was almost as if the dance arbor was already there. It just hadn't been built yet.

I looked at Ellen, and I asked her permission. Again she said "yes." I put my hands on the earth and I asked permission from the earth in that space to dance the Fire Dance here, and I was brought to tears. Once again I felt the earth speak to me. I heard what she said.

"It is time for the ceremony to come back to this land. It is time to dance here again."

I had found a home, a place to birth the Fire Dance.

Fire Dance Final Crew

At last I had a place to dance. Once everything fell into place, I could quit being distracted by location and other things, and I could focus on the actual dancing of this dance. There were a few crew members I had not yet asked to be a part of this, and Trai was one of them. He had only been to one dance and had no idea what to expect. He had kept fire for me at several lodges, but in reality he was new to this.

One of the things, Trai had discovered about himself over the past few months was that not only was he a drum builder, he was also a drummer. When I first I asked him if he would drum at my Fire Dance, he said that he would be happy to. Then, I asked if he would be the drum chief, the one to hold the energy of the drum altogether. He had never seen that before, apart from being at the one dance. I knew that he could do it. I felt that he could do anything. I think that he felt that he could do it, too, but he didn't say yes right away. He said he wanted to think about it. That showed me that he did take it seriously, and it was not about his ego. It truly was about whether or not he could do what I asked.

Being the drum chief of a dance is a huge undertaking. Granted, this was a small dance. There was only one dancer. Me. I told him it wasn't going to be that hard because there was just me, not an arbor full of dancers. After a few days went by, he said yes, he would. That felt good and solid to me. I was used to him playing the drum. I had played the drum with him at different events. We had done shamanic journeys together, playing the drums. It felt like a good fit.

Prior to the Fire Dance, I had not had a strong connection to Charlaine Jones. In fact, I didn't understand Charlaine at all.

She spoke to the star people. She got her information from the cosmos. I got my information from the earth. I spoke to the trees and the plants. She spoke to the stars and the beings out there. I didn't understand it at all. In fact, I struggled quite a bit with it, and I think she struggled a bit with me. It was like we were two people who spoke completely different languages. We were saying the same thing but neither one of us really understood the other.

What I did know was that Charlaine did spiritual work on a level that I didn't know and understand and that she would gain understanding and information about this Fire Dance as it was being birthed into this reality that I could never get, and even though I was the one dancing it and even though the ancestors had given this to me I knew she would be an interpreter of a different kind.

I asked Charlaine if she would come, if she would be my witness and my cosmic interpreter. That is the best way I can describe it. We never did find the exact words for what I was asking her to do and be. She said yes.

Everyone else that I had asked had said yes. All the drummers, the fire keepers, the fire mother, my chief, Sammye Jo, and Charlaine.

The only crew position that was not in place and not ready was the spirit fire keeper, the one that would be close to the center. I knew who I wanted to do it, but I was a little afraid to ask. I knew I wanted to ask LB Best, Sammye Jo's partner. Like Trai, she had not been coming to the dances for long, maybe a year longer than Trai. I had, along with Sofia, a dear elder from Germany, held the wedding ceremony for Sammye and LB, and I was so honored to have done that.

I watched LB at the different dances. I watched her step up, just as I watched Trai. I watched her step into her own power, and into who she truly is. She had never been a fire keeper before. The night before the dance LB arrived to support me and to support Sammye Jo, and to do whatever she could do to help, to serve as a dog soldier. She just wanted to help. I asked her if she would be the fire keeper for the spirit fire the fire that holds the energy of all-that-is, that represents everything; the past, present, future, love, cosmos, the earth. Her answer to me was a quiet "yes."

My crew was complete. I had five fire keepers: Candy, Teresa, Jamie, Big Bob and LB. I had four drummers, Annie, Scott and Ellen, with Trai leading the drum. I had Charlaine watching over, listening and interpreting. I had Marty as a fire mother, and I had Sammye Jo to take care of us all.

I knew I was safe, and I knew it was complete. I knew something amazing was going to happen. I don't think I slept at all the night before my dance.

Honoring an Elder

Brenda Sue was the visionary of the Women's' Web of Life dance. She was a woman of few words, and when she did have something to say it was usually something profound. When I met her for the first time at Joseph's Mystery School, she barely said anything to me during the whole weekend, but I remembered her constant, strong and protective presence towards Joseph. I was always a bit cautious in my approach with her. She knew so much more about these traditions and teachings than most people. She had spent more time with Joseph than probably anyone else except his family. I was quite intimidated by her, and I always worried and wanted to make sure I would say the right thing or honor her in the right way.

I received a message from her on Facebook, saying, "Do I understand that you received a vision while you were dancing the Women's Web of Life dance?"

When I received that message, it shot right through me. I realized at that point that because she had been the visionary of the Women's Web of Life dance that it would have been appropriate, and a way to honor her as an elder, to speak to her about it. For her to reach out to me made me wish that I had realized that I needed to go to her and have a conversation with her. I said, "Yes. I did. May I call you?"

She was gracious and responded, "Yes, absolutely, it is better to talk on the phone."

We arranged a time for the call and she asked me quite simply to explain to her what happened. I told her that I had not shared the actual vision, and the details of it, with anyone. She said she didn't need to know the details, and that my vision was mine and that she honored me for not sharing those details in a big way. She told me that I should hold onto them.

What she wanted to know was more of my experience and what happened to me when I put the shawl over my head. What did I feel? I explained all of those things to her, what I felt, being transported completely into a different space and while I didn't talk to her about the experience in that other place I did tell her what it felt like and that in the vision I experienced several days with the ancestors. I explained to her that when I came back into the Women's Web dance arbor, in this time and this space, it had only been maybe half an hour – not long at all. She asked me if I had fallen down, or gone into a place of surrender. I told her that when I came into consciousness the two moon mothers were standing on either side of me, to hold me up. I can only assume that my knees had buckled and I had started to go down but I didn't have a memory of that.

She paused for a long time and then she said, "Yes I do believe that you have experienced a vision." She asked me to give her more details about what I felt and what I thought. Then she asked me to write down a few words as we spoke. As I told the story of my experience, she would say would say words like, "Yellow, write that down." Then I would go on, and she would give another word, and I would write that down. These words seemed to be so arbitrary and out of the blue. I didn't think they had anything to do with what I was telling her. At the end of the story, she asked me to read the words to her, one by one, which I did. As I read them out loud, she wove a beautiful web from the words that came to her in a way that made so much sense.

She spoke about yellow being about new beginnings, the sun rise and new days, and stepping into a new life, the beginning of a new day. She explained a lot more about my own vision and about what I had experienced. She opened a door in a way that I could step into it and see things more clearly. It was a beautiful and powerful way to gain more understanding. What was so astonishing was that she didn't even ask me to give her the details. She wanted me to keep those details for myself. She told me they were mine. She just wanted to know about my feelings, my thoughts, and my experiences.

Once we had shared all of that, she opened up, and we started speaking as if we had been best girlfriends for years, decades, even, and it was so wonderful to feel this loving, giving, nurturing side of her. She gave me advice about where I could get sage and where I could buy cornmeal in bulk. She told me where to get special items that had been grown in a good way and had been blessed for ceremony use. We talked about so many things, the details of ceremony and what I would need to move forward. In that conversation she gave me her blessing as the visionary of the web dance. In essence, she passed on to me the permission to be able to move forward with my own vision. It was empowering and loving. I felt her connection to what I was saying to her, and I felt her support and encouragement.

Birthing the Fire Dance

It was three years to the day since I had had the vision. Finally, after holding on to the vision for so long, and after being in denial for so long, and feeling like I was in labor for so long, it was finally here. I was so excited and relieved. I had told myself that I had to dance it so that I could understand it and feel what it felt like to be a fire dancer, and after I danced it, I would know how to be the chief of this dance. I would know how to hold the space of this dance for others, how to give this dance to the people and to the world, which is what the ancestors were asking me to do. On many levels I thought this was going to be like a classroom. I didn't realize the full extent to which I would be dancing. I didn't realize that I wouldn't just be tutored and trained in these things, that I had to live them and experience them and embody them.

The next day, on Friday, when my dance was to start, Trai and I drove out to Sacred Grove. There was no real arbor built yet. My dance was to take place inside a medicine wheel and so I placed the stones of the medicine wheel in a circle to create the space. One by one the crew started showing up.

The firewood had already been delivered. Usually the firewood that Ellen ordered for Sacred Grove was neatly chopped. For some reason this time it was a lot of scrub wood, and it was not chopped. It looked almost as if it had been collected out in the woods. There were some long pieces and some short pieces. Some were cut, some were split. Most were not. Even though it was difficult to work with, all the fire keepers said they would make it work. When I spoke to them about it, they said, "Robbie, you don't have to worry about the wood, you can focus on your dance."

Each fire keeper created their own circle around their fires in each of the four directions. The spirit fire ring was created. Everyone was busy at work and Marty, my fire mother, was busy taking care of me, making sure I had what I needed. I was busy trying to be in charge of everything. I was telling everyone what they needed to do, and how best to do it, instead of being busy being a dancer.

Looking back that was probably my way of avoiding the fact that I could feel my spirit stepping into that dance arbor, readying itself for what was to come. We created a space for me to sleep under a tiny little backpacker shade tent. I didn't want to be in a tent. I wanted to be able to see all five fires. My plan was to sleep out in the open with just a little bit of shelter over me that would protect me if it rained.

The fire keepers prepared their spaces and the sweat lodge. I had heard stories years earlier about Joseph building a sweat lodge out of pvc pipe. There were lots of jokes about it. It was not the first time I had ever had a lodge built out of pvc, and it held up really well. It is not a traditional structure, but I remembered what Joseph taught us about not getting stuck in form. I figured if it was good enough for Joseph, it was good enough for us.

We covered the lodge with blankets and the fire keepers got ready. We would all go into the lodge together for purification to ready me as the dancer, and the crew for the ceremony before we lit the fires in the arbor and before we started the drum.

The fire keepers had the stones ready, so we all crawled into the lodge. The door to the lodge faced east, which is the way that Black Elk taught us, so that when you come out you face the new day. When I crawled into the lodge, I sat directly opposite the door, in the west. Jamie, who was the west fire keeper sat in the west. Teresa, who was the south fire keeper sat in the south. Bob sat in the north and Candy sat in the doorway near the east, to lead the lodge. The rest of the crew sat in between.

The stones were brought in, and the lodge became hot. Candy closed the door to the lodge. I believe Candy put one ladle of water on the stones, and within minutes, the lodge began to bear down on our heads and our backs. It felt like it was coming down altogether. Jamie put her hands up to hold the lodge up and said, "Okay, we've got a problem. Open the lodge door!"

As the lodge door was opened, I could see a rush of steam going out of the door. The lodge was collapsing on us from the west. I said loudly, "Everyone out!" and Jamie said, "Yes, everyone out of the lodge!" and we helped each other get out.

When we were all out of the lodge, it was clear that the collapsing was starting in the west, and then the north and then the south collapsed. The last to collapse was the east. We pulled the blankets off quickly so that they didn't touch the hot stones in the center. There was a bit of chaos as everybody rushed around.

I turned to Candy and asked her if she had cornmeal and tobacco. She said that she did. I took a handful of cornmeal in my left hand to honor the feminine energy and a handful of tobacco in my right hand to honor the masculine energy in that plant, and I walked up to the lodge fire, just to the east of the lodge.

I said all my prayers that I would have said in the lodge and offered my prayers to the fire. As I finished my prayers, I realized that everyone was watching me in silence. One by one they came behind me and each got a handful of cornmeal and tobacco. I offered my tobacco and cornmeal to the fire and I walked round it in a full circle. I honored the fire for the work that it had done and for the work it was doing.

Each person stepped up and honored the fire and offered their own prayers for the ceremony and for me, as the dancer and as the future chief and visionary, and for themselves as they held the space for me and as they were in service to the dance. Each one walked a full circle around the fire and back. Once we were all complete with that, I realized that was the ceremony that needed to happen. That was what we needed to open the dance. The lodge represents the womb of mother earth and it had literally had contractions that birthed us out to this new ceremony into our prayers with the fire.

One by one we walked the few paces over to the medicine wheel that had been created as the arbor. I waited in my space as the fire keepers took coals from the sweat lodge fire to the spirit fire to light it using those coals. Once the spirit fire was blazing and was rooted in and fully engaged, they took coals from that fire and lit the east fire. They took more coals from the spirit fire and used them to light the south fire. They took more coals from the spirit fire and lit the west fire. And finally they took more coals from the spirit fire and lit the north fire. The sun started setting just as all of this happened. It started to get dark, and the arbor lit up with fire. That is when I saw the Fire Dance arbor that I had seen in the vision.

The drummers started playing. I felt my emotions well up. I felt the tears coming, and I almost couldn't move, but my body started to move, and I felt the earth calling. I danced around and around and around. I danced from one fire to another over and over and back and forth. I went to all the fires, and when I reached the spirit fire, I would dance all the way back round to the other side, just as the ancestors had shown me to do.

The drum was going; the crew was chanting and singing. It felt like they were cheering me on even though I know that is not what they were doing. I don't know how long I danced on Friday night. I danced until I was exhausted. And then it was time to sleep.

Early the next morning when I woke up, the fires were all burning, and I realized the crew had been around all night. There were no dog soldiers, so they took turns to sit and watch over me. The drummers stayed with me. The fire keepers stayed with me. They kept the fires burning through the night, and I was safe.

I stood up, and we sang the morning song in honor of the new day. We offered cornmeal in honor of new beginnings. I saw Sammye Jo and LB walk up to the arbor in the light of the morning, and I burst into tears. I don't know why I cried. I cried because I felt safe. I cried because there was something that I needed. I didn't know what I needed, but I felt like Sammye Jo had it.

I just cried. I started shaking. I recognized that old familiar feeling from the first time that I had danced, that thing that was coming up. I knew. I had not felt this in so long. I felt it coming up and then the drum started. I started running. I started moving and dancing and I felt it coming up. When it came up, there was no stopping it this time.

I went to the spirit fire, and I started screaming. I was screaming and yelling. I wanted it out. Whatever it was that was in me, whatever it was that I was holding on to, I wanted it out. All I knew was that this was my last chance. This was it. I had to get it out.

I danced and I screamed and I danced. And I sang. And I danced and I screamed. I dropped down to all fours. All I wanted to do was to crawl inside that spirit fire. I felt like there was relief inside that spirit fire. Freedom. There was something inside that fire that I needed. I didn't know what it was.

I put my hands on the rocks around the fire. They were hot, and it felt like my hands were burning, but I wanted to crawl in anyway. I put my hand down into the ash that was inside the fire ring. Then someone grabbed me around my waist, and I realized that Marty had hold of me, and she was pulling me back.

If Marty had not grabbed me, I would have crawled into that fire without any question. She pulled me out. I lay in her arms and cried and cried, like a baby. I don't know why I cried. Then I got mad. I got angry. I was so angry.

I stood up and stomped away, and I started running. Around and around the arbor and again I was yelling at the fire.

"What else do you want from me? I have given you everything," I screamed at Spirit. "You took my home. You took my work. You took everything. You took my security. You took my relationship. You took my business. You took my identity. You took everything from me. What else do you want?"

What I heard was, "You have to be willing to give up everything. You have to be willing to give it all up. Your community, your friends, your family, your loved ones, Trai, every person who is here today. You have to be willing to give it all up."

I got even angrier, because I wasn't willing. I didn't want anything else taken away from me. I didn't want to lose anything. I felt like so much had been taken already. I just kept dancing, and I said, "No, no! There's got to be another way! This can't be the way."

I kept dancing and dancing, and the spirit fire got bigger and bigger. It reached a point where I couldn't move. I felt like I was dancing in quicksand. Everything felt so thick. The air felt like mud. It felt like peanut butter. I couldn't move. I just kept trying and trying to move and then I felt someone on my left and someone on my right. Marty and Teresa were holding me up. They were standing on either side of me, and they started dancing with me. They held me up and they helped me push through. They helped me move beyond the muck and mire of my own creation and let go of my own anger and my own resistance. They helped me, and as they danced around with me, it started getting a little easier.

When I could stand up on my own again, they moved away and I went back to the spirit fire. I just surrendered. I got down on my knees and I said, "I'm done. You can have it all. You have already taken so much, you can have it all. Whatever you need from me, you can have it."

I heard clearly, "All I want is the willingness, just the willingness." I sat there staring into the fire and I realized that Spirit wasn't asking me to give up anything else, to walk away from my community, my friends, my loved ones, or Trai. It was not asking me to give up anything. Just to be willing.

I felt something open up in those moments. It was some kind of recognition that I wasn't really going to lose everything, but just asking the question, "Are you willing to let go of it all?" And I surrendered, and I said, "Yes. I am willing."

Spirit told me that it is in the willingness that I will find the ability to truly love, and to truly be loved, because as long as I am willing to lose everything, then I am loving without fear and allowing myself to be loved without fear.

It was my fear of not being loved and my fear of not being able to love, that had been blocking me my whole life from having that one thing that we all want, from experiencing the love that we come here on this planet to experience. I became willing in those moments with the fire. My willingness to let go of anything and everything is the one thing that's true.

Once my surrender was complete, it was time for me to walk across the coals, to walk across the spirit fire, across the bridge. It was time for me to complete the dance, to complete the circle, to complete the hoop. I had given everything I had to give. I had given my surrender and now it was time for me to receive.

I lay down in my space while the crew prepared the spirit fire for me to walk across. I pulled a sheet out and put it down on the ground under a tree that was in the arbor. It was the only place I could find relief from the heat. Once again the temperatures were near 100 degrees in May, which was extraordinarily high for that time of year in North Carolina.

I rested in the shade. I allowed the experience with the spirit fire to integrate, to become my truth and to become real.

I allowed for that to happen. I lay there watching the fire keepers working the spirit fire to make it ready. I saw Trai outside the arbor. He had been quite moved, I think, by what he had witnessed. I thought how hard it must have been for him to see me screaming and yelling and crying and crawling. How strong he was to still be there. To still want to be there.

I watched him as he sat outside the arbor, and he watched me, and I felt safe. I felt loved. He simply put his hand over his heart and looked at me. I knew that I would be able to love him completely and that I would be able to allow him to love me. To see it visibly there on his face in those moments was the most precious gift I had ever received.

I fell asleep under the tree with those thoughts. When I woke up maybe an hour or two later, the fire was mostly coals, but there were still some big pieces of logs in the fire. The fire keepers were raking and moving the coals around. I thought I could tell they were preparing for the fire walk ceremony when I would step across the fire.

I needed to move my body again. I needed to feel the fires. I needed to feel the rhythm. I needed to feel the earth. I asked if the drummers could drum so that I could dance. I danced around and around as they were busy working. I kept dancing. I went around to the spirit fire and then turned around to go around in the opposite direction back to the spirit fire, and then around again. This time it felt different. I knew I was preparing myself for something.

I was dancing around and around. I danced up to the spirit fire and saw flames on some small logs off to the side. As I looked into the flames, I saw two hands holding a sacred pipe come towards me. The pipe was being presented to me by these hands coming out of the fire. I turned around and turned back, and it was gone.

I kept dancing and moving around. Sammye Jo had moved off and turned her back. She was preparing a sacred space for me to sit after I walked across the coals so she had her back to the spirit fire. The fire keepers had stepped to the side of the fire, and suddenly the path across the fire looked open. The bridge looked ready to me.

I didn't ask anyone. I didn't ask permission. I didn't ask Sammye Jo. I kept dancing, and the drummers kept drumming. Before I knew it, I was walking across the fire. I didn't know it at the time, but I walked across a live fire. I didn't know that Sammye Jo wasn't ready. I didn't know that it wasn't time for me to walk. Something in my heart said 'go across the coals' and I did. When I reached the other side, I heard everyone cheering and laughing. I looked around, but I didn't see everyone. I didn't see Candy. Sammye Jo was caught by surprise. She came up to me and looked at me. Suddenly I realized that my feet were burned, and I was in pain.

I whispered to her, "Don't let anyone know, but I'm hurt." She pulled up a chair for me to sit in, and I sat down. Marty got down on her knees in front of me and lifted up my feet. The look on her face told me that something was wrong. I looked down; my hands were shaking.

Sammye Jo grabbed one of my hands. I said to her again, "Please don't tell anybody." I looked at Marty and said, "Please don't tell anybody." Then LB came up, and she got down on her hands and knees and looked at my feet. Then the others started gathering around. The drummers had come in, and Trai had come in. Everyone had come in and gathered around me.

I sat in the chair, and Sammye Jo held my one hand. It was shaking. My other hand was also shaking. I knew Trai was going to try to hold my hand, and so I sat on it because I didn't want him to know. I knew my body was shaking because I was going into shock because I had been burned. Marty was doing her best to tend to my burns without scaring anybody.

I don't know why I was so worried about not scaring anybody. I didn't want anybody to… I don't know what. I didn't want to hurt anyone? LB said that she had some salve. She went and got it, and she spread it on my feet. I said to Sammye Jo, "I can't dance anymore. I can't walk."

"I know," she said. "Your dance is done. You're complete. You crossed the fire. You're done."

After putting the salve on my feet, Marty and LB helped me try to slip my shoes on, but I couldn't. My feet were greasy and slippery with the salve and with the pain from the shoes. At that point Trai realized that something was wrong. He got in front of me and he said, 'Let me carry you."

He picked me up and carried me out of the arbor. As he was carrying me, I looked down and saw a container of cornmeal on the ground. I knew that cornmeal held the nurturing and magical energy of unconditional love. I said to him, "I need to put my feet in the cornmeal."

He didn't question anything. He put me down in the cornmeal, and I stood there for just a minute. Because I had the salve on my feet, the cornmeal just coated and stuck onto my feet. Trai carried me into the guest house. I sat on the floor, and then everyone else came in, too. I still didn't want anyone to know how badly I was hurt. I thought I needed to go to the hospital, but I decided I could wait till the next day.

Trai gave me his socks to put on, which I did. It was the strangest thing to put the socks on over the cornmeal and the salve.

I sat there with all of the crew and talked and laughed. We had such a wonderful time. We all agreed that we would spend the night and gather together the next morning when we would have a feast and breakfast and that I would have my giveaway for all of them. I had made gifts for everyone. We would celebrate that the Fire Dance had been birthed into reality.

I told Trai I needed to take a shower, so he waited for me while I went into the shower. Somehow I was able to stand in the water. Even though the lukewarm water hurt so much, I needed to get my feet clean. I washed my hair, and it still smelled like smoke. I put Trai's socks back on and came out. I was able to walk. It hurt, but I was able to walk.

Trai and I were staying in a small cabin at Sacred Grove, and I said I wanted to go and lie down in the cabin. I knew I couldn't put my shoes on, and I knew I couldn't walk all that way, and so Trai carried me to the cabin. When we got there, we lay down and didn't talk much. We just slept.

I slept with his socks on my feet all night, and when I woke up the next morning I had just a few small blisters. There were red spots on my feet that were tender, and it hurt to put shoes on, but I could walk. I couldn't believe it. Marty told me the day before that the bottoms of my feet were covered in huge blisters. I didn't look at them because I couldn't. Not until the next day.

They were healing. It was the most amazing thing.

We all came together and shared with each other. We talked about our experiences, about what we saw and what we felt. I didn't tell them the details about what the fire had said to me. I didn't tell them what my lesson was and what it was that I released or what my commitment and my agreement was or what my surrender was about. That was personal.

I did tell Sammye Jo in private about what I saw right before I crossed the fire, about the hands that were holding out a pipe. She told me that it meant I was to be a pipe carrier, and that one day a pipe would come to me and that when it did I would have the responsibility of being a pipe carrier for the people.

I knew, through everything that happened, the lodge collapsing, the gut-wrenching dance, my own personal dance, my surrender, and even the pain of the fire walk, I knew that I had to give this dance to the people. I knew this was not the end. It was not just for me to dance. My dance was just the beginning. It was the birthing of the Fire Dance.

Feeling the Fires

Once I knew that I was to take the Fire Dance to the people, things moved quickly. We scheduled a dance to take place at Sacred Grove in the fall. As I planned the Fire Dance, it became clear to me that the elders would be crucial and important to this ceremony. The elders hold the wisdom, and they hold the traditions. They know. They connect so quickly and so easily to the medicine, to what is happening, and to the healing. They can see it like no one else can. I honor them for the experiences, wisdom and teachings they bring to us.

Somehow in this society we have lost connection to our elders, and it is a sad thing because they hold the key to everything for us. One day we will be the elders, and we will hold the keys for the generations that come after us.

The ancestors shared with me the importance of honoring the elders, of being able to listen. I knew that as the Fire Dance chief and as the visionary that if I was to hold the space for many dancers to come at one time and dance this dance together, I needed a team working with me. I needed a team larger than the drummers, fire mothers, fire fathers and fire keepers. I needed the elders, and I needed a team of elders that would understand this dance.

I invited five or six of the elders who I knew would connect into this first Fire Dance; some of them were able to come and some of them were not. The elders that came showed up in an amazing way for me.

Pattie McFee, who had made the fire shawl, came and brought with her not only the fire shawl but also all the other elemental shawls that she had been working on that carried the same wisdom that the fire shawl carried.

I reached out to Ula Rae, which took a lot of courage, because I had not spent much time with her before this. She had been to almost every dance and almost every ceremony. In fact she taught me how to make prayer ties for my first dance back in 2001. She was a little bitty fireball of a woman, and she scared the bejeebers out of me. I can't tell you why because she was kind and loving but she carried something powerful deep down inside of her and it scared me. And so, over all these years, I didn't spend much time talking to her.

Every time I saw her at a ceremony, I would hug her hello, and tell her how happy I was to see her – and that was it. That was probably about as much as I could take of her power, her strength, and what she carried within her. From the other side of the dance arbor, I would wave to her, or from the other side of the table during breaks, I would say hello to her. But I never spent time really talking to her and connecting with her.

When I knew I needed to reach out to elders to come and support the Fire Dance, she was at the top of my list. I needed to reach out to her; I just needed her to be there. I didn't know how much I needed her to be there until she showed up. She said yes and that she wanted to know what this was all about.

I asked other elders to come. I asked Jeanne and Perry Robinson from the Center for Peace, and Steve and Nan Citty and many of my other teachers to come. For various reasons many of them could not be present for the first Fire Dance for the people. But Ula Rae, Patti and several others who had been part of this community for so many years, came in support of me, in support of the dance, in support of the ancestors, and most importantly in support of the dancers.

When Ula Rae arrived with Charlaine, who had been with me at the first Fire Dance, I felt as though the queen had arrived at Sacred Grove, and I gave her the grand tour. All Ula Rae wanted to do was step into the dance arbor and see where the fires had been during my dance. She wanted to feel what that felt like and connect with the ceremony that had been there about five months earlier. She wanted to know what the Fire Dance was. She could do that just by stepping into the arbor where I had danced.

I stood in the east, between the trees that framed the entrance into the arbor and watched while Ula Rae walked up to the place where the east fire had been. She held out her hand over the top of where the fire had been as if there was still a fire there. I think she could feel the heat from the flames that had been there months before. She stood there with that fire, and then she walked in a circle around it.

She moved to the next fire, in the opposite direction that I usually go in, honoring the tradition of the Cherokee – she comes from the mountains in Tennessee, in Cherokee country. She went to the north fire. She stood there with that fire, and in the same manner she put her hand out and held it over the space where the fire had been. She walked in a circle around the fire. She felt the guardian energy there. She felt the protector.

When she was done, she walked around to the west fire, and when she put her hand out as if to feel that fire too, she jumped back a bit. Then she looked back at me in the east gate with a little smile on her face, like she knew something. Putting her hand over the west fire space, she moved quickly in a circle. I knew she was feeling that call to action fire and she could feel the manifestation of that fire.

After that she walked over to the south fire, the fire that nurtures the dancers, that holds the emotions of the dancers. She put her hand out over that fire, and as she did she started to cry. I knew that she was feeling all the feelings that I had felt before. I knew she was feeling my fear of being soothed, my fear of being comforted, my fear of being weak. I knew she could feel the fire that wasn't there anymore. I knew she was feeling me.

She walked into the center and stood with the spirit fire. She stayed with that fire the longest. She walked around and around where that fire had been. I knew that she was listening.

I knew she didn't have to ask me about my experience of the dance. I knew she didn't have to ask me what Spirit had given me or what my surrender looked like. She didn't have to ask me what I learned. She didn't have to ask me any of those things because she got it all from holding her hand out over the spaces where the fires had been. She felt how the fires had turned me inside out and had transformed my life completely. She felt it. She walked back to me and put her arms around me.

"I love you, and I am happy to be here," she said.

Fire Dance for the People

I made a commitment to spirit, to the ancestors, and to the people that I would take the Fire Dance wherever and whenever I was asked to take it. I just knew that I wouldn't have to seek out anything, that the requests would come, even from people who didn't know exactly what this was. And that is what happened.

We danced the first Fire Dance for the people at Sacred Grove in the same place where I danced. And one month later we danced in South Africa. After that, over the next two years, we danced the Fire Dance eleven more times, in the United States, South Africa, Germany, and Norway. The dance has been invited to Hawaii, the Pacific North West and England, and all of those are in the planning stages.

Every time we dance this dance, every time I say "yes," the gifts that come to me are immeasurable. The blessings come from meeting so many different people, so many people who trust me. I have no idea why people who don't even know me will write to me and ask if I will bring the Fire Dance there.

A woman from Germany sent me a message on Facebook and said, "A friend of mine danced the Fire Dance in South Africa. Would you be willing to come to Germany?" I didn't even think about it. My answer was "yes." Immediately everything just opened up and opened the way to go to Germany. It is the way of it, and how this works. I went to Germany with six people from the United States, and there were also two people from Croatia, six people from Norway and one from Ireland. The rest were Germans. These people are all my family now.

As we continued to move forward and as I continued to hold this dance and to step up over and over again, the lessons kept coming. Lessons in humility, community, vulnerability, strength, and guidance. The idea that I would be welcomed into a place, a land that I had never been to, welcomed into the homes of people who had never met me, that they would take the time and the energy and the effort to build a dance arbor so that we could do this work, so that we could open up the space for people to connect with their own ancestors and with the roots of their own being in all of these places, was so thrilling.

I don't know how it happens. I just keep saying "yes." I keep in mind what Jeanne White Eagle said to me, "Just say yes, and show up." I show up for Spirit, for the people, and for myself.

Good Company

After I started saying "yes" to take the Fire Dance wherever it was called, we started having four or five Fire Dances every year. That was in addition to the teachings that I was doing and my private work with clients. I was also doing shamanic and spiritual work, pouring sweat lodges every month, and making drums. Things were moving forward in such a good way, and I felt like I was on solid ground. I felt as though I was standing on top of a mountain, and I could just feel Spirit moving through me.

I stayed busy. Even though I did not have a big business to run anymore, I found that making myself available to the community and to anyone who needed me kept me occupied. If there was someone in the hospital, if someone needed advice, or counsel, or a shoulder to cry on, or if a baby had been born or there was a death or illness in the family, I was there. That is what happened when I said "yes" to Spirit.

I enjoyed being active and having so much going on. In the midst of all of that, Ellen invited me and Trai to live at Sacred Grove Retreat. It happened at the point that Trai and I decided to make the commitment to live together and to leave the city to create a life together that was centered on the spiritual work that we were doing. It was one of the greatest blessings.

It was also a huge decision and commitment because moving an hour out of Charlotte meant there would be no more interior design work, no looking back, no falling back on that old way of earning a living. It meant looking at life in a completely new way, trusting Spirit and trusting the community. It was absolutely fabulous.

Trai immediately went to work remodeling some of the spaces at Sacred Grove to accommodate more people. We did whatever we could to give back to Sacred Grove. The blessing of living in such a special, sacred place where people come from all over the world to be here was immeasurable.

I helped in the ways that I could to create new events and open doors for other facilitators to come in. We invited some of the other dances to Sacred Grove.

Trai and I made a home with each other and realized that what we wanted in life was simple and yet also incredibly powerful. We wanted to live simply, to be on the land, to contribute in every way that we could and do whatever work that we could do and build a better community. We wanted to help Ellen in all she was creating and to see her dream come to reality and for the two of us to create our own life and our own path together.

I was absolutely thriving. I loved the work I was doing. I loved the place that I lived. I loved the man that I was with. I loved my life and my community. In the midst of all of that good, something happened that I never could have foreseen.

A group of Native American activists found out about my work, and they resented it because I am not a full-blooded Native American. In fact, with my red hair and my blue eyes, I look like I am anything but Native American. Their objections came in the form of a systematic and relentless attack on my Facebook page. Initially, I was utterly devastated.

My great-great-grandmother was Cherokee. While I know that she was Cherokee, I also know that she married a white man and assimilated fully into living in the white culture. She did not pass on anything to her children – neither teachings nor her spiritual practices. The only thing she passed on from one generation to another was her blood.

Something similar happened on my mother's side of the family. That great-great-grandmother was Creek, and we don't know much about her. The only thing we know for sure is that she was on the census form in the mid-1800's that refers to the Indian Creek Roll, which is the list that they made when they were trying to annihilate the Native Americans from the South East. This was a list of all of the Native Americans that were put onto the Trail of Tears and sent west. That great-great-grandmother also assimilated into white culture and married a white man because my great-grandmother was only half Native American, and so it goes all the way down.

So it is true that according to the legal definition, I am not Native American. Some of my teachers have been Native Americans who taught people no matter what color their skin or their hair or their eyes. It never occurred to me that anyone would have a problem with my spiritual connection to the creator.

Ula Rae proved to be a pillar of wisdom and strength. She told me that there were others who had experienced the same thing. When I told her what these people were doing and that they had added my name to a website that supposedly exposed spiritual frauds, she laughed and said, "Well you know, Joseph is on that website – you must be doing something right!"

The objections to my work and to me were upsetting, but Jeanne White Eagle told me that she had also experienced something similar a few years earlier via email, before Facebook. I felt a little better, knowing that I was in good company.

Ula Rae told me not to worry, to hold my head up, and that the work I was doing in the world was too important to let anyone bring it down. She told me stories about people she has known throughout her eighty-something years who have had the same things happen to them. She said there are traditional Native Americans who feel that people who are not full blooded do not have the right to practice any of these spiritual ceremonies or rituals, that it is reserved only for those with pure blood. And yet there are so few people of any race with pure blood anymore. If a spiritual practice was reserved for only pure blood Natives, then the culture and the spiritual path could die out.

I did understand that people could feel the way these activists did. But if I was to honor their feelings around this, then I would be denying who I am. I would be denying my own deepest connection to the Creator. I would be denying my soul. I started asking questions, and I learned there were more Native Americans, full blooded or not, who supported the sharing of these spiritual ways and who truly believe, just like Joseph believes, that sharing these beliefs will save this planet. That's what I choose to believe.

What I came to understand through this experience is that no one, no other soul on this earth, has the right to tell another one what their spiritual path should or shouldn't be. No one has the right to tell me that my path to the creator is wrong. It is not theirs to give, and it is not theirs to take away. It is mine. I cannot deny what I know in my soul.

The Sacred Pipe

Almost exactly a year after birthing the Fire Dance at Sacred Grove, we held another Fire Dance for the People, also in Sacred Grove.

Marty invited a friend of hers, Kathryn Leeman, a medicine woman from California, to come and dance at this Fire Dance. When Marty told her about the dance, Kathryn knew she had to be there. She came, trusting, not knowing anything about the work that I was doing, not knowing me, but trusting Marty to share with her the medicine and healing of this dance.

It was a powerful dance, with sixty people gathered, and it was beautiful for all of the dancers who came. At the end of the dance we had a feast and then the giveaway ceremony. At the giveaway, in front of everyone, Kathryn came to me and handed me a bundle.

"This is a gift for you," she told me, and then she leaned in and whispered in my ear, "It is your pipe."

Chills went over my entire body, and in that moment all I could remember was a year earlier in the Fire Dance arbor, feeling so distraught and worn down at my point of surrender and looking into the spirit fire and seeing those hands reaching towards me with a pipe.

I was shocked. I had almost forgotten about that. I had forgotten that Sammye Jo had told me that a pipe would come to me. It took me a few minutes to catch my breath. I sat with the bundle in my lap as we continued with the sharing. I was a little scared, and I was anxious to speak to Sammye Jo about it.

When everything had come to its conclusion and we were done, everyone came to hug and say their goodbyes. I quickly went over to Sammye Jo and asked if she would come with me to a private space. We went into the Grove House, and I sat down with the bundle on my lap again. I told her that Kathryn said it was a pipe.

"Have you looked at it yet?" she asked me.

I replied, "No."

"Do you want to open the bundle?" Sammye asked.

"Yes, I do."

It was wrapped in red cloth and had a narrow strip of red cloth tied around it to keep it together, which I untied. Then I peeled back the larger piece of red cloth to reveal a large leather pouch. It had a beautiful fringe on it, a braided leather strap to hold it, and a deer antler button keeping it closed.

Opening up the leather pouch, I pulled out a bundle of sage that was in the pouch. Next I reached in and pulled out a bundle of sweet grass. Sammy said, "Pipes are always carried with sweet grass and sage."

I pulled out the pipe. It did not look like any pipe I had seen used in sacred ceremony before. It was strikingly different. The bowl of this pipe was carved out of wood, and it was shaped almost like a spinning top that you would have played with as a child. It was pointed on the bottom, and in layers it got wider and wider as it got to the top. At its widest point it got smaller and smaller until you could see the bowl and the opening in it. The opening had a little silver rounded hinged lid that you could pop open and look inside.

The bowl inside was beautifully carved. It looked hand-hammered with metal. Attached to the bowl was a stem, but instead of the stem coming out perpendicular to the bowl, it came up against the side of the bowl. I realized that the stem was missing a piece, so I reached into the pouch and found an additional extension for the stem that could be put in place. I remembered that the tradition says that the bowl and the stem stay separate, and it's when they come together that we smoke the pipe. I realized that as different as this pipe looked, it still had the bowl and the stem separate

Except for the bowl that was hand-hammered and carved, everything else was wood. It was beautifully finished. I could tell it was carved with care – it was perfect. It was painted with stripes and patterns in beautiful bright colors which reminded me of the colors and patterns I had seen on many Native American weavings.

Sammy Jo looked at me and said, "That's a different pipe!"

"It's not what I would have thought!" I said.

Sammye looked at me with her familiar little grin and told me, "You have to sleep with this pipe underneath your pillow for 30 days. Then you will know if it's yours, and you will know how to use it."

I packed it up exactly as I had found it and did not attach the stem to the pipe. I closed it back up into the pouch with the sweet grass and the sage and wrapped the pouch with the red cloth and tied it up tight. After that I went to find Kathryn to ask her about it. She told me that her daughter had given her that pipe years earlier and that she had never smoked it. Her daughter had gotten it when she went into the mountains of Russia to volunteer at an orphanage there. Someone had given her the pipe, and she knew that she had to bring it home to her mother.

Now it had been passed on to me, just as the fire had told me I would get a pipe, and I knew this was not a small thing. I knew the importance of receiving a pipe. Sammye Jo told me that I needed to seek out another pipe carrier, and I needed to learn and understand, but I remembered that Joseph told me that I was not to have a teacher.

I did what Sammye Jo told me to do. I slept with the pipe under my pillow for 30 days. Two weeks after that dance Trai and I headed back to South Africa, and so the pipe made the trip with me. Wherever I put down my head, the pipe was under my pillow. During those 30 days, my dreams were strong and vivid, and it became clear to me that the pipe was to do healing work, specifically healing work for the children.

Whenever it was smoked, prayers were to be offered for the children first, and after that for the people.

I knew this pipe was mine and that I was to use it in a good way and that the pipe would use me and teach me. I knew this was a new path to walk. I knew the importance and the sacredness of this. I knew other people who were pipe carriers, but because Joseph had told me that I was not to have a teacher, I never asked for a teacher with the pipe.

About a month after I came back from South Africa, Brenda Sue came to Sacred Grove for the Women's Web of Life dance. I told her about the pipe, and she asked me if she could share some things with me about the pipe. I was grateful that she asked, and I was grateful for her teachings and her sharing.

She told me I should carry it for another year before I smoked it. I thought, 'I can do that.' I didn't feel an urgency to open up the pipe and smoke it. I felt that there was something more powerful there, something deeper, and I was willing to learn what I needed to learn from the pipe. Brenda Sue said I would learn, and she told me to take it to every ceremony, and at every sweat lodge to put it on the altar. She told me how to work with it while it was bundled.

I did that for a year. I took it to every Fire Dance and every ceremony. I trusted the pipe and learned to listen to it.

Exactly a year after I had received the pipe and two years after I had seen the pipe come to me in the fire, Kathryn came back to Sacred Grove to another Fire Dance. I sat with her and Ula Rae and told them my year of time with the pipe was up, and Kathryn said it was time for me to be initiated. After the Fire Dance, Kathryn and Ula Rae did ceremony with me. They initiated me as a pipe carrier, and I smoked the pipe for the first time with my honored elder and with my sister.

Medicine of the Fire Dance

In birthing the Fire Dance, the Fire Dance also gave birth to me as a Medicine Woman. Even though I may not have fully understood it then, and I may not fully understand it now, I know that's what happened. I know that by dancing the Fire Dance I have become who I am. I have stepped into my power. I have become Otter Woman Standing. I understand, to some degree, what my name means. I have clarity about standing in my own truth, in my own power, for the people, to serve the people and to serve Creator.

I am standing out publicly, standing firmly on the earth. Standing tall. Standing. I am Otter Woman Standing.

What an amazing gift to feel that, to feel how real a shift it is, and to see how my life has changed. All those years I knew I was headed to something different, but I didn't know what it was. I knew there was more, but I didn't have clarity on what that "more" was. After I danced the Fire Dance, I was called a visionary. I was called a chief. And I was called Otter Woman Standing.

I know the power of this dance. I know what the ancestors gave me was more than magical and powerful and life-changing. I know this dance could be everything. I know that if a dancer comes to dance this dance, it is completely unpredictable. There is no knowing how their life can change or what will open up on their path.

We, the people, have become so clouded by the 'should haves' and 'could haves' and the societal demands. We have become so confused by all of the lies that we believe about ourselves. We forget who we are. The things we believe about ourselves, about not being good enough, not being strong enough, not being pretty enough, not being smart enough, or not being clever enough. We believe all of those lies from society and all those 'others' about what we should look like or be like. Somehow, on some level, we all believe something about ourselves that isn't true. We believe something that stands between us and our most divine selves.

I know the medicine of this dance is exactly what the ancestors promised. When a dancer steps into the dance arbor and gives themselves to the medicine of the Fire Dance and surrenders completely, there's no more holding onto the lie, there's no more believing the lie. There is no more opportunity to hide behind something that isn't true, that doesn't serve, that keeps us small, that holds us back, and that holds us in the illusion that we are not full and amazing beings. There is no more believing the lie that keeps us small. That is the medicine of the Fire Dance.

When a dancer steps into the Fire Dance, that lie is exposed and the dancer has a choice to see it for the lie that it is, and let it go, or to hold onto it. It is in that choice that the dancer steps into their own power, into the truth of their own being. When the lie is exposed, even the choice becomes an illusion because you can't unknow something that you know.

So the dancer can let it go and move forward and call into their lives all that they want, all that they desire and want to create. The dancer can step into the power of who they are with passion and excitement. They can create their lives, whatever it looks like, whatever they choose.

When a dancer walks across the fire, that's what they choose. They choose to let go of the lie. They choose to live in passion. They choose to create with God. It seems simple, but this dance is not simple, because once the dancer makes a choice to let go of the lie, to see the truth, then everything that they allowed to come into their lives that supports that lie and that they believed about themselves will be removed by Spirit.

Those things will disappear and move away. They will be pulled away, if necessary, stripped away.

All of the things that supported the mistaken beliefs I had about myself were removed before I danced. They started being plucked away from me one by one once the vision was given to me. It took three years to completely dismantle my life as I knew it. I see now that it was dismantled methodically, painfully, and beautifully. When someone says 'yes' to dancing with the fires, the same thing will happen for them.

It is part of the 'yes.' It is part of the truth. As painful and messy and scary as it is, it is also beautiful and empowering and strengthening. I have been given the gift and what sometimes feels like the burden of holding the space for others, of witnessing the transformation, the letting go and the rebuilding. To me it's a place of honor to be the witness for so many people.

Sometimes sitting in a place of honor is difficult, but I do see it as honorable, and I do see it as a gift. Joseph said a long time ago that it is the witness that makes our experience real.

I am honored to be the witness for so many.

Acknowledgements

This book has been an amazing process and a learning experience. I didn't want to write it, but I knew I had to. Some parts of this story were hard to tell, some painful. Some parts of it make me sad to remember while I'm still laughing at others. It is my hope that you have laughed along with me. Now that it's done I feel both relief and pride.

This book would absolutely not have been possible without Susie Spies, who lovingly transcribed my recorded memories, pelted me with questions from across the Atlantic, encouraged me and partnered with me, and who laughed and cried with me through the writing process. Susie, you are my soul sister and I love you. Thank you so much.

Thanks also to my editor, publisher and cheerleader, Trish MacEnulty, who held my hand through the editing process and continually reminds me that I'm not crazy. Trish, thank you for walking through fire with me and helping me keep my head on straight as we do this dance together.

The beautiful painting on the cover of this book was intuitively created by Renae McGuire after I told her the title of the book. Renae is an amazing and generous artist.

Also a big thanks to Katie Mattson for her creation of the cover art and layout. She knew exactly how to capture the art and the feel of the book.

Jeanne White Eagle has been an inspiration and a source of tremendous support for me as I walked the path that made the stories in this book. Her willingness to write the foreword was such a blessing. Jeanne, words can't express my gratitude for your presence and guidance over the years. Thank you so much.

Thank you to Joseph Rael, Beautiful Painted Arrow, for seeing me.

Last but not least, thanks to Trai, my partner in life, my anchor who keeps me tethered to the ground and who knows when it's time to either turn down the crazy, or turn it up and dance with me. Trai, my sweet man, I promised it would never be boring.

About the Author

Robbie Warren, Otter Woman Standing, is a modern day Medicine Woman and a traditional Shaman who serves as an intermediary between this world and the spirit world. She holds ceremonies, rituals and healing with the aid of Spirit Guides following the cultural traditions passed down through generations. Her journey along this path has given her many opportunities to work with renowned spiritual teachers and other visionaries. She was given the Medicine name Otter Woman Standing by her Ancestors and Spirit Guides, who work with her in the other realms.

Made in the USA
Charleston, SC
23 June 2015